Shattering the Denial

Protocols for the Classroom and Beyond

KAREN B. McLEAN DONALDSON
Foreword by Christine Sleeter

BERGIN & GARVEY
Westport, Connecticut • London

1002715485

Library of Congress Cataloging-in-Publication Data

Donaldson, Karen B. McLean.
    Shattering the denial : protocols for the classroom and beyond / Karen B. McLean
    Donaldson ; foreword by Christine Sleeter.
        p.   cm.
    Includes bibliographical references and index.
    ISBN 0–89789–777–3 (alk. paper)—ISBN 0–89789–778–1 (pbk. : alk. paper)
    1. Discrimination in education—United States.   2. Racism—United States.   3.
    Multicultural education—United States.   I. Title: Protocols for the classroom and beyond.
    II. Title.
    LC212.2.D64   2001
    305.8′00973—dc21   00–057929

British Library Cataloguing in Publication Data is available.

Library of Congress Catalog Card Number: 00–057929
ISBN: 0–89789–777–3
        0–89789–778–1 (pbk.)

First published in 2001

Bergin & Garvey, 88 Post Road West, Westport, CT 06881
An imprint of Greenwood Publishing Group, Inc.
www.greenwood.com

Printed in the United States of America

The paper used in this book complies with the
Permanent Paper Standard issued by the National
Information Standards Organization (Z39.48–1984).

10 9 8 7 6 5 4 3 2 1

In Loving Memory of Mrs. Grace Lymas Clark

Mrs. Grace Clark was born in New York City, February 24, 1936, and died on March 17, 1997, shortly after being diagnosed with cancer. "Ma" was my mother-in-law, my second mom, and a true friend. She supported me and the rest of the family in all that we did. In writing this book, I owe my confidence and persistent spirit to my gracious mother-in-law. While sick in bed with cancer she still encouraged me to remain steadfast in my work because it was an important contribution. Certainly she knew best about hard work because she raised five children while working full-time jobs all her life. She was very proud of me and my accomplishments but not half as proud as I will always be of hers. I love you and I miss you, "Ma." This book is a testament to your hardworking spirit and your righteous love for all people.

Contents

Foreword

In *Shattering the Denial: Protocols for the Classroom and Beyond*, Karen B. McLean Donaldson argues forcefully that data can serve as ammunition for reforming schools to serve well the very diverse student populations that attend them. This book provides a rich resource of intervention models and data about changing how teachers think and teach. I would like to contextualize the issue of school reform and teacher education for anti-racist multicultural education within some additional data. Consider the following:

1. The population of students in schools, particularly public school, continues to become more and more diverse. In 1976, the K-12 public school population in the United States was 75 percent white, 15 percent black, 6 percent Latino, 1 percent Asian, and 1 percent Native American. By 1995, it was 65 percent white, 17 percent black, 13 percent Latino, 4 percent Asian, and 1 percent Native American (U.S. Department of Education, 1998). In twenty years, school populations had diversified markedly. These figures, however, oversimplify the complexity of diversity in classrooms. Racial and ethnic categories mask huge within-group differences; for example, a first-generation Chinese student and a third-generation Japanese American are both Asian but very different from each other. The categories also presume distinct racial groups, and they hide growing numbers of bi-racial or multiethnic students. Further, racial and ethnic categories do not address other forms of diversity in classrooms such as social class, disability, or sexual orientation. The average teacher can anticipate

teaching in fairly diverse classrooms, and any new teacher over her or his teaching career can anticipate classrooms that become more and more diverse.

2. Although schools historically have best served students who are white, English-speaking and middle class, a growing research base documents schools and teaching practices that work for diverse student populations. For example, Reyes, Scribner and Scribner (1999) studied eight high performing schools along the Texas–Mexico border, which serve primarily low-income Hispanic students, and have produced high achievement scores on the Texas Assessment of Academic Skills. Their research identified four clusters of "best practices" that these schools had in common. The schools, a) proactively involved the community and families, b) were organized around collaborative governance and leadership that was clearly focused on student success, c) used culturally-responsive pedagogy extensively, and d) used assessment to advocate for student needs and stronger teaching practices, rather than merely to assign grades or describe achievement levels.

There are other examples of teaching practices that "work" but that are not widely used. We know that students in dual language programs perform better on standardized tests of academic achievement than they do in English as a Second Language or transitional bilingual education programs (Thomas and Collier, 1999), yet ESL or transitional programs continue to dominate. Well thought out, culturally centered programs can serve students of color better than traditional Eurocentric schools. For example, the African American Immersion Schools Evaluation Project, working through University of Wisconsin–Milwaukee, is finding gradual improvement in student achievement as measured by various standardized achievement tests, as well as improvement in school attendance, in an African American immersion school (AAIS Evaluation Project, 1996). African-American independent schools educate more than 70,000 children from low- and moderate-income families. Most of these schools spend less per child than nearby public schools spend, yet students achieve at a much higher level in them. One study shows that students in 64% of these schools score above average in reading and 62% score above average in math (Ratteray, 1992). Culturally-centered programs have successful track records with other cultures as well. Gallaudet University is structured around use of American Sign Language and Deaf culture. A survey of its most recent graduating class found that within the first year after receiving their degrees, 95% either secured employment in their chosen field or were seeking an advanced degree; 48% had entered graduate school (www2.gallaudet.edu). In other words, although schools generally do not serve students of color, language minority students, and other "non-mainstream" student populations nearly as well as white middle class students, this is *not* because there are no models of successful schooling and successful teaching.

3. The population of teachers increasingly does not reflect the students. In the United States, currently about 90 percent of the teachers are white and

about three-fourths are female. Teachers tend to come from working or middle class backgrounds, and from small towns and suburbs.

4. Studies of white preservice students in varied geographic areas of the United States have found consistently that although a large proportion anticipate working with children of another cultural background, as a whole they bring very little cross-cultural background, knowledge and experience (Barry and Lechner, 1995; Gilbert, 1995; Larke, 1990; Schultz, Neyhart & Reck, 1996; Su, 1996, 1997). For example, Schultz, Neyhart and Reck (1996) found most white preservice students in their sample to be fairly naïve and hold stereotypic beliefs about urban children, believing that culture does not affect education, and also that urban children bring attitudes that interfere with education. White teachers bring little understanding of discrimination, especially racism (Avery & Walker, 1993; King, 1991; Su, 1996). Su (1996, 1997), for example, found white preservice students, most of whom came from middle to upper middle class backgrounds, to have little awareness of discrimination inside or outside schools. Many saw programs to remedy racial discrimination as discriminatory against whites.

Further, white teachers often question whether they can actually teach students of color. In a survey of preservice and inservice teachers (74 percent white, 26 percent of color) in southern California, Pang and Sablan (1998) found almost half to believe that school has little influence compared to the home, and two-thirds to believe that even a good teacher might not reach African American youth. As a group, then, white teachers tend to be ignorant of or resistant to using strategies and programs that work for culturally diverse student populations.

5. Predominantly white institutions have been very slow to respond to the need to recruit and prepare teachers for the students who are actually in the schools. For example, Fuller (1992) reported a survey of nineteen Midwest Holmes Group teacher preparation programs. Their students and faculty were about 94 percent Anglo. Only 56 percent of these institutions required elementary education students to complete a multicultural education course; one institution did not even offer such a course. Preservice students generally were placed in field experiences "reminiscent of their childhood" (p. 192).

These data illustrate a tremendous problem that does not need to exist—the growing gap between the commitments and knowledge of professional educators, and the children in the schools. Although it is possible to educate most children well, schools are not doing this with any consistency, and most of the teaching force is not prepared to do so. Further, most educators do not recognize their own complicity in perpetuating school practices that do not work well for the children who are actually in the schools.

In this book, Karen Donaldson directly and forcefully challenges these problems. She examines white teacher denial of problems in schools in different regions of the United States. She then goes on to document strategies that help white teachers to address and move beyond denial, and she illustrates creative ways to reconstruct both schools as well as teacher preparation. Donaldson is a gifted teacher and teacher educator who has a strong and compelling vision of how schools could be, and how teacher education can look. She also offers very important data documenting the link between multicultural teaching and student learning. Her ultimate goal is to improve schools for the students who are actually there. Her strongest tools for school reform are creative thinking and research data. Readers who share her vision of school reform will find her data to be extremely useful in their own quests, and her creative thinking refreshing.

Christine Sleeter

REFERENCES

AAIS Evaluation Project. (1996). *AAIS Newsletter*, Issue No. 5. Milwaukee: AAIS Evaluation Project.

Avery, P. G., & Walker, C. (1993). Prospective teachers' perceptions of ethnic and gender differences in academic achievement. *Journal of Teacher Education* 44 (1): 27–37.

Barry, N. H., & Lechner, J. V. (1995). Preservice teachers' attitudes about and awareness of multicultural teaching and learning. *Teaching and Teacher Education* 11 (2): 149–161.

Fuller, M. L. (1992). Teacher education programs and increasing minority school populations: An educational mismatch? In C.A. Grant (Ed.). *Research and multicultural education: From the margins to the mainstream* (pp. 184–200). London: The Falmer Press.

Gilbert, S. L. (1995). Perspectives of rural prospective teachers toward teaching in urban schools. *Urban Education* 30 (3), p. 290, 16p, 2 charts.

King, J. E. (1991). Dysconscious racism: Ideology, identity, and the miseducation of teachers. *Journal of Negro Education* 60 (2): 133–146.

Larke, P. J. (1990). Cultural diversity awareness inventory: Assessing the sensitivity of pre-service teachers. *Action in Teacher Education* 12 (3): 23–30.

Pang, V. O., & Sablan, V. A. (1998). Teacher efficacy. In M. E. Dilworth (Ed.), *Being responsive to cultural differences*, pp. 39–58. Washington, DC: Corwin Press.

Ratteray, J. D. (1992). Independent neighborhood schools: A framework for the education of African Americans. *Journal of Negro Education* 61 (2): 138–147.

Reyes, P., Scribner, J. D., and Scribner, A. P., eds. (1999). *Lessons from high-performing Hispanic schools*. New York: Teachers College Press.

Schultz, E. L., Neyhart, K., and Reck, U. M. (1996). Swimming against the tide: A study of prospective teachers' attitudes regarding cultural diversity and urban teaching. *Western Journal of Black Studies* 20 (1): 1–7.

Su, Z. (1996). Why teach: Profiles and entry perspectives of minority students as becoming teachers. *Journal of Research and Development in Education* 29 (3): 117–133.

Su, Z. (1997). Teaching as a profession and as a career: Minority candidates' perspectives. *Teaching and Teacher Education* 13 (3): 325–40.

Thomas, W. P., and Collier, V. P. (1999). Accelerated schooling for English language learners. *Educational Leadership* 56 (7), p. 46, 4p.

U.S. Department of Education. (1998). *Common core of data.* Washington, DC: U.S. Department of Education, National Center for Education Statistics. http://www.nces.gov/pubs98/Condition98/

Preface: Voice of an Antiracist Education Practitioner

This book is centered on antiracist education practices and findings; however, the term *antiracist* causes many people in education, generally whites, to avoid this concept at all costs. The fear of being accused of being a racist, of breaking the taboo of discussing race issues, and of becoming downright uncomfortable has for the most part led every level of education to ask for a less-threatening term. A number of techniques and practices involve hard-hitting activities to have whites realize their privilege in society. Yet, those strategies are not the thrust of antiracist education. Antiracist education is a concept and discipline that focuses on the reduction of racial injustice through historical and institutional perspectives, inclusion of racial ethnicities' traditions and experiences in school curricula, and so on. As a practitioner sensitive to how our society has contributed to the racist conditioning of its people, I strive to address race-related issues in ways that are nonthreatening, but nevertheless effective. On numerous occasions I have been asked to change the title of a course, presentation, or written work to eliminate the word *antiracist*. For example, "Enhancing Racial/Ethnic Understanding" was a title that a co-presenter and I came up with after an hour of debate with a committee employing us to prepare antiracist seminars, yet adamant about our not using the term *antiracist* in the seminar title. The title we agreed upon worked well for registering more participants. However, the impact that the term *antiracist education* is meant to have had to be compromised in order to conduct and fill the seminar with participants. As a practitioner in this field, I see the term as an important step to recognizing that we must stand firmly against racist practices, and that there is struggle and battles still waging to end racism. Taking a stand against any injustice is not easy, but until equity is available to all, those with a conscience should be willing to assist in eradicating social ills within our society. Using a term that describes the intensity of this work should be acceptable.

ANTIRACIST EDUCATION DEFINED

Beginning with a contemporary view of antiracist education in theory and practice will enable readers to use this definition as a guide for understanding the context of the antiracist education research and protocols for educators, the classroom, and beyond given in this book. Furthermore, the definition will describe the interchangeable and individual uses in the book of the terms *antiracist* and *multicultural education*. The definition shares the views of the United Kingdom (where the term *antiracist education* is used more readily) and the United States. Permission to use the following section, *Antiracist Education Definition*, has been given by Oryx Press.

Antiracist Education Definition. McLean Donaldson, K., & Verma, G. K. In *Dictionary for Multicultural Education*, ed. Carl A. Grant & G. Ladson-Billings. Oryx Press, 1997.

Antiracist education is a critical pedagogy that seeks to take a stand against racial injustice and oppression. In the United States, many scholars of multicultural and non-Eurocentric education, or others with these perspectives, have sought to develop antiracist education as a part of their projects. In the United Kingdom, the antiracist movement has been described as a development of multicultural education and a reaction to it (Verma, 1994). It grew out of a realization that simply focusing on cultural diversity did not ensure that more subtle forms of racism, particularly at the institution level, would be addressed. Central to the concept of antiracist education is the need to deal with racial discrimination and to develop a more critical approach to all teaching methods and materials. As Rex (1989) puts it, "anti-racism has a moral purpose going beyond multicultural education."

Attempts to "bridge the gulf" between antiracist and multicultural models by Grinter (1985) and others produced a concept of *antiracist multiculturalism*. In his later writing Grinter argues that the gulf is unbridgeable and "the philosophies do not meet" (Grinter, 1990). In practice, Grinter argues terminology is perhaps less important than the practical responses of teachers.

However, in the United States many theorists-practitioners have used the framework of multicultural education to address the ills of racism in U.S. schools, seeing antiracist education as an integral component of multicultural education. Whether standing alone or in conjunction with multicultural education, antiracist education seeks to combat the racial intolerance that is evident in schools in numerous educational biases.

These biases are apparent in standardized testing, curriculum that excludes or minimizes various cultural contributions, student organization that promotes tracking and ability grouping, high suspension and detention rates for students of color, inequalities in school financing, and lower teacher expectations of students of color. Racism in schools is also manifested in school policies such as failure to hire people of color at all levels and the omission of antiracist regulations in faculty and student handbooks. Racism also surfaces in schools through individual acts of bigotry and lack of understanding.

Antiracist education practice begins with educating administrators and teachers to understand racial oppression and racial identity issues, as well as racist conditioning and internalized oppression. Antiracist education challenges the total school environment to understand the ways in which racism is manifested in schools and society. It encourages educators to integrate antiracist concepts into all subject areas. Through recent research studies with students, antiracist education attempts to reveal the adverse effects of racism on student learning and development (Donaldson, 1996; Lee, 1996; Murray & Clark, 1990). Furthermore, a number of studies of antiracist education teachers have been conducted, and some teacher preparation programs now offer antiracist-education courses. Tatum (1992) has researched and designed psychology of racism and racial identity development theory models for undergraduate students.

In an antiracist program at the elementary level, students are taught to appreciate the contributions and experiences of racial groups and to become aware of racial injustices. At the secondary level students may explore issues of racism and seek solutions for reducing it.

The challenge of accepting antiracist education as viable pedagogy is dealing with fear and resistance. Schools often refuse to use the term *antiracist education*. Many schools, in an attempt to feel safe, choose the term *multicultural education* because they assume that antiracist education is not a major characteristic of multicultural education. This misunderstanding frequently causes a wedge between antiracist and multicultural education in practice. For many students, antiracist education is a high priority. As cultural diversity and curriculum reform take shape in our schools, all indications point to the emergence of antiracist education as an important educational approach.

Acknowledgments

The motivation for this work comes from my family first and foremost. To ensure the production of this book, they have sacrificed the time we would normally spend together. I'm noted to have many extended children; the five children I was blessed to birth (Wayne, Nyanda, Devin Marie, Chris Jr., and Courtney Simone), as well as my grandsons Dominque and Stephen, all understand the importance of reducing racism in schools and society. Without my parents encouraging cultural exploration, human rights, and love, this book would probably never have come to be. I thank my loving parents, Calvin V. McLean (deceased) and Maria Cardoza McLean, as well as my in-law parents, Raymond Clark and Grace Lymas Clark (deceased), and my closest aunt, Dorothy Cardoza Cooper. Coming from a large and loving family, I have also had the support of my brothers and sisters—Shirley (McLean) Houston, Barbara Ann McLean (deceased), Calvin McLean (deceased), Lois (McLean) Jones, Anthony McLean, Antoinette (McLean) Leoney, Paul McLean (deceased), Lynwood McLean, Trudy (McLean) Lowery, and Raymond McLean. My siblings have given me pride and the courage to go to fight the "good fight." May we all continue to prosper in love and to stay strong to pass on these qualities to all our many children.

Thanks go to Brenda Jones for her art illustrations, Christine Sleeter for writing the foreword, and Sherron Roberts for suggesting the title of the book. Thanks also go to the friends, colleagues, graduate research students, and research investigators without whose continued assistance this book would never have materialized. This list includes Carlie Tartakov, Theresa McCormick, Sonia Nieto, Anita Rollins, Anthony Stevens, Maurizio Visani, James C. McShay, Guisela Ana Chupina, Linda Benson, Phyllis Labanowski-Cantillo, Jose Cantillo, and Phyllis Brown.

Teachers and their students, educational institutions, parents, and communities have all made this book possible as well. It has been my distinct pleasure to work with teachers such as Mary Hulleman, Bruce Antion, Dwight Herold, Wayne Clinton, Larry Middleton, and Reggie Greenlaw; administrators such as Karen Simms, Barbara Jefferson, Mary Lynne Jones, and Suzanne Mendelson; and counselors such as Mary Worthy and Parris Howard.

It is perhaps unusual for those of us in academe to acknowledge God as the source of strength in our work and personal life, but here I must do so. This book was originally scheduled to be published in fall 1998. Following my review of the manuscript, one grave hardship after another challenged the lives of my family and me. These hardships retarded the publication of this book. Yet, through my belief in the grace of God, my perseverance and my strength were lifted. I was able to update and finish this book knowing, through reviewers' comments, that its content makes an important contribution to addressing the devastating effects of racism on students by way of the exploration of teachers' perceptions on race, staff development, and implementation of antiracist education strategies. My personal passion to reduce racism and to allow every child to experience education at its best fueled the research efforts of this book. "The voice of the author" precedes each of the four sections in the book to acknowledge the humanity necessary for this work and the need for research to accept openness in personalizing the issues. I give all glory to God for the production of this book.

Introduction

Shattering the Denial: Protocols for the Classroom and Beyond follows a previous publication, entitled *Through Students' Eyes: Combating Racism in United States Schools.* In the latter, youths revealed that they are looking for real-life education. Understanding that racism is part of our society, they desire to know more about its history, its current manifestations, and ways to combat it.

In recent years thousands of ethnically diverse students from around the country have shared tormenting stories of racial injustices in schools (Nieto, 1999; Cleary and Peacock, 1998; Daniel-Tatum, 1997; Lee, 1996; Ford, 1996; Donaldson, 1996). As numerous students experience racism firsthand, they have high expectations of educators to learn of its ill effects on them and of the damage it does to society. For the most part, though, they feel that educators cannot do this because educators deny that racism exists. Therefore, students are requesting that their teachers, administrators, counselors, and school communities become educated about the racism that exists in schools and on strategies to integrate antiracist education into curriculum and policy.

What the youth are asking for on the grassroots level has simultaneously been expressed as a national concern. Former president Bill Clinton in a weekly radio address stated that "the divide of race has been America's constant curse" and that the future depends upon "laying down the bitter fruits of hatred and lifting up the rich texture of our diversity and our common humanity" (*Washington Post*, 3/30/97). The appeal followed the surmounting racial hatred evidenced by the Lenard Clark beating on March 21, 1997. Awakening from a coma, 13-year-old Clark is slowly recovering from massive brain damage caused by three white teenagers motivated by racial hatred (Associated Press, 5/2/97). The president's comments were most likely spurred by events such as the burning of black churches, successful movements to dismantle affirmative action, the call for a national apology to African Americans for the wrongs of slavery, the controversy with Merriam-Webster Dictionary to acknowledge the ill effects of its definition for the word "nigger," findings of sociologists such as Dr. David R. Williams of the Institute for Social Research, University of Michigan, that "racism can affect health by giving rise to racial discrimination at the individual and institutional level" (*International Journal of Health Services*, vol. 26, no. 3, 1996, p. 497), and the racial unrest within educational institutions.

Despite the downplay by many, racial hatred in the United States remains explosive. Many Americans choose to believe that racial incidents are infrequent and isolated, but in reality, blatant and physical acts occur repeatedly throughout the nation. Part of this rude awakening to this national epidemic can be realized from the following incidents that occurred over just a five-month period: (1) On May 4, 1997, a 62–year-old Korean American woman was thrown against a wall and kicked by a white male in his twenties shouting racial obscenities, after she walked out of a bookstore in San Francisco's Union Square. She had to have a hip replaced while the assailant remains at large (*San Francisco Chronicle*, 9/9/97). (2) In Virginia on July 25, 1997, two white men dragged 40-year-old handyman Gainett P. Johnson from a trailer, doused him with fuel, burned him alive, and beheaded him (Associated Press, 8/27/97). (3) On August 9, 1997, Abner Louima, a 33-year-old Haitian immigrant, was beaten by New York City police officers. The officers shoved the wooden handle of a toilet plunger into Louima's rectum, causing a ripped bladder and punctured lower intestine. This abuse was followed by their forcing the plunger into his mouth while shouting racial epithets (*New York Times*, 8/13/97). (4) In Kansas City on August 22, 1997, Liza Costa of Cape Verdean descent experienced a cross-burning episode on her front yard. Ironically, Costa had held racial prejudices against blacks and hadn't realized that many whites view anyone with dark skin as unacceptable citizens (*Kansas City Star*, 9/8/97). (5) Three white teenagers used a baseball bat and a steering wheel lock to beat Kevin Teague, a 27-year-old black man, as he walked from a subway station in Carroll Gardens, Brooklyn, to his home (*New York Times*, 9/22/97). (6) A retrial was ordered for the white officers who stopped Jon Gammage (31 years old) for a flickering brake light in Brentwood, Pittsburg (1995). He suffocated while the officers restrained him (Associated Press, 10/5/97).

In the "Summary of Hate Crime Statistics for 1997," the number of race-related incidents far outweighed crimes related to religious and sexual orientation. The number of incidents for anti-black crimes was 3,120 compared to anti-white crimes of 993; keeping in mind that whites in the United States comprise about 76% of the population and blacks about 13% (Almanac Society–Law Enforcement & Crime, 1997). Racial incidents continue to occur in the United States, with nationally publicized incidents such as (1) the James Bryd Jr. murder (Jasper, Texas) of whites dragging Bryd two miles by automobile until his death in June 1998; (2) the murder of Charles Lovelady, 26 years of age at the time of his death, said to have been beaten to death by two nightclub bouncers on February 26, 2000, in Des Moines, Iowa ; in the wake of his death two Des Moines men have filed a race discrimination compliance grievance with the Iowa Civil Rights Commission against six local nightclubs (Lee Rood, *Des Moines Register*, 4/16/2000); and (3) the February 25, 1999, shooting of African immigrant Amadou Diallo, shot at by New York City police 41 times, with 19 shots hitting their mark. The four police officers involved claimed to have misinterpreted Diallo's reaching inside his pocket, believing he was retrieving a gun, rather than his his wallet to exhibit his identification. All the officers involved were acquitted (*Time Magazine*, 3/6/2000).

Additional numerous incidents involve what is known as racial profiling by police. Racial profiling and minority victimization by state troopers persists and continues to be debated in places such as Trenton, New Jersey. It was a case in New Jersey that helped bring racial profiling to national attention, introducing to white America the acronym DWB—"Driving While Black." New Jersey state troopers stopped a van carrying three men of color. During the stop the van began rolling backward toward one of the troopers. The troopers fired 11 shots, wounding all three men (*New Jersey: North*, 9/8/99). The U.S. Justice Department is currently investigating state police discrimination allegations against New Jersey, Florida, Maryland, Connecticut, and other states (Associated Press, 4/21/99).

On the education front a professor of law teaching race relations courses, Lino Graglia, of the University of Texas (UT), insisted that the black and Mexican students of his university enter college through the lowering of university standards. He stated that "blacks and Mexican Americans are not academically competitive with whites in selective institutions" (*Houston Chronicle*, 9/16/1997). Consenting to become a faculty advisor for a student anti–affirmative action group, Professor Graglia teaches that students of color are not motivated academically because they have cultural deficits—this is, despite the fact that numerous scholars of color have graduated from UT. Continuing in this vein, within academic papers Professor Glayde Whitney of Florida State proudly asserts that blacks are generally less intelligent than whites (McMurray, Associated Press, 4/19/99). If such misinformation is taught within educational institutions, what is the fate of future racial harmony and justice? And what about teachers who view children of color as lowly objects? Consider these incidents: (1) A teacher in North Charleston, South Carolina, wrote with an indelible marker, "Where are my glasses?" on the face a five-year-old girl. A similar case was being investigated in South Carolina's Aiken County, where a teacher wrote on a young boy's face because he was late for class (*South Carolina News*

Summary, 10/23/97; Associated Press, 1/8/97). (2) A teacher in Cambridge, Massachusetts, taped her third-grade student's mouth (*Cambridge Chronicle,* 3/27/97; *Boston Globe,* 3/20/97). (3) Another kindergartner was placed in the rest room as a "time out" for his disruptive behavior and was made to eat his lunch there (*Des Moines Register,* 2/22/97).

Students themselves carry out racist practices, such as the three teens who wore Ku Klux Klan costumes to school in Clifton Forge,Virginia (*U.S. News,* Associated Press, 4/1/1997). In Torrance, California, at West High School, students of color were appalled at the joking manner of white students during a mock slave auction activity (Associated Press, 11/4/97). More recently Eric Harris and Dylan Klebold, students claiming to belong to the "Trenchcoat Mafia" opposed blacks, Hispanics, athletes and others, to the extent that they went on a shooting spree killing 13 people and wounding 23 others before kill-ing themselves at Columbine High School in Littleton, Colorado, on April 20, 1999 (*APBNews.com,* 5/15/2000). With the existence of such racial violence, discrimination, and insensitivity, how can all students feel safe, respected, and academically motivated in schools?

Blatant atrocities such as those mentioned above are matched by devastat-ing subtle forms of racism that threaten the academic success of students of color. One recent incident is the controversial tests in Massachusetts. These high school graduation tests were criticized because of high failure rates among blacks and Hispanics (*USA Today,* 11/26/99). As a result, the U.S. Department of Education is expected to review the state's new exams to deter-mine if the tests indeed discriminate against minorities. Prejudice, stereotyp-ing, and discrimination exist through the very denial of racist acts and attitudes and through biased education, policies, and hiring practices. These factors are present in schools, where they adversely affect student learning and develop-ment. Students of color in U.S. school systems are generally the targets of rac-ism (Donaldson, 1996; Murray and Clark, 1990). As it is used here, the term *students [people] of color* typically identifies and links racially oppressed cultural groups. For example, African American, Latino American, Asian American, American Indian students—all students of color—have experienced bigotry and unequal access to education because of their darker skin color, ethnicity, or race (Donaldson and Verma, 1997).

Although this book offers outlooks on racism from a variety of educational studies and projects, it pays particular attention to successful re-education for teachers in order to make a difference for students. It reports actual data show-ing that teacher development in antiracism can affect what teachers do in the classroom strongly enough for students to notice the difference. Most studies of teacher education collect data on the impact of teachers; and very few re-search studies measure the affect of teachers' professional development on stu-dents (Nieto, 1999; Donaldson, 1997). What matters is not so much what the teachers learn but what their students learn as a result and that we offer re-search on that.

This book highlights multicultural education as antiracist education and concentrates on teacher education in this context. Antiracist teacher education data connect staff development with student learning. Three main ideas inter-weave throughout this book: (1) how teachers (in-service and preservice) think about race, (2) what strategies work to develop their thinking and ability to implement antiracist teaching, and (3) the impact antiracist education has on students. The research approaches used for this book include quantitative (e.g., data interpreted through statistical programs), qualitative (e.g., recogni-tion of common themes or patterns through the collection of various tran-scribed interviews, etc.), and action (e.g., educators study their classrooms, students, schools, school districts, parents, and/or communities in order to improve their teaching practices) research.

Various research genres are infused in a holistic attempt to view perceptions from numerous angles. For example, ethnographic approaches (participatory lessons, storytelling, dramatic scripts, focus group interviews, etc.) are used to grasp the depth of what teachers and students feel about their experiences in understanding racism and its implications. Whereas written surveys (t-tests, ANOVAs, regressions, path analyses, frequencies, etc.) reveal numerical evi-dence that despite the geographical region, many teachers believe that racism exists in schools, but they admit not knowing how it is manifested.

Shattering the Denial: Protocols for the Classroom and Beyond features a geo-graphical antiracist education teacher study conducted in four regions of the United States over a two-year period. To address antiracist education efforts from a nation wide viewpoint, racial awareness, attitudes, and antiracist educa-tion intervention among 512 teacher participants from different parts of the country are explored. Teacher profiles, antiracist curriculum development and implementation strategies, as well as student responses to the implementation, and student-designed antiracism curriculums are presented. One purpose of this book is to demonstrate the degree of racism in schools and society. A fur-ther aim is to demonstrate that educators and students can be proactive against racism, thereby becoming change agents to assist in the reduction of racism.

This book will specifically speak to, but is not limited to, the issues of *white racism* and institutional racism in education. *White racism* is a term that delin-eates the role of European and Caucasian American white culture as collectively oppressing people of color and controlling the wealth and power of the United States (Feagin and Vera, 1995; Sleeter, 1994). White racism is tied to institu-tional racism through the gateway of white majority dominance of power and control. Nieto (1992) states that "institutional racism is manifested through es-tablished laws, customs, and practices that reflect and produce racial inequalities in society" (p. 37). Recognizing that students of color are generally the victims of racism and that they perceive racist attitudes more from white teachers, this book strives to bring antiracist teacher studies to the forefront to encourage ed-ucators at large to reduce racism and to impress upon white teachers to take ownership of and responsibility for their own antiracist education and growth, as they are the majority both within the study and within public schools through-out the United States (87.2%; National Center for Education Statistics, 1990–91). It is important to address here the issue of teacher-student racial and cultural misunderstanding and mistreatment. It is, however, also important to note that white educators are not by themselves synonymous with racist prac-tices in schools. Multiple studies reported in this book confront the practice of racism in schools from grade school through college. *Shattering Denial* presents antiracism models for the classroom and beyond.

The book is divided into three parts with one to five chapters in each section. In Part I (chapters 1–5), "Shattering the Denial: A Geographical Antiracist Edu-cation Interdisciplinary Curriculum Development and Implementation Study with K–12 Teachers," provides baseline figures of teacher perceptions about rac-ism in schools. It reviews the five data collection components of the study: a pre and post race awareness survey for teachers, an antiracist pilot curriculum hand-book (instrument) for teachers, focused group antiracist education workshops with midpoint surveys, and implementation action research. Furthermore, these components of the teacher study are analyzed, with major findings pre-sented. A central finding of this study was that regardless of region, teachers were in great denial. Hence, the title "Shattering the Denial" seemed an appro-priate choice. The majority of white teachers were resistant to the term *antiracist education*. Perceiving that the term implied "against whites," sug-gesting that whites are the sole cause of racist acts in the United States, white teachers generally refused ownership of personal bias. Their lack of self-aware-ness, their racist conditioning, and their failure to recognize the racist experi-ences of others impeded their recognition of racism in education.

The Geographical Antiracist Education Teacher Study was created because of the requests of many students who wanted to have teachers assessed and re-educated. They wanted teachers to implement antiracist concepts in regular classroom settings (Donaldson, 1996). The researchers took these requests one step farther to explore whether the teacher-participants' enhanced knowl-edge of racism in schools, curriculum development, and actual practice would make a difference to schoolchildren; it did.

The research team succeeded in that exploratory journey with teachers which circled back to benefit students with the help of ongoing findings from the race awareness teacher survey (baseline of how teachers perceive racism in schools), antiracist education staff curriculum development workshops, and the monitoring of the implementation process. For teachers who participated in the implementation segment of the study, we were able to administer pre and post student surveys in their classrooms.

Chapter 4, about a few courageous teachers, documents 11 teacher profiles taken from the final one-to-one interviews. These profiles exhibit proactive at-titudes toward addressing racism in schools. Although 512 teachers com-pleted the pre and post surveys, general denial explained why only 8–15 teachers per region volunteered for antiracist education workshops. These teachers became cohort groups in the study. For the most part, these cohort group members displayed some form of kinship to diversity efforts. Featured in this section are 11 teachers from the midwest and northeastern regions. These teachers went on to implement antiracist education strategies in their classrooms and in guidance settings.

Pre and post surveys were disseminated to the students of these teachers. The results of the student survey indicated that proper intervention does produce change in the classroom, certainly not change the students appreciated. The findings from the student pre and post surveys, as well as antiracist teacher implementation video analyses, will be discussed in this section.

Chapter 5 attempts to bring the teacher study full circle. The teacher study was motivated by requests to re-educate teachers made by students involved in previous antiracist studies. The students' hope was to make teachers aware of how racism negatively affects student learning and development, to address racist conditioning with teachers and others, and to discover ways to develop and implement antiracist education within basic subject areas and special programming. Each teacher who completed the implementation process by conducting antiracist education lessons and/or units had students participate in a pre- and posttest survey entitled *Student's Perceptions of Teacher Race/Diversity Awareness* (see Appendix A). In this way we were able to examine the effect antiracist teaching has on students.

To understand the organization of this book (e.g., moving from students' requests to re-educate teachers, to an awareness and methods study for teachers, and then back to students' perceptions of their teachers after the re-education process), a brief sample of the findings of the pre- and posttest given to the students will now be mentioned.

Using the Likert scale model, we attempted to bring the antiracist teacher study, a re-education experience, back to students through a students' perception survey of their teachers implementing antiracist curricula. The student survey consisted of ten statements (see Appendix A), among them Q2, I feel comfortable around my teacher(s); Q4, My teacher(s) use classroom activities that reflect the history and contributions of my racial group; Q5, I respect my teacher(s); Q6, My teacher(s) won't allow students to make jokes or talk bad about people who are not of the same race; and Q7, My teacher(s) only pay attention to students who are the same color that he/she is. The objective of this survey was to measure students' perceptions of teacher race relations and antiracist curriculum implementation in the classroom setting before and after implementation.

Analyses were conducted using SPSS-X mainframe version 4.1. The frequencies were listed by school in terms of the percentage of student agreement with each question. The breakdown begins with a total sample pretest, total sample posttest, students of color pretest, and students of color posttest. Responses from the students were separated into two groups for the analyses. The two categories, children of color and Caucasian children, were necessary in that this study was conducted to discover the presence of racist behaviors by teachers toward students of color. Whereas it has been found in earlier studies that children of color are often targets of racism (Murray and Clark, 1990; Lee, 1996; Donaldson, 1996; Daniel-Tatum, 1997), we were interested in detecting differences between the responses of the children by race. Consequently, t-tests were conducted to assess differences between the two groups prior to and immediately following antiracist curriculum intervention by the cohort teachers and the principal and by on-site investigators.

Through the pretest we found that students of color did not feel as comfortable around their teachers as did their white counterparts in this study, and they did not feel that their culture's contributions were mentioned enough in the classroom. The results overall suggest that there are strong discrepancies between the satisfaction levels of students of color and Caucasian students in predominantly white scholastic institutions.

Only one test question remained significant after the intervention (i.e., Q1, My teacher(s) mention contributions made by people of color in class). The implication here is that proper intervention does foster attitudinal change and appreciation in the classroom. Such change may result in increased interest and belongingness for children of color, especially for those who are in predominantly white educational settings. Nationwide, this could serve to reverse many of our nation's downward trends in race relations.

The student findings presented in chapter 5 encouraged the efforts produced in Part II. These following sections adhere to the view of many multicultural education scholars such as Sonia Nieto, James Banks, Christine Sleeter, Carl Grant, and Christine Bennett that the total school environment—that is, students, teachers, administrators, parents, and the community—must contribute to the empowerment of the education of students by "many means necessary"(adaptation of a quote by El-Hajj Malik El Shabazz [Malcolm X]).

Part II (chapter 6), "Students Empowered by the Antiracist Teacher Study," demonstrates the impact that antiracist education can have on students. This chapter describes specific courses designed and implemented by the principal investigator, in specific contexts. The implications of these course discoveries suggest what can be done at the secondary education level to assist teachers to recognize which teaching processes make the most difference when attempting to present an antiracist curriculum.

The secondary level was selected because many high school students have reported that multicultural concepts are often omitted during these last years of required schooling, a time when such students are especially interested in social action–based curriculum.

This section initially investigates disturbing findings presented by a Time/CNN poll that racism does not affect the education of U.S. students. It explores an experimental antiracist human relations 15-week course taught at a high school within one of the regions of the study. Classes were videotaped and used as an instructional tool for participating teachers. In this segment of the book the human relations course content will be presented for teachers wanting models for implementation. Furthermore, this section examines the "difficulties and elation" of teaching and learning antiracist education. Ultimately, we are trying to meet students' needs regarding multicultural acceptance and learning. This section discusses what can happen when we do that and explains why we need knowledgeable teachers if we are to reach students.

The course was followed by a drama production for a national multicultural conference. Students from the course and from the drama class of a teacher-participant (Geographical Antiracist Education Teacher Study) performed antiracist education vignettes for multicultural educators from across the country. Along with the students' original script is a description of the grueling process of working on issues of racism.

It is essential to connect all levels of education (Teacher Education, Education Administration, and K-12 Education) if we are to penetrate and shatter the denial of racism. In Part III (chapters 7–9), "Protocols for the Classroom and Beyond," higher education and primary education are the focus. Antiracist education projects on a college campus are described to demonstrate the ability to make a difference within Teacher Education. Part III also includes descriptions of an antiracist education experimental graduate course, a faculty antiracist education project, international field trips in an antiracist-multicultural education study abroad program to South Africa, and an experimental antiracist-multicultural education K-6 research project. This section pulls together the antiracist education studies and programs presented in this book with one common theme, to demonstrate strategies and research that develop consciousness and abilities to implement antiracist teaching. It focuses on issues educators grapple with regarding multicultural teacher education, distance learning, and the impact that antiracist-multicultural education has on student learning and development. As mentioned previously, interspersed between parts of the book is the personal "voice" of the author. The conclusion ends with this "voice" in an appeal to open the doors of discourse, research, and practice. It follows with implications and recommendations for shattering the denial of the devastating effects of racism on students and society.

Throughout the book anonymity is maintained. This book aims to present issues, strategies, and research in antiracist education from the point of view of educators, students, schools, and society, both at home and abroad. To expose or point the finger at participating schools and educators is not necessary because attitudes and situations are similar nationwide and beyond. The purpose is to expose the deep, ingrained existence of racism in schools and suggest solutions for eradicating it.

The unique aspect of this book is that all the antiracist education projects and research were generated by the efforts of the author. This book attempts to demonstrate the unlimited possibilities to change racist views and actions;

beginning with just one person and one idea, change can take place. Of course, a multitude of people have participated in these efforts, and in the case of the antiracist-multicultural experimental school research project there is a co-principal investigator, Professor Carlie C. Tartakov. Nonetheless, the content will render an unusual approach to the scholarship of this book in that I as the author served as a researcher, teacher, curriculum developer, concerned citizen, and parent of four public school children. These roles will demonstrate various styles of discourse in this presentation, such as that of parent, that of empirical researcher, and that of antiracist-multicultural scholar-practitioner. As with *Through Student's Eyes: Combating Racism in United States Schools* (Donaldson, 1996), this book reaches out to all educators, secondary and college students, and the general audience.

I

Shattering the Denial: A Geographical Antiracist Education Interdisciplinary Curriculum Development and Implementation Study with K–12 Teachers

Teachers are some of the most dedicated professionals in the world, yet the societal conditioning of biases often prevents them from successfully educating all students. This section will focus on the two-year (1995–96) Geographical Antiracist Education Teacher Study administered in four regions of the United States. The importance of exploring various regions was to discover any differences in attitude and to investigate which particular region had developed and implemented models of antiracist education that other regions could emulate. Instead, we discovered that the school district selected for each region had its own particular resistance toward antiracist efforts; and where there were state mandates for multicultural education, gross neglect of curriculum integration existed at the school level.

Within each region there were distinct forms of denial of racist attitudes presented by teachers. For example, many of the northern region teachers believed they were exempt from racial bias because the North had historically been liberal and recognized as a "great supporter of the abolishment of slavery," whereas teachers in the southern region, much more conscious of racism because of the nation's accusation of southern racial hatred during the civil rights movement of the 1960s, were working hard at reducing it. The western region teachers perceived that their demographic pluralism made it impossible to be racist. Teachers in the midwest, in contrast, thought that because they were not as racially diverse as elsewhere in the nation, they lacked the opportunity to be racist.

On a number of occasions we found one or two teachers committed to eliminating racism, but they were without full staff support and frequently felt alienated by others. Often these were teachers of color, who were frequently accused of being overly sensitive about the issue of racism in schools, or white teachers fitting a liberal profile because of their positive experiences with diversity.

One finding was that teachers working on the individual level incorporated antiracist-multicultural concepts directly in their classrooms without advertisement, fought in staff meetings for greater diversity efforts by the school, and/or grew discouraged and bitter that their efforts could not make change in isolation. Study strategies that seemed to combat these disappointments were professional development that included the positive role of whites in antiracist-multicultural education; awareness of students' perceptions of racism in schools; experiential exercises to dismantle bias conditioning; open, nonthreatening discussions of responsibility; examination of stages of racial development and understanding the doling out of privileges and penalties within society; and knowledge enhancement of antiracist-multicultural theoretical, philosophical, historical, and practical foundations. The study ultimately created cohort groups of teachers who felt more empowered by this "ally" approach.

The process of the Geographical Antiracist Education Teacher Study included pre- and posttest surveys, focus group antiracist workshops, and follow-up implementation support in the classroom. For those teachers who went on to attend the workshops, much was revealed in the awareness segments, such as childhood racist experiences making an impact on adult life, anger, disappointment, disbelief, and tears of relief for being allowed to get things out in the open.

Chapter 1 begins with background information on the rationale and guiding research questions for the Geographical Antiracist Education Teacher Study. Further, it presents an introduction of the study instruments, the methodologies, and social context of the study. Chapters 2 and 3 focus on the instruments in detail, the actual process of administering the study instruments, direct teacher responses, and major overall findings. Chapter 4 features the profiles of teachers who implemented antiracist teaching practices.

Voice of a Parent:
Caught in the Midst of It

My heart cries out to see the pain racism has caused my children and other children. To hear them be called names, shut out, stereotyped, and sometimes physically attacked because of their race has fueled me with the fervor to stand up and stand strong. I recall the day I was forced to sit my four youngest children down to explain what they couldn't understand—racism—for their protection at school and in the neighborhood. I wondered how many white parents had ever been forced to discuss racism with their children before the youngsters could really understand it? I thought perhaps that because they had never seen the tears and pain some children have to go through, they never realized that *"it"* exists or how important it is to end racism and other prejudices.

Reflecting on this "race issue" took me back to my own childhood experiences: 1960s elementary school in the black community, a rundown school operated by an almost all-white teaching staff and administration with low expectations of students and resulting lowered self-esteem in students; middle school (Catholic school), same lowered expectations scenario, except corporal punishment was added; high school, with a volunteer busing program to a suburban white school with daily ridicule from students, teachers, and the local community, and later a public high school bordering the black community and the poor white community. Most of the teachers there despised or ignored the black and Latino students. Reprieve in the late 1970s to 1980s! I sent my eldest son to African-centered (Afrocentric) schools; he was taught to be proud of his heritage and his brilliance. Yet now, living in a predominantly white setting, my other four children struggle to maintain their identity in the school setting where they seldom see themselves reflected in the curriculum. I ask myself, how many whites are forced to see racism synonymous with school as I do?

As a parent I am a stakeholder, and as an educator I hold myself accountable to assist in the reduction of racism in our schools. Many educators are parents whether we have children of our own or wear the hat of a parent while teaching in the classroom. All parents, teachers, and the total school environment are stakeholders of educational institutions. We can stand together to reduce racism in schools by seeking to uncondition our own racist views and by requiring our schools to enforce rules of tolerance and equity. We can see to it that our children receive education that is antiracist and multicultural. And in whatever capacity we are able to stand up against racism, we must. By sharing the personal pain of racism, the voice of this parent is seeking to open the door for other voices to join in and help to make this more of a nationwide effort; the hatred that hurts many of us today will eventually hurt all society.

This parent has been given the opportunity to share information on the presence of racism in our schools from the student and teacher point of view. Part I spreads the word on the ways in which many teachers are responding to racism in schools today, in most cases denying the devastating effect it has on student learning and development. As a parent, I know that attitudes will not change without our strong voice present. The research in this section will, I hope, "shatter the denial" of educators, educational institutions, and the total school environment, thereby enabling us to move forward in the reduction of racism in our schools and in society at large.

1

A Description

Many teachers, having lived the privileged side of racism, do not or cannot accept that they have internalized racist attitudes. Because they truly believe that they are inherently better than the students they serve, they transfer those beliefs to the students. This may or may not be a conscious act; however, the students end up disliking school, the teachers, and themselves. In my opinion, it all boils down to respect. We must, individually and collectively, practice respect for all ethnic groups. Different does not mean wrong or inferior; it means different. (northeastern high school teacher, reflection notes, June 1996)

RATIONALE

The sentiments of this teacher echo the concern of numerous students facing racism in schools today. Directly or indirectly, students from all major racial ethnic groups—American Indian, African, Latino, European, and Asian American—have reported discomfort, anger, depression, embarrassment, decreased interest in school, isolation, and so on, as a result of the presence of racism in schools. These observations stem from nearly two decades of antiracist education work with elementary and secondary students. A number of studies on student views of racism in schools also acknowledge the presence of these negative effects (Donaldson, 1996; Lee, 1996; Murray and Clark, 1990).

The Geographical Antiracist Education Teacher Study (1995–96) follows a student study that sought to identify how students perceive racism and its effects on student learning and development (Donaldson, 1996). The qualitative student study included focus group and individual "telling their stories" interviews, as well as action research through a social action project. This student study was requested by a northeastern school district after a race relations survey of 2,000 eighth and eleventh graders indicated that 88% of the student respondents perceived racism in their schools. Major findings of the qualitative student study included that racist attitudes and institutional racism (1) belittled student self-esteem, causing diminished interest in school; (2) pressured and heightened students' perceived need to overachieve academically; and (3) made students, especially European and Caucasian American students, feel guilty and embarrassed at seeing other students victimized (Donaldson, 1996).

This student study concentrated on approximately 40 secondary students who were high academic achievers of various cultural backgrounds. The advantage of working with this group was that it helped to dispel the myth that racism is an imaginary occurrence. Each of the students interviewed had humiliating experiences with racism; this was a contradiction to the popular belief that students of color use racism as an excuse to fail or to give up on schoolwork and that white students are not affected by racist teaching practices.

Students in the qualitative study identified teachers as greater threats of racist attitudes than their school peers. For the most part, this is because they felt educators were in authority positions and were seldom questioned about their cultural know-how or sensitivity. Yet, aware that teachers are facilitators of learning and spend the most time interacting with them in schools, students perceived teachers as direct conduits of racist ideals and treatment (Donaldson, 1996). It was for this reason that the Geographical Antiracist Education Teacher Study was designed.

As educators committed to ensuring that all students receive an equal and comprehensive education, we must further evaluate the effects of educators' racism on students and the ways to combat them. With the development of antiracist education curriculum and assessment instruments for educators in several geographical areas, movements toward reducing racism in schools create greater opportunity for change and become more widespread.

STUDY AND METHODS DESCRIPTION

The Geographical Antiracist Education Teacher Study used both qualitative and quantitative data. Data were collected and analyzed to address some of the following research questions shown in Table 1.1.

In retrospect these research questions were prompted by inquiries and investigations done in previous student studies. Numerous teachers are doled bias curricula to teach, or they enter the teaching force tainted with stereotypi-

Table 1.1
Research Questions

QUESTION 1	Is there a change in teachers' attitudes toward racism during the study or after exposure to curriculum?
QUESTION 2	Is there a difference in attitudes toward racism by geographical area?
QUESTION 3	What problems do teachers have implementing antiracist curricula?
QUESTION 4	What forms of denial are common among white teachers, and what strategies seem to get them past denial?

cal views, along with other racist conditioning. Therefore, it was essential to begin by examining teacher attitudes about racism in schools. Understanding that we live in a racist society, the decision to do a geographical study could assist in discovering if there are differences in attitudes according to region and, if so, learning how to help educators dismantle racism in schools based upon their own region, state, and district needs. As this study was formulated, prior research and experiences guided the need to develop questions that would explore, introspectively, the role teachers play in continuing racist attitudes and schooling and whether or not staff development intervention could make a difference for teachers and students. We are aware that teachers have reservations about teaching multiculturally and addressing biases such as race discrimination. In addition, in many parts of the country teachers deny the existence of racism. We understand that these issues exist, but to what degree? What attitudes and inabilities to implement antiracist teaching are we specifically dealing with here, and what will spark change? Through the investigation of the above research questions, perhaps concrete evidence can be made available to heighten the efforts for change, and perhaps the requests of many students to have their teachers assist in the reduction of racism in schools would be more forthcoming.

The methods of data collection and analysis included statistical inquiry (frequencies, ANOVAs, regressions, t-tests, and path analysis), teacher workshop focus group interviews using the Sorenson and Sweeney model (1995), individual interviews and "telling of stories" (Lancy, 1993; Seidman, 1991; Guba and Lincoln, 1989), action research (reflective field notes of the teacher implementation component) and "Teachers Are Researchers" (International Reading Assn., 1993), and a video ethnographic and tool approach for recording field notes and behavioral observations.

The purpose of using the varied aspects of methodologies and investigation was to fully examine common themes and issues regarding the major research questions. The common themes and comparison approach used within each of the data collection methods helped to solidify these findings. Using various research methodologies helped to strengthen the empirical evidence that is needed to address the paucity of formal research. These sundry investigative methods assisted in the expansion of sound evidence in this area, opening a bit wider the door to scholarly discourse on teachers' perspectives of racism in schools and what teachers are willing to do about it. For those teachers willing to become change agents, this approach encourages determining what kind of professional development would give them confidence to address the issues squarely and to introduce antiracist concepts in their classrooms.

To explore the research questions selected, a series of study instruments and components were devised. Each component explored the study research questions, but in its own ways. Because these components contain volumes of data, it was best to present our research findings through the instrument or components rather than by framing the findings under each of the study research questions. Furthermore, the components include social context, preparation, and content information, enabling a holistic approach to viewing research and practice. The findings of this study are organized according to the sequential order of the study components, and the research questions are addressed within each of the components presented. Common themes and comparisons of the various sets of data are analyzed, and major findings highlighting the research questions are documented. Table 1.2 highlights the instruments and components used.

These instruments were given in five sequential stages. A brief overview of the stages and instruments follows.

Table 1.2
Assessment-Study Components

1	Teacher Pre + Post Racism Awareness Surveys
2	Antiracist Curriculum Guidebook for Teachers (reflection sections after each chapter; four chapters included)
3	Antiracist Education Teacher Workshops (Focus Group Interviews took place during each workshop; Video Analysis used)
4	Implementation (including Pre and Post Student Surveys to measure teacher implementation success by students' perceptions; and a Midpoint Survey for Teachers was also distributed)
5	One-on-One In-depth Interviews for Teachers (who completed the above four components; action research journals were also collected at this time)

(1) Teacher Pre and Post Racism Awareness Surveys

The purpose of the pre and post racism awareness surveys was to acquire racial views of teachers with regard to self and institutional awareness and to measure ideological movement, if any, after intervention. In addition, the aim was to compare the cohort groups receiving intervention to teachers who participated only in the race awareness survey (see Appendix B).

(2) Antiracist Curriculum Guidebook

The teacher review component began the intervention process that would continue until the end of the study. The unit was co-designed by high school students and approved for testing by curriculum validators (experts in the field). Teachers could choose to continue to this phase after the completion of the survey. The Antiracist Curriculum Guidebook consisted of four chapters with reflection response pages after each chapter. The chapters were (1) "Examining Attitudes about Racism," (2) "Racism in United States Schools," (3) "Racism from the Student Perspective," and (4) "Antiracist Lesson Ideas for K-12 Schools." Media teachers were asked to review antiracist lessons developed from the unit during this time in order to measure the feasibility of creating a similar software unit (see Handbook Questionnaire, Appendix D).

(3) Antiracist Education Teacher Workshops with Focus Group Interviews

Interested and available teachers followed the review of the unit handbook with three to four antiracist education workshops. Each workshop was designed to follow the sequence of the unit. Hands-on, experiential activities were used to draw upon the empathy of the teachers and to demonstrate strategies that could be adapted for their own classrooms. Focus group interviews were integrated into the workshops as reflective session discussions. Midpoint surveys were given during the administering of this component in order to consider any suggestions and/or issues from the teacher-participants (see Midpoint Survey, Appendix C). A video analysis was also conducted. Workshops and teacher implementation were videotaped and analyzed. Body language—behavioral reactions—were recorded as per focus group interview literature. Verbal discussion and interaction were also transcribed for analysis.

(4) Implementation Sessions with Pre and Post Student Surveys

The fourth component allowed teacher-participants to chose the length of unit implementation to be observed and assisted. Furthermore, their students completed pre and post surveys (before and after the standard curriculum adapted–antiracist units were presented (see Appendix A).

(5) Teacher One-to-One Final Interviews

The teachers in the study were interviewed following their unit implementation. The interviews lasted 1 1/2 to 2 hours and focused on unit preparation, implementation, student reaction, and effect of the professional development workshops (i.e., how the workshops assisted or limited the success of their unit implementation). Action research journals reflecting on daily class outcomes were also collected at this time.

Background Information

The study instruments were developed at Iowa State University (ISU) (a research 1 institution). The principal investigator (Donaldson), serving half time in the Research in Education Studies (RISE) Program of the College of Education (1995–96) solicited the research design capabilities and staff support of the RISE Program. The Teacher Race Awareness Survey was designed with the assistance of this program and validated by statistical faculty, staff, and pilot-testing dissemination. In addition, the ISU Department of Curriculum and Instruction Multicultural Education Program faculty, including Theresa McCormick and Carlie Tartakov, and other national multicultural and antiracist education scholars such as Sonia Nieto (University of Massachusetts, Amherst) and Beverly Daniel-Tatum (Mount Holyoke College) assisted with review and validation. This particular group reviewed and validated the teacher survey and the pilot antiracist education teacher handbook on the accuracy of content and needed exploration in the field.

Data collection was made possible through graduate research assistants with specializations in multicultural education and educational testing and through the Diversity Consultants Network (DNC), Amherst, Massachusetts; also both teams served as on-site investigators. These teams worked to disseminate and facilitate education workshops, surveys, interviews, and field observations made through video notation entries.

Through the various research resources, a pilot study was conducted to gain reliability for the study instruments (Donaldson, 1996); 119 teachers participated. The pilot study was administered between March 1995 and June 1995 in the northeastern and midwestern regions of the United States. The pilot study encouraged the feasibility of administering an official study because it revealed significant findings, such as that many teachers acknowledge the existence of racism in schools and that antiracist education is a key to addressing this problem. Furthermore, many teachers denied that racism is manifested in biased curriculum and instruction, but those who participated in the curriculum components tended to change their view.

The pilot study branched into the official study, which began August 1995 and ended June 1996. The goal of the official study was to broaden teacher participation, thereby developing greater baseline figures. The aim of the wide coverage was to discover and compare outlooks and needs of U.S. teachers in a variety of geographical settings with diverse population demographics. All the study instrument components remained intact, with slight modification made in accord with the pilot study analyses and recommendations.

SOCIAL CONTEXT: AN OVERVIEW OF THE OFFICIAL TEACHER STUDY

The Geographical Antiracist Education Teacher Study was a two-year research project. The purpose of the study was to explore and enhance teacher awareness of racism in schools, as well as to provide and research instructional alternatives to monocultural education. The purpose was also to examine the abilities of teachers to address racism within themselves, their students, the curriculum, and the total school environment. Furthermore, the study was to create baselines regarding how teachers perceive racism in schools and to develop ways of dismantling racism through antiracist education curricula.

The official study included research and data collection in four regions of the United States: northeastern, midwestern, West Coast, and southern. Within these regions, the study included responses from teachers in urban, suburban, and rural schools. The goal of this wide coverage was to discover and compare outlooks and needs of U.S. teachers in a variety of demographical settings.

It is important to note that even the process of finding schools willing to become involved in the project told something regarding attitudes about racism. There were many obstacles to getting the different regions to participate. In the Northeast, two predominantly white suburban school districts decided to postpone and eventually cancel the antiracist study in their areas. This was because racist incidents that had occurred in both school systems had subsided and racial discrimination lawsuits were settled; school administrators feared bringing racial issues to the forefront once again. This is the "If it isn't broken, why try to fit it?" syndrome that is pervasive in school districts throughout the country. In addition, financial considerations were often the argument; for instance, arranging for teacher substitutes was said to be too costly.

When the first choice for the Southern region was approached, the curriculum superintendent accepted our invitation. He agreed that there was a need to assess the attitudes of teachers regarding race and to assist them with developing antiracist curriculum. Later he was advised by the school board committee to decline the invitation. In confidence, the superintendent explained that although his school district consisted of 70% black students, approximately 40% black teachers, and 50% black administrators, the school board committee (all white) maintained control of the major decisions for the district. The researchers then attempted to locate a school in a second southern state; and again, although the district-area superintendent agreed to do the study, because of the racial tension in her district, her superior advised her to refuse. The third southern state we approached agreed to participate in the study. Six years earlier, its state supreme court had ruled the public school system unconstitutional, thereby proposing the Education Reform Act to give every child in the commonwealth an equal opportunity to have an adequate education. In many regions of the state, the Confederate flag remains strongly embraced, and white supremacist views and actions often threaten the well-being of teachers and community activists who promote antiracist views. The goal of the state and federal laws to provide an adequate education, in these cases, often omits "age-old" racist promotion and practices.

In each of the regions the teacher-participants represented all grade levels and disciplines: 344 were female and 155 were male, and their ages ranged between 21 and 70. The teachers' racial makeup consisted of 340 European and Caucasian Americans (70%), 33 African Americans (6.8%), 32 white Hispanics (6.6%), 24 Latino(a) Americans (4.9%), 13 Asian Americans (2.7%), 2 Native Americans (.4%), and 10 who reported "other" (7.6%). The teacher participation breakdown by region was as follows: (1) Northeast, urban school district, 63 teachers (12.3%); (2) Midwest, urban school district, 190 teachers (37.1%); and Midwest, rural-suburban school district, 50 teachers (9.8%), (3) South, suburban school district, 103 teachers (20.1%); and (4) West, suburban school district, 106 (20.7%). A close participation balance was produced regarding urban and suburban participation. These cross-cultural characteristics, coupled with the varied geographical locations, provided an opportunity to gather diverse views of teacher attitudes about antiracist education.

The following four chapters feature the Antiracist Education Teacher Study findings and are arranged in the sequential order of the study components. For example, chapter 2 focuses on the Teacher Race Awareness Pre and Posttest major findings, chapter 3 highlights the Antiracist Curriculum Unit development work done by teacher-participants who reviewed and participated in the awareness and curriculum methods workshops, chapter 4 features teacher implementation profiles gathered mainly through in-depth interviews, and chapter 5 presents the students' view of the teacher implementation segment. Each of these chapters helps to address the main research questions presented in the Antiracist Education Teacher Study. Chapter 2 addresses change in teachers' attitudes before and after exposure to the curriculum, reflecting attitude differences according to region as well as the pervasive denial found among white teachers. Chapters 3 and 4 respond to all the research questions, especially those asking what strategies appear to help teachers move beyond denial and those pinpointing problems teachers experience attempting to implement antiracist curricula. Chapters 5 and 6 focus on student perspectives and empowerment gained by the Antiracist Education Teacher Study. Students were found to be the driving force in assisting teachers with overcoming denial, as we will come to recognize in Part II, chapter 6.

2

Teacher Race Awareness Survey

OVERCOMING RELUCTANCE

Five hundred twelve teachers volunteered for the first component of the study, which was the preliminary race awareness survey; of these, teachers 243 completed the posttest. The majority of the teachers asked to participate in the survey did so with great reluctance. In fact, the process of gaining permission, recruiting volunteers, and disseminating and collecting surveys is an important aspect of the study because it became a method of early detection of antiracist education resistance throughout a number of regions in the United States.

In order to begin the first phase of the study, superintendents, research departments, and school principals all had to give their permission. In most cases superintendents and principals who approved the study failed to advocate to their staff the need and importance of participating; as a result, the task of getting teachers to volunteer rested with the team of investigators.

The antiracist education team consisted of a principal investigator-developer, a project analyst, and six on-site investigators. Often team members would be allowed to make appeal presentations to teachers during staff meetings. The presentations were carefully delivered in order to avoid contamination of the study, but teachers required justification of its importance. Therefore, in as general a way as possible investigators highlighted the need to share individual views and experiences with racism in order to assist in countering students' perceived negative effects of racism on learning and development. As teachers raised their hands to receive the survey, investigators frequently heard expressions of dissatisfaction such as "This is waste of time, what good will it do?" "Teachers are blamed for everything that goes wrong in a school" Or "Yeah, we're all thought to be racist, so why bother with these surveys?" This resistance continued during written completion of the surveys.

The survey addressed the opinions of teachers in areas such as racism awareness in self and others, racial biases in curriculum and instruction, racist childhood experiences, and interest in reducing racism in schools. These constructs were congruent with the major research questions for the overall survey. The survey consisted of 34 statements with a Likert scale answer format. The survey items were validated by Dr. Gary Downs, Professor of Curriculum and Instruction, and the RISE Program at the College of Education, Iowa State University.

The six possible responses to each statement included 1 = strongly disagree, 2 = disagree, 3 = somewhat disagree, 4 = somewhat agree, 5 = agree, and 6 = strongly agree (see Teacher Race Awareness Survey in Appendix B). Since 79.7% of the 512 pretest teachers who responded to the survey agreed that racism existed within most schools, it was puzzling to witness teachers hesitating to confront issues of racism, responding angrily, or detaching themselves from this social disease. Many teachers felt a need to add comments along the survey margins. These comments revealed a tremendous amount of denial. A number of teachers sought to place blame elsewhere. For instance, some remarked that the survey was flawed. One added to the scale "7 = survey flaw," and such comments as "you need a professional to help you with formal definitions [referring to Myer Weinberg's definition of racism (1990) that it is a system of privilege and penalty based upon one's race]." This respondent suggested, "Also see *affirmative action*," and he gave a "7" rating to statement 14, "Racism affects students' learning and behavior in numerous ways." For the demographic section he described himself as "other" American, and for age he listed "old." On the bottom of the survey he wrote, "Such a wasted opportunity."

A number of the respondents had difficulty understanding the term *students of color*. In most cases this term was defined before the survey was disseminated by the investigator; nonetheless teachers defensively replied, "Are there people with no color?" Another demonstrated his racist views as he stated in response to statement 14 that "students of Asian heritage might be considered of color but they are succeeding in school due to family influence." Many of the respondents often took offense to the ethnic identification section. Many preferred to be called "white" or "American." However, one opposite view was shared, "Just for the record I find your ethnic categories inadequate [the categories were standard U.S. Census Bureau ethnic identifications (U.S. Department of Commerce, Bureau of the Census, 1997)]. I am of Irish/Swedish descent and do not consider myself 'European.' If we must categorize maybe the 'other' category is the only one we should have." Perhaps this concept is a useful one because scientists now say that we have over 2,000 racial mixtures in the world today (*Prejudice: Answering Children's Questions*, ABC Broadcast,

1994), but including all these racial ethnicities on demographic surveys would be extremely difficult. School systems and other institutions grappled with revising racial and ethnic categories as the U.S. Census Bureau prepared the Census 2000 (Statistical Policy Directive No. 15). The directive proposed slots for Hispanic subgroups such as Puerto Rican, Cuban, and Mexican American/Chicano; at least 10 subgroups for Asians; tribal affilation for Native Americans; white; and black, African American, or Negro categories (white and black are still recognized as one-dimensional). Yet, biracial persons were allowed to check more than one box, and a "some other race or ethnicity" section was also included. Despite the fact that for many race is seen as a social construct, we must remember that discrimination on the basis of race (skin color) still exists and that one rationale for creating a racial-ethnic census was to ensure that racially oppressed groups are afforded equal opportunity for employment, education, and housing.

STATISTICAL TESTS

The statistical tests administered in this study addressed all the research questions quantitatively. The tests were able to probe results for explaining differences of attitudes toward racism by geographical area, forms of racist denial that exist, changes in attitudes after exposure to antiracist education staff development, and problems that prevent teachers from implementing antiracist curricula. The statistical section is organized according to each statistical test explored.

The statistical tests results, produced by project analyst Anthony Stevens, will be presented in part, along with infused qualitative reflections by the author. Very often the legitimacy of multicultural and antiracist education as an academic discipline has been challenged because of the lack of empirical research. Although the concept of antiracist and multicultural education dates back to the works of such scholars as Carter G. Woodson (mid- to late 1800s) and W.E.B. Du Bois (early 1900s), national recognition in public schools did not begin to take place until the late 1960s. Education scholar-practitioners such as James A. Banks, Carl A. Grant, and Geneva Gay began to lay foundations for teaching multicultural education in schools during this period, but these disciplines remain a part of our new century's curriculum reform movement. Understanding this progression, we must remember that antiracist and multicultural theoretical frameworks are new in comparison to other areas of disciplines practiced within U.S. curricula for several centuries.

This section attempts to further demonstrate that research is important to those of us in the field of antiracist-multicultural education. With these data we are able to indicate perceptions, create baselines, test models, and gain support for future courses for teachers and antiracist-multicultural education integration in all schools, grade levels, and subject areas.

The teacher pre and post race awareness survey statistical analyses included frequencies, ANOVA, structural equation modeling, t-tests, and regressions. To prevent alpha inflation problems and thereby results that would be contaminated by capitalizing on chance, only the most pertinent questions were addressed in our analyses. We chose those questions capable of "telling the story" of the individual's racist views (or lack thereof) and racist curriculum at once. The project analyst used the interitem correlation technique to measure the scale's internal consistency (reliability). The alpha coeffient was equal to .83 and was considered acceptable. Many "well-established" questionnaires hold alpha coefficients equal to .80 and are deemed reliable (Anastasi, 1988).

DEMOGRAPHICS

Most participants were white females (67.2% of the total) who taught at the high school level (40.9% of the total). The remaining ethnic categories were African American, White-Hispanic American, Hispanic-Latino American, Asian American, and Native American (American Indian) teachers (listed in descending order).

It must be noted that in essence, in this study we were dealing mainly with white adults in the teaching profession. Most survey participants recognized the existence of racism in schools but not the avenues through which it surfaces or the devastating effects racism has on student learning and behavior, especially of students of color. If many of a nation's individuals fail to learn the most basic skills (e.g., reading and math), then we should not expect the *nation* to thrive. If teachers maintain racist ideals or choose to ignore racism, so the ultimate learning environment cannot be created to ensure the success of all students, then should we expect the *nation* to thrive? This is the question that must be asked by all who desire to teach in these United States.

ANALYSIS OF VARIANCE (ANOVA)

Given the large number of ways to interpret data, ANOVA models were used to analyze differences between groups on selected questions. Only those tests that resulted in statistically significant findings are reported. The results of the ANOVAs are explained in the following sections.

Birthplace

An effect was found for the birthplace of the interviewee in relation to response to question 25, "During your teaching career, you unintentionally made a racist/stereotypical comment to a student, parent, or fellow teacher" (F, 5, 468 = 3.6888, p = .003). Mean scores for the regions indicated that teachers from the South reported the strongest disagreement with this statement, followed by teachers in the East, internationally born teachers, and then teachers in the West and the Midwest. Note that all of the mean scores are below 4, indicating that all of the teachers report rarely if ever making racist comments.

Various data collection by geographical area permitted several distinct forms of denial to surface—denial as a result of fear, isolation, race solidarity, disempowerment, and so on (Sleeter, 1994; Feagan and Vera, 1995; Daniel-Tatum, 1997). The geographical study revealed these attitudes: (1) Northeast, "Liberal states are less likely to have serious racist attitudes"; (2) South, "We are always accused of racial bigotry, for many of us those times have changed," and "White superiority views are ingrained from one generation to the next; therefore it is a matter of white pride and not intentional racism"; (3) Midwest, "Not much exposure to diverse settings, therefore we are ignorant of having racist attitudes"; and (4) West, "We are a multicultural state, how can we be racist?"

Additional action research exploration of geographical differences in attitude and cultural experiences may assist in drawing further conclusions. Data collected from field notes and observations indicated that the southern teachers tended to be more cognizant of racist practices. This may be attributed to the nation's attention to southern states regarding their historical struggles to maintain the institutions of slavery and segregation. Yet, often attitudes of white superiority made it impossible to recognize personal racist statements. Instead, such statements are frequently seen as "a fact of life." In the case of the Northeast, teachers repeatedly held on to the liberal "impossible to be racist" attitude. For example, "It was the North that fought against slavery." "Slavery was not practiced in the North." "My parents taught us that we were all equal." And "Minorities are too sensitive when it comes to race issues." Many northeastern teachers felt that their students exaggerated racial remarks or incidents. In contrast, the teachers from the West pointed out that the diversity of their state made it nearly impossible to be racist and that there existed more intraethnic (i.e., Korean vs. Japanese) or interethnic (i.e., Mexican and African American) hostility than white racism.

On one survey from the Midwest, a teacher responded with an additional comment in the margins, "Would I know [if I made a racist or stereotypical comment]?" This may be a true reaction for other teachers as well, who have not been exposed to antiracist education. Middle and high school students and teachers of color often affirm this possibility when they consistently remarked that "most white teachers haven't got a clue on the racist comments they make" or that "many teachers are ignorant when it comes to recognizing racist attitudes and behavior."

Ethnicity

An effect was found for question 3, "Racism is largely manifested in schools through biased curriculum and instruction" ($F, 4,456 = 4.783, p = .000$). The lowest three mean scores were from Asian, European American, and Caucasian teachers in that order (white teachers varied their identification within these two latter classifications). Furthermore, their mean scores were well below those teachers whose ethnicities were African American and Latino American. For the most part, the white teachers (and the small sample of Asian teachers) did not recognize the racial biases present in schools, nor did they see how those biases alter the success of students.

Region

A significant effect was found for region and question 3, "Racism is largely manifested in schools through biased curriculum and instruction" (F, 4,456 = 2.61, p = .035). Teachers from the midwestern urban school district disagreed with this statement the most (mean = 2.69), followed by the southern suburban school district (2.73) and the West Coast suburban school district (2.97). The most disconcerting fact here is that none of the means for the four regions analyzed manifested means above 4, the minimum level of agreement. These teachers apparently do not grasp that racism can be manifested through curriculum or instruction.

A significant effect was found for region and question 4, "Racism exists within most United States schools" (F, 4,456 = 3.557, p = .007). Here the midwestern suburban teachers scored higher than all others, with a mean score of 4.98. They were followed by the northeastern urban teachers, then the West Coast, the midwestern urban, and the southern. Contrary to question 4, a significant main effect was found for region and question 5, "Racism in schools ended with the civil rights movement of the 1960s" (F, 4,456 = 4.073, p = .003). The mean scores on this question were very similar for all the groups. Midwestern suburban scored the highest, with a mean score equal to 5.76, followed by the midwestern urban teachers, West Coast, northeastern, and the southern. All the groups scored in the "agreement" range with means over 4. This agreement implies that all the groups believe that racism ended in the 1960s. With question 4 indicating the opposite view, teachers were contacted randomly, without code identification, to investigate how the question was interpreted. The original intention of the survey developer was to solicit further explanation of the respondents who disagreed with question 4, asking whether they thought racism ended in the 1960s with the civil rights movement (Q5). Instead, many respondents interpreted question 5 to mean that segregation and blatant racism ended with the civil rights movement.

The ANOVA results point out limitations of administering an "untouchable topic" quantitative survey. Interpretations can vary, and without deeper probing results can often be uncertain. Understanding these possibilities, we used various statistical tests, as well as qualitative and action research.

T-TESTS

The data were coded so that categories would exist for the cohort variable. The group means were then analyzed for pre- and/or posttest differences on pertinent questions for the intervention group. The value of that practice lies in the identification of significant attitudinal or belief change for those teachers exposed to proper intervention. The statistically significant findings (questions one and three) are as follows:

Question 1: Racism Is Defined as a System of Privilege and Penalty Based on One's Race

A significant positive change occurred in the understanding of the definition of racism for the teachers who participated in the intervention group. Keep in mind that this is the definition employed by multicultural education teaching professionals (Weinburg, 1990). Their pretest mean score of 4.46 changed to 5.17, indicating that the definition of racism was clarified for them by the intervention(s) these teachers did. Such intervention should be sought out by our school officials if the racism epidemic is to be quelled.

Question 3: Racism Is Largely Manifested in Schools Through Biased Curriculum and Instruction

In this test a significant difference was found between the pretest mean scores of the teachers who participated in the intervention(s) and those who did not participate. As might be expected, the teachers who participated had the higher of the two mean scores (3.55 vs. 2.80). However, there are two problems with this fact. First, the teachers with the lowest score did not receive the intervention. Feasibly, their score would be the same today as it was when they were given the pretest survey. Second, a score of 3 indicates that the person "somewhat disagrees" with the statement, whereas a score of 4 indicates that the person only "somewhat agrees" with the statement. So, both groups of teachers failed to agree convincingly with this statement before the intervention, and only a small group received any intervention.

REGRESSIONS

It is often desirable to determine how well a variable or attribute may be predicted from another for a particular sample. Given the nature of the present research, several regression equations were tested to determine if attitude or behavior predictions would be possible for an intervention group subsample.

Question 25, "During your teaching career, you unintentionally made a racist/stereotypical comment to a student, parent, or fellow teacher," was used as a dependent variable with questions 1, 3, 4, 5, 6, and 27 serving as independent variables. Significant regression weights were found for question 1,

"Racism is defined as a system of privilege and penalty based on one's race," and question 4, "Racism exists within most U.S. schools." The regression weights (standardized) were .274 and .700 respectively. The p values were equal to .04 and .001 respectively. In both instances awareness of racism (Q1 and Q4) is most likely enabling these teachers to understand racist comments.

It should be noted that for the total sample, not just for the intervention group, there were significant regression weights for question 4, "Racism exist within most U.S. schools," and question 27, "As a child, your family members promoted racist beliefs" (using question 25 as a dependent variable). The standardized regression weights were .199 and .238 respectively. The p value was .001 in both instances. This is a telling find. Question 4 in essence deals with a teacher's awareness of racism. Therefore, it is understandable that the more teachers agreed with question 4, the better they understood question 25. That is, teachers who are aware of the racism in U.S. schools would also be aware of their own racist comments. The reverse would also be true.

Question 27 deals with a teacher's personal experiences with racism. Regrettably, the more teachers experienced racism at home, the more they engaged in racist activity. To stop racism, then, we should focus intervention at the home and family level as well.

STRUCTURAL EQUATION MODELING

The unique capabilities of the linear structural relations program (LISREL) were used to determine the paths of nine constructs resulting from a factor analysis of the questionnaire. LISREL is considered by many to be the most general program available for estimating structural equation models and can be used to analyze data from surveys, experiments, or even quasi-experiments (Hayduk, 1987). LISREL allowed us to pose a "pictorial theory" about the relationships of our constructs and then revamp that theory in stages.

The predictor constructs are (1) childhood racist experiences, (2) racism awareness, (3) antiracist education, and (4) awareness of the impact of racism in schools. The predicted constructs are (1) racist teaching tendencies, (2) awareness of antiracist teaching techniques, (3) openness to antiracist teaching aids, (4) awareness of antiracist curriculum, and (5) openness to antiracist curriculum. These nine constructs served as the infrastructure by which we were able to model the relationships between participant attitudes and awareness (predictor constructs) and racist outcomes (predicted constructs) (see Appendix E). The Goodness of Fit index for the model was equal to .981 ($p = .418$) with an Adjusted Goodness Fit index equal to .916 and a root main square residual equal to .032. We viewed the indices as proof that our model represented the depicted relationships very well.

QUANTITATIVE SUMMARY

In summary, the quantitative analyses allowed many unique perspectives to be uncovered by this research. We have gone to great lengths to give as detailed a quantitative report as we dare without boring the reader with useless numbers. Too often researchers in education are criticized for their lack of empirical research. It is apparently believed by many that "numbers do not lie." Numbers may not lie, but we must admit that they can be misinterpreted. As we moved forward with our research, we found that the qualitative findings were supporting the quantitative findings and vice versa, and each was serving as a sounding board for the other. Lest critics misunderstand the importance of that statement and accuse us of bias, it should be known that the project analyst did not conduct the qualitative portion of the research. Nor was he aware of the principal investigator's hypotheses until the data were analyzed. We believe, therefore, that what we have "discovered" and reported in this research is a true and stable social phenomenon.

These are social phenomena that must be attended to. To recap, we have found that in the teaching profession here in the United States, there are professional people who are aware of racism in our schools but are not aware of the avenues through which racism is manifested in our schools. These individuals are unlearned of those avenues to the degree that they are unaware that they themselves engage in racist behaviors. We also found that the racist environment in our schools may be positively affected by the intervention of antiracist professionals capable of addressing racism with teachers and administrative personnel. Finally, the reported significant regression weights showed that those individuals who understood the formal definition of racism also knew that they had made racist comments in their past. The reverse of this is the root of the problem; perhaps those who do not understand what racism is are racist and do not know it. This is one of the problems we want address.

As whites were the dominant group within the study, the underpinning research question, "What forms of denial are common among white teachers and what strategies get them past denial?" is examined poignantly through the statistical tests. For example, we were able to determine that white teachers, especially, did not recognize the racial biases present in schools and the negative effects that biased attitudes have on schoolchildren. Yet, through intervention many white teachers are able to conclude that their possible racist biases and comments link to learned behavior and racist conditioning and/or upbringing. A learned behavior, spawned by a racist society, is nothing to be personally ashamed of. This release of personal guilt allowed white teacher-participants to address the issue of denial more openly.

3

Antiracist Curriculum Development
Work with Teachers

This information provides us all a way to look at ourselves and how racism ef-fects us. (northeastern elementary teacher, curriculum guidebook re-sponse, 1996)

INTRODUCTION

This chapter begins with the *Antiracist Education Interdisciplinary Curricu-lum Guidebook for K–12 Teachers* (henceforth abbreviated and referred to as the curriculum guidebook), the second assessment component of the Antiracist Education Teacher Study. This section presents the rationale for us-ing this method of inquiry, a description of the curriculum guidebook with validators' feedback, the process of dissemination of the instrument and meth-odology, and teacher-participants' reflective review of the curriculum guide-book (assessment and study component data). This chapter also includes the third assessment component, "Antiracist Education Teacher Workshops." A design description of the workshops, methods for collecting data, and findings that relate to the major research questions are documented.

WHY THE CURRICULUM GUIDEBOOK COMPONENT?

Racism is a leading deterrent to the educational success of students of color and threatens the well-being of our nation. In a curriculum and implementation study it is imperative to have samples of curriculum to be tested by curriculum experts, teachers, students, and others. Moving beyond the Teacher Race Awareness Survey preliminary assessments, the curriculum guidebook assisted interested teachers in filling the void in becoming more proactive antiracists. Many educators have revealed that because the topic of racism has been "taboo," little attention has been paid to wholeheartedly addressing the issues of racism in school. Therefore, a curriculum guidebook for instructors is important to help them see the degree of need to accomplish self-awareness and infusement strategies for the classroom.

It was important to use this method of inquiry for the reasons stated above. In addition, this method was the tool used to actively begin the qualitative intervention. The curriculum guidebook component was the next step in exploring each of the study research questions.

A DESCRIPTION OF THE UNIT GUIDEBOOK WITH VALIDATORS' FEEDBACK

The curriculum guidebook consisted of four chapters: (1) "Examining Attitudes about Racism"; (2) "Review of Racism in U.S. Schools"; (3) "Racism from the Student Perspective"; and (4) "Antiracist Lesson Plans for K–12 Schools." After each chapter, open-ended reflection pages followed, enabling teachers to critique each of the sections. The guidebook was approximately 75 pages in length, with double-spacing for participants to write editing suggestions between lines.

Chapter 1 of the curriculum guidebook incorporated a number of activities that I often use in multicultural-antiracist college courses and in-service teacher professional development seminars, such as "Building a Racist Society" (an activity designed by the Council for Interracial Books), which allows participants to create an imaginary society, giving power to the dominant group through perceived superior characteristics, customs and laws. However ridiculous the imaginary societies seem to be, they always contain elements of privilege and penalty (oppression) reflective of the realities in our actual society. Participants are asked to reflect on deliberate laws and customs in our society that weave racist views and practices, and so on. This chapter also highlighted activities from *Living Our Commitments: A Handbook for Whites Joining Together to Identify, Own and Dismantle Our Racist Conditioning* (Fry, 1990). Participants were asked to recall their first encounter with a racist act directly or indirectly and tell what they did, if anything, as a response to witnessing or experiencing this act. Other activities such as imagining a world without racism and what it would take to make that happen, as well as creating a timeline of activities to help reduce racism, were included. In addition, the Stages of Racial Identity model created and adapted by Beverly Daniel-Tatum for participants to review was in this section.

Chapter 2 of the curriculum guidebook featured the research documented in *Through Students' Eyes: Combating Racism in United States Schools* (Donaldson, 1996). The purpose of this chapter was to allow participants the opportunity to understand how pervasive racism is in schools today and how students are affected by it. Chapter 3 used the same book as chapter 2, but highlighted students' social action approaches to address racism in schools. The intention here was to motivate teachers, using the efforts of students, to become multicultural and antiracist. Chapter 4 of the guidebook consisted of two lesson plan ideas dealing with understanding the roots of racism from the American Indian (Native American) and African American perspectives and experiences. The guidebook appendices included other suggestions for lessons, resources, and articles addressing racism.

The design of the curriculum guidebook sought to define antiracist education, share research on the effects of racism on student learning and development, and heighten awareness of racist conditioning and the need for understanding the racial identity development stages of various racial and ethnic groups. The high school students involved with antiracist education social action endeavors suggested examining the historical roots racism from various cultural perspectives in the United States and proposed ideas for lesson plans, all strongly supported by the curriculum developer. Suggestions from validators (Prof. Sonia Nieto of the University of Massachusetts, Amherst, and Prof. Carlie Tartakov of Iowa State University) and pilot study teachers assisted with the further development of the guidebook for the study.

Changes and suggestions were slight. For example, one of the validators suggested obtaining more facts on the ethnic groups, such as contemporary experiences for Latinos; another suggested using "Americas" in place of "New World," to change "Hispanic" to "Latino(a)" and "Native American" to "American Indian." The validators also suggested incorporating modern views of the government's relationship to American Indian nations and the impact of historical events today. Teachers reviewing the curriculum unit during the pilot study expressed satisfaction with all the chapters and were grateful to have such a guide to expose racism through research and to give solutions through antiracist education strategies.

PROCESS OF DISSEMINATION OF INSTRUMENTS AND METHODOLOGY

During the Teacher Race Awareness Survey, teachers were further encouraged to sign up for the curriculum, workshops, and implementation phases of the study. They were asked to put a check mark at the right-hand corner of the survey if they were interested in reviewing the antiracist curriculum guide for teachers, which was the beginning phase of the next study component. Only 42 teachers of the 512 participants volunteered (not including 22 mandated elementary teachers and support staff) for the curriculum guidebooks and the antiracist workshops. With such a small sample of volunteers, a dismal outlook for the number of teachers interested in enhancing antiracist education techniques for the classroom and discovering ways to reduce racism in schools became evident.

Sixty-four guidebooks were distributed to the teachers who signed up for them, but only 16 were returned with comments. Teachers were invited to write critiques and ways to share the ways that they were able to use the guidebook. Many of the teachers who did not return the guidebooks on time requested to keep them longer.

The curriculum guidebook component made various stages of control group development apparent. For example, some teachers only did the Teacher Race Awareness Survey; others did the survey and reviewed the curriculum. The next control group completed the survey, reviewed the curriculum guidebooks, and attended the workshops. The full-treatment group (cohort groups) participated in the surveys, review of curriculum guidebooks, workshops, and implementation. The approach of varied control groups was a natural response to the levels of interest demonstrated by the participants in the Antiracist Education Teacher Study. As a qualitative component of the research, the study was able to have flexibility and build upon the availability and interest typical of the participants. As most of the school administrators advocated a one-step-at-a-time approach for the volunteering process, before distribution of the Teacher Race Awareness Surveys we could not anticipate how the volunteering process for the other components would go. Would all the survey participants volunteer or just a few? There was no way of knowing this, until after completing the preliminary surveys. We could not anticipate how the control groups would materialize.

With each control group we were able to examine how level of exposure enhanced the antiracist-multicultural education knowledge base of the teachers. The second-level control group (survey and curriculum guidebook reviewers), which included participants from various geographical regions, gives a glimpse of teachers' technical and personal outlooks on antiracist curriculum guidebooks for teachers.

Some general teacher-participant comments about the curriculum guidebooks were as follows: (1) Pages 3–5, *Definition of Terms,* was considered very good information. (2) Chapter 1, pages 8–12 and exercises were usable at the middle school level to make students aware but would need to be simplified. (3) Pages 19–20, *Common Stereotypes,* and pages 52–60, *Let's Stop Racism in Our Schools* script, could be used at the eighth grade level and above. (4) Pages 62–74, *Antiracist Education Lessons K–12,* could be adapted to their subject areas: "This section was useful to me. My concentration as an English teacher might be to emphasize literature, poetry, plays written by authors of other backgrounds (I would appreciate suggestions for sources of such literature)." Another English teacher, of African American descent, said that the guidebook "motivated me to use even more multicultural resources than I currently use.

It motivated me to use various teaching strategies and to look at myself more closely." In addition, she said, "I would include additional exercises for people of color who are educators. These exercises could serve as a tool to help us remain focused while dealing with racism on a daily basis." It became apparent early on that based on race and cultural differences, there would be significant differences in the way teachers perceived and/or experienced the components of the study.

Teachers reviewing the guidebook also answered quite candidly with regard to racist conditioning that affected their lives. For instance, when asked if they had ever successfully tried to interrupt racism, many made statements such as "No, tried but to no avail." When asked what next steps they would take to end racism, some replied, "Trying to communicate with others [adults] but not so easy." Another teacher (African American) wrote, "Though I've only been teaching for three years in the public school system, I have pledged to educate myself regarding other cultures and share that knowledge with my students. From an economic viewpoint, we are in a global society where the more diversely we prepare future leaders of this and other countries, the more successful they will be. They must understand and take part in a highly competitive and interdependent world society. By miseducating our students, we are doing them a great disservice and we, as educators, will be, and should be, held accountable." One teacher commented in her curriculum guidebook, "Some of the implications on society if we do not change racist ideals are death to a nation, racial genocide, civil war/disobedience, and negation of wondrous possibilities."

Many teachers did not have time to participate in the next phases of the study but held on to the guidebooks. It was presumed that because the teachers retained the guidebooks, they must have been interested in them. Study evaluators preferred to collect the guidebooks with comments. However, teachers were permitted to keep them because the guarantee of anonymity of study participants made it difficult to enforce returns. In addition, some teachers signed up for guidebooks but never stopped to pick them up from the main offices. Again, these situations influenced the control group approach.

Participation was categorized according to willingness to "build antiracist education skills," the lowest being completion of pre- and posttests, and highest was the implementation of antiracist education in the classroom. Researchers worked with teachers as far as they were interested in going. In some cases, this meant co-teaching antiracist education concepts within general subject areas in the classroom to lessen teacher anxiety about teaching multiculturally.

Through the review of all the guidebooks turned in, second-level teachers displayed some movement in change of attitudes toward racism. Common themes were drawn out according to their reviews and analyzed based on the research questions of the study.

The idea of providing teacher-participants with a curriculum guidebook that addressed self-awareness, national research, and sample antiracist education lessons assisted in creating further ideological movement. It also indicated problems that teachers have with implementing antiracist curricula. One issue was feeling as if there was insufficient time to develop new philosophical and pedagogical strategies for teaching; another was that the work is sensitive and too difficult to tackle. White teachers at this stage continued to demonstrate denial that racism was manifested through a biased curriculum, but the guide-book appeared to challenge these beliefs. Overall, the teachers who reviewed the guidebook said it was informative, and this was a start.

ANTIRACIST TEACHER EDUCATION WORKSHOPS

The curriculum guidebook was used to frame each of the workshops, and assignments from the handbooks were given. Each workshop focused on each of the four chapters in the guidebook in sequential order. The workshops were conducted by the researchers, who were diverse facilitator professionals. Workshops were scheduled according to school district, school, and workshop volunteer teacher arrangement requests and lasted anywhere from two to four hours each, depending on what the teams could handle. Some schools used professional development funds or grants to gain paid release time; others used staff meetings and/or volunteer evening meetings.

At this point, each geographical region set up its own arrangement for staff development workshops. According to these arrangements, each region received more or less time for professional development. The teams of teach-ers who attended the workshops became known as the antiracist teacher co-hort groups of the study. Table 3.1 indicates each geographical region's level of involvement.

Seven cohort groups were created: (1) an urban northeastern high school; (2) an urban northeastern elementary school; (3) a suburban southern school district (varied grade levels of teachers); (4) an urban West Coast special educa-tion middle school; (5) a midwestern suburban school district (varied grade levels of teachers); (6) a midwestern urban secondary schools (two high schools and one middle school); and (7) a midwestern urban elementary school. Group membership ranged from 7 to 22 teachers in a group. The co-hort groups varied in the number of seminars that they received. Often grants would not cover all the release time requested, or the number of staff meetings allowed would be limited.

DESIGN OF THE WORKSHOPS

The design of the workshops was a hands-on awareness and methods ap-proach using the curriculum guidebook as a syllabus of instruction. Samples of workshop activities included the "Africa to America" lesson done during the first workshop, to look at the roots of racism from another culture perspective. This workshop was created over 12 years ago and has been done with at least a

Table 3.1
Regional Antiracist Workshop and Implementation Cohort Groups

Northeast	• Completed all components • Variations: ex: 3 workshops, shorter implementation • Teacher designed units—less effective (worked in isolation)
Midwest	• Completed all components • Variations: ex: 4 workshops, longer implementation • Team teaching of units—greater effect; leadership confidence
West	• Completed all components • Variations: ex: 2 workshops • Alternative school; different approaches used • Teacher units not designed or implemented
South	• Did not complete all components • Variations: ex: 2 workshops • Late start and no financial support to complete study

few hundred groups, most often with outstanding reviews. The significance of using dance was to exhibit various teaching strategies that can be taught in the classroom to reach out in different ways to all students. The teachers learned of African culture, became an African extended family, and reenacted a West African village during the kidnapping of Africans to labor in the New World. The workshop began with a celebration dance that was interrupted by raiders (both black and white). Participants were put into imaginary chains and forced into the hull of the slave ship. Arriving at their destination, they were sold on the auction blocks "like a piece of meat" and then forced to work on plantations from sun up to sundown without any compensation and without freedom. The workshop sought to give a hands-on experience using the arts and physical movement to create empathy for the racist treatment of African people. It sought to enable participants to understand racism as a system of power, privilege, and oppression. Discussions centered on the roots of racism as the foundation for racist practices today. Workshop 1 also highlighted antiracist education student and teacher research, definitions, implications, and methods to reduce racism in schools through curriculum and instruction.

Workshop 1 had the same content for each region. Workshop 2 included a recap of the first workshop, activities such as "*Building a Racist Society*" and "*Perceptions*" (self-awareness activities taken from the handbook), "*Ethnic Studies Exploring Five Major Ethnic Groups in the U.S.*," and antiracist curriculum development small group work with sharing of ideas and goal setting.

The antiracist workshops also used visuals, such as films, to further demonstrate and discuss issues with the teacher-partcipants. Teachers were exposed to students' views, through antiracist education student performances and student interviews, and to contemporary films, such as *The Chamber* and *A Family Thing*. In sharing video excerpts of *Let's Stop Racism in Our Schools* by Students against Racism in Schools (SARIS), teachers were able to grasp the depth of anguish that students experienced because of racism in schools. Often teachers would reply that hearing the students' voices helped convince them that racism was an epidemic plaguing many students. This had been the intention of the original SARIS group from the student antiracist study project (Donaldson, 1996), which aimed to make students' voices heard by teachers, administrators, and counselors. Excerpts from *The Chamber* assisted in discussions about extreme and generational racist conditioning by the Ku Klux Klan; and *A Family Thing*, in which a middle-aged southern white man finds out that his mother was black, brought forth dialogue on racial identity. Revelation of this heritage "shook up" and eventually changed the man's whole being and way of thinking.

DATA COLLECTION

The purpose of the third Antiracist Education Teacher Workshop component was to assess how the active intervention process could make a difference in addressing the major research questions. Data collection consisted of audio- and videotaped focus group discussion and interviews. The use of video for critique and analysis is a highly effective curriculum and research tool. We were able to document and code differences and similarities regarding points of view and the participants in practice. Each set of data from the Antiracist Teacher Education Workshop component was transcribed and analyzed using a common theme approach and was searched for differences according to region and ethnicity. The workshop component data are reported by geographical region. For the benefit of understanding the needs of various regions regarding re-education for teachers, a comparative geographical analysis will be drawn at the end of this chapter. Differences and similarities in the "learning and teaching" aspects of antiracist education curriculum development workshops will be discussed. The following section will begin with the southern and West Coast regions.

THE SOUTHERN REGION

The southern and West Coast regions are the focus here, as they were the regions to receive less time for staff development and for the most part did not complete the implementation component. Focusing on these regions from the start may explain why these areas did not continue. The southern and West Coast regions revealed interest, but policy, budget, and administration shaped the extent of their participation in the study. This order of reporting mirrors the organization of the study findings. For example, the southern region had the least participation for the workshop component of all the regions and consequently had the least data. The West Coast followed.

The suburban southern school district participated in two workshops but did not, for the most part, return the guidebooks or Midpoint Surveys (distributed generally after the second workshop) and/or complete final interviews because we expected to conduct a third seminar.

The southern cohort used the workshops to understand racism in schools as a national problem and not just for their state or community. They dialogued openly about their perceptions about race, some going deep into the history of their racist upbringings and how to rid stereotyping promoted by them and their students. Some of those stories included being raised in Klan territory and taught to embrace the Confederate flag, or understanding the isolation and hurt that black schoolchildren felt as they were required to sing school songs about pride in the Confederate flag, Jefferson Davis, and so on. The one African American teacher in this cohort group was able to share the isolation he had felt while actually attending the district high school as a student. Sharing these stories gave great insight: Teachers were becoming more sensitive and more interested in infusing antiracist curriculum. This school district was predominantly white middle class and had few experiences with teaching students of color; but witnessing increasing integration, they felt it necessary to become prepared. During the two workshops teachers realized that antiracist and multicultural education is for all students, not just for students of color.

THE WEST COAST REGION

Originally 94 teachers from the West Coast participated in the pre and post study surveys. The area cluster leader, an on-site school district administrator, was instrumental in getting schools involved. Despite her efforts, only eight teachers volunteered to engage in the seminars from the West Coast suburban area school district, and only one teacher out of eight attended the first scheduled seminar. This teacher said, "One of the main reasons why the other teachers changed their minds about coming was because other school teachers reacted negatively to them signing up." The teachers who did not show up feared there would be repercussions for affiliating with antiracist education training. When asked why she came, this teacher said she was free from the fear of alienation and backlash because she was due to move back East in a week's time. Given this poor turnout, researchers turned to the special education school that volunteered for the workshop data collection.

The special education school director strongly encouraged all her teachers to participate. This school was a public alternative school. Special education programs and schools warrant antiracist education investigation because of the disproportionate number of students of color referred to such programs throughout the United States. This was also the sentiment of the school's director. Student makeup was 95% African American. Many of the students, she felt, whose behavior was often misread, belonged in mainstream schools. Furthermore, there was a diversity awareness imbalance regarding instruction. Since they entered the study late, however, time and funding ran out before additional workshops could be given. Although this West Coast cohort had little time by the end of the study to review the guidebook, cohort members were interviewed about their workshop participation. (The following names are pseudonyms to protect the identity of the participants. Three partial West Coast interviews reveal sentiments about the first workshop:)

Stacey. Most of my experience is in early childhood. I've been teaching about eight years; I'm Hispanic. Having mostly African American students influences my lesson plans, especially since this training. I'm taking a multicultural education class and it's bilingual and I'm trying to bring understanding to all students. I haven't had time to implement the antiracist component yet since we just had the workshop last week, but it has made me more aware of how I present things. I recognize that there is a problem with racism so I was interested in the study. I needed ideas for the population I'm working with. My impression of the questionnaire, my reactions: well it was asking questions about all different areas of teaching and where racism could show up. I hadn't seen that before. The workshop was touching on things like eye contact and not being aware of cultures. It was different than racism discussions in textbooks. The antiracist workshop gave me a lot of hands-on training and more information for going to students and finding out how far back this started. I found it very eye-opening and uplifting. We all said we wanted more of these.

Can the workshop be an aid to teachers? I can see it definitely helping me. I don't know if that would be the majority response. I could say that I think it can help. Overall, I was impressed; overall, I was motivated. I would like to learn the handbook and use that information. I do think that the whole package should be marketed to the general public. I like the way our facilitator presented it, so maybe it could be videotaped. That would be nice. I do think that our school should pursue funding for this. I also know that there is funding out here.

Sam. My areas are behavioral management and I've been teaching approximately eight years. I'm from Nigeria originally. My interest in the study? If the topic is not well presented the students do not respond to it. Having the antiracist topic taught in a positive way is best. That way the students do not have to learn about this in a negative way. If we design the curriculum correctly then it will be understood, and it must reflect all of the ethnic groups. I thought the workshop was wonderful and great. It should be taught in all the schools. Me? Yes, I do think I'll have a positive impact on other teachers' antiracist learning. I don't have any plans for developing my own antiracist works, but it is possible that I could collaborate with others. I think that the products here should be packaged because they are good for the students. I also think that funding would be cost effective.

Monica. I'm the director of the school. I specialized in bilingual education K–middle school previous to being here. I've been teaching for seven years. I'm Caucasian, but I've worked most with Latinos. I'm bilingual, and I feel real comfortable in that setting.

The students' background definitely influences my selection of materials for the classroom. I'm not in the classroom right now, so I haven't taught anything for quite a while. I won't be implementing the antiracist techniques because I'm not teaching. [Here she did not realize her role and influence to implement antiracist education techniques administratively and through her teachers.] My interest in the study was sparked by the fact that I've seen a lot of multicultural curriculum over the years but I hadn't seen any antiracist. When I saw the antiracist I thought that was a new twist to it and that it should be interesting. I'd never put the two together—the reason we do the multicultural is to become antiracist. I'd never seen the connection before now, even though I should have. We'd been enlightening each other regarding our backgrounds, but we had never taken on the evil racist issue.

The facilitator taught us that the students need this. I think that has to be addressed in a gentle way to be able to touch all involved. I love the fact that there was a lot of good research background involved too; it's not just the feelings of it all. Workshops like this will bring together teachers in understanding racism in schools. Having multicultural and antiracist education books, as well as updating book information and software, must happen. We need this in the suburbs, too, where you still have a mom, dad, dog, and station wagon. Teachers do what the state mandates, so if it is not mandated it doesn't get done. The curriculum lessons should be extended to tie them better with U.S. history lessons. If you share with teachers where to implement these topics, that way they'll be better prepared to use them.

THE NORTHEASTERN REGION

The suburban Midwestern cohort and the urban northeastern elementary school were the only cohorts to complete 3–4 seminars. This was partly because the midwestern and northeastern regions were able to get a head start through participation in the pilot study.

The northeast high school cohort group consisted of 13 members, 7 of whom expressed dissatisfaction with the seminars. Examples of this resistance are as follows: For question 1 on enhancing antiracist education through understanding the roots of racism in the United States from African American cultural perspectives and experiences, teachers wrote: "I am fairly aware of the roots of racism so I have not had my awareness substantially increased"; "The workshop really didn't increase my awareness of racism. I know it exists. I failed to see the importance of the ritual [traditional and cultural dances are often interpreted by whites as ritualistic] and enslavement enactment in relationship to racism as it exists today." This last quotation refers to the "Africa to America" workshop. Despite the open and engaging deliverance of the workshop, responses from the same northeastern group continued to express denial: "Frankly I felt patronized. I also was offended by the implication that 'we white folk' are racists." Another statement focused on a different form of denial: "I am aware and understand, but I feel that it was so painful and so long ago, *dwelling* on it is not the answer." The feeling of "*dwelling on it*" as opposed to feeling what it was like and examining the past to understand it as a continual problem revealed the teacher's lack of wanting to acknowledge the pain and suffering that racism causes. One other teacher also expressed disappointment in these constant reminders: "I am sure there are some real racial problems, even in Branchard [ficticious name for the location]. However, I don't see many, and I don't think constant reminders of what happened centuries ago is productive. I agree with one of the statements in the book—"We are members of the race of mankind!! Let's focus on this." Another teacher-participant didn't want to accept that racism existed in her town: "I think racism exists. I know that it does. However, I feel that it is more dominant in older generations and in nonurban areas. I personally feel that Branchard is outstanding in the area of antiracism; I honestly feel that the majority of teachers (not all) judge a student on personality rather than color."

Some of the Northeastern high school participants demonstrated more open views in this workshop. For example, one teacher wrote, "It is in the area of historical omissions and misinformation that I feel needs to be corrected for students and myself in particular." "Anytime someone introduces concrete examples from experiences and situations, my awareness and understanding is heightened. Thus the presenter's examples have helped." It is worthwhile to hear all points of view to comprehend the extent to which antiracist education is needed and to determine how to encourage all U.S. teachers to accept that something must be done about racism in schools. We as teachers share in that responsibility, although racism is a difficult topic to address.

The northeastern urban elementary school and the midwestern were more receptive to learning about research on racism in schools, stages of racial development, racist conditioning, and the roots of racism. However, the northeastern elementary school did part on racial and cultural lines within some of the workshops. One white male teacher felt the "ritual dancing" (as he called it) went against his Christian religion; he was unable to connect the cultural significance for his students. Most of the teachers of color at the same school shared that they were concerned about these attitudes projected by white teachers who are working in predominantly Latino and African American settings. For instance, an African American male educator remarked, "My interest in the study comes from my concern for my colleagues. I know that many have problems working with African American and Latino children."

THE MIDWESTERN REGION AND THE MIDPOINT
SURVEY RESULTS

The midwestern section will be reported differently because their cohort completed the full study and had the most success because of the team teaching process they used. This cohort will be profiled extensively in the following chapter. Therefore, this section will combine the Midpoint Survey results of the midwestern and northeastern cohorts. The Midpoint Surveys (see Appendix C) were generally distributed after the second workshop and served to evaluate the success of the workshops midway through this study component.

Basically, the Midpoint Survey began as a two-question narrative on how the workshops increased awareness of racism in schools and societal racism. They were also asked if they would recommend these workshops to others. However, questions were added to the original Midpoint Survey.

The cohort groups that participated in at least two workshops were asked to complete Midpoint Surveys. The evaluation design of the Midpoint Surveys came from the teacher discussions through observation field notes recorded during the workshops. The Midpoint Survey was expanded to include the following questions: (1) How have the antiracist materials/workshops increased your awareness and understanding of the roots of racism? (2) How have the materials you've been exposed to increased your understanding of how children of color may feel threatened in today's "mainstream" educational system? (3) After viewing the materials/workshops, do you believe that racism actually exists? Or do you believe that people who make claims of racism are more or less "crying wolf?" (4) Now that you have been exposed to these materials/workshops, would you like to be exposed to other multicultural education seminars and training programs?"

The cohort groups that completed the Midpoint Survey were the northeast urban high school and elementary school, the midwestern urban secondary group, the midwestern urban elementary group and the midwestern suburban multigrade group. The Midpoint Survey responses varied according to geographical area, grade level, and racial ethnicity. For example, many of the white northeastern cohorts expected to gain immediate skills in addressing racial remarks between students and what they saw as students' reverse racism toward teachers. The teacher-participants tended to be very much on the defensive even though throughout the workshop they visibly demonstrated appreciation and understanding for multicultures. With regard to the Midpoint Survey, many said that they had known about the roots of racism, racial stages of development, and racist conditioning before the workshop; but when asked if they had received formal antiracist and multicultural education, they replied that they had not and that this was why they had signed up for the workshops.

The midwestern Midpoint Survey indicated that teachers were fairly open to trying new things. For example, one respondent mentioned that "being exposed to racism through the workshops helped bring old feelings and ideas to the surface to be worked on." Another said, "It has given me confidence in recognizing areas of need within myself. I am less nervous about verbalizing this issue"; yet another declared that "the workshops reinforced and updated previous exposure, brought much thinking to the front burner; had an excellent role model and good material."

Out of 28 Midpoint Surveys collected, 9 teachers declared they were not satisfied with the workshops. These nine appeared to want to focus on immediate remedies that would not have included much self-reflection on their part. Other participants overwhelmingly understood the need for antiracist education and agreed with the antiracist education approaches and teaching strategy models of the workshop.

REVIEW OF THE GUIDEBOOKS VERSUS GUIDEBOOK REVIEW WITH WORKSHOPS

There were noticeable differences between teachers who took the antiracist education workshops and those who only reviewed the guidebook. Teachers who only reviewed the guidebook spoke about the "desire" to incorporate the antiracist approaches in the guidebook or to have discussions and planning time with other teachers, whereas many teachers who took the workshops actually tested the lessons with their students and took the opportunity to synthesize the guidebook with other teachers. For white teachers especially, less change in attitudes occurred when they only participated in the review of the guide. For instance, one teacher stated that "by celebrating one's heritage that sets the races apart." Teachers in the workshops discussed whether multicultural education merely celebrates differences and whether affirming diversity divides the races further. It was acknowledged that with antiracist and multicultural education skills, along with more cultural exchanges, people are brought closer together in understanding and appreciation.

A comparison of the levels of exposure to antiracist education concepts was used to determine if the combination of workshops with guidebook held greater benefits than review of the guidebook only. It was found that for many teacher-participants, a greater degree of exposure lead to a change of attitude and teaching style. The degree of exposure did make a difference in most cases in the study. The more phases the teachers participated in, the more of antiracist instructional strategies and awareness of the extent of racism knowledge they demonstrated. The teachers who reviewed and responded to the curriculum guide displayed changed attitudes after completing the guidebook, and the guidebooks were central in enhancing their awareness of racism in schools and in self-development. Yet, they did not appear to give much assistance in implementing daily antiracist education concepts in the classroom. The workshops appeared to give more preparation and confidence for awareness and classroom methods. The basic curriculum argument, that professional development education must go along with curriculum reform guides, holds true here.

Faculty who chose to participate in the workshops demonstrated that the teachers receiving additional workshops were much more prepared to integrate antiracist education into basic subject areas than were those who did not participate in the seminars. The exception to the previous statement is that those teachers with deeply ingrained denial needed more than the four workshops provided in the study to work through the more personal issues before they could really be effective in a classroom. For instance, after being exposed to research on students of color being the targets of racism, a number of the northeastern white cohorts still had this to say in response to a discussion about the Midpoint Survey. The question was asked, *"How have the materials you've been exposed to increased your understanding of how children of color may feel threatened in today's 'mainstream' educational system?"* Some answers: "Frankly I don't feel that the students of color in the city of Branchard [pseudonym] feel threatened. [This comment was made in spite of the fact that the city had a long history of racist incidents against students of color; including higher detention and suspension rates, disproportionate enrollment in special education classes, and racist actions by teachers.]" "I feel their 'color' is not an issue and, if anything, they use their color to intimidate." "It hasn't. The high school students use their color as a threat against white teachers." "Not at all, no change in my understanding."

SHATTERING THE DENIAL

Various forms of denial of racism in schools existed throughout the four regions investigated. During the curriculum review and components, white teachers revealed many aspects of denial, such as (1) not believing that racism existed within their schools and communities; (2) feeling it was too painful and embarrassing to look at racism; (3) projecting blatant racist beliefs and conditioning; (4) expressing white privilege, which overshadowed the oppression experienced by others; (5) believing that underrepresented groups "made a mountain out of a molehill" regarding racist treatment; (6) feeling immune to racism if working with students of color as the majority; and (7) not participating out of fear of alienation from colleagues, family, and so on. Nonetheless, there were white teachers open to exploring issues of racism and developing solutions for the classroom.

What helped to open white teachers to addressing racism in schools was the research presented in the guidebook and workshops. These white teachers were committed to combating racism, but many had expectations different than those of teachers of color in the study. As mentioned previously, white teachers desired skills to address students' racial remarks and "reverse racism." Differences in outlooks according to ethnicity surfaced in the responses of African American and Latino teachers. African American and Latino teachers always spoke and wrote about racism in schools being evident on a daily basis. Their perceptions often intersected with awareness of classism and linguicism. Each of these teachers stood firmly for antiracist education being integrated into school curriculum but may have varied in the style of implementation. These teachers were also open to exploration of the problems and solutions suggested by the "experts."

The curriculum guidebook and workshop research components helped to determine what teachers want, need, and perceive regarding antiracist curriculum development. These components illuminated the lack of interest for this cause and the bigotry that exists within the teaching communities. It also demonstrated the problem of why teachers choose not to become involved and the courage of those willing to take risks to ensure change. These study components were useful in identifying teachers who wanted to go beyond antiracist education and professional development. The curriculum guidebook and professional development data collected and analyzed matched closely with the pre- and posttest quantitative survey results.

4

Antiracist Education Implementation and a Few Courageous Teachers

To get all teachers "on board" would take more than an act of Congress. More than an 11th commandment. It's never going to happen. Some people believe their job is just to give information out and race has nothing to do with it. I don't agree, but some teachers will live and die by that rule. (Caucasian male teacher with 31 years of teaching experience [Donaldson, 1996])

THE SIREN

This teacher gives reason to "sound the alarm" as we reflect on the ever-increasing racial diversity among students within U.S. schools (National Center for Education Statistics, 1990–91) but the lack of antiracist instruction and policy. Antiracist education is an important approach that addresses racial intolerance in schools. In practice, students are taught the contributions and experiences of racial and ethnic groups and ways to combat racial prejudice (Donaldson and Verma, 1997). Educators interested in teaching antiracist education concepts in schools have a common view in regard to this challenge; they are just too few. This conclusion comes after the two-year antiracist curriculum and implementation study administered in four regions of the United States (Northeast, South, Midwest, and West).

Of the 42 midwestern and northeastern curriculum and workshop volunteers (plus 22 mandated), only 11 volunteered for the implementation segments of the study, and only 7 completed the full implementation process, thus completing the study. When the researchers asked administrators and teachers about the lack of follow-through on the part of other teachers, responses were mainly "inundated with work" and "it is impossible to add one more project to my schedule." Basically, racism was still not viewed as a national crisis negatively affecting students and their education. However, the 11 teachers who volunteered for the implementation component felt that the completion of the study was important and would benefit both students and teachers nationwide.

As principal investigator, I call the few who volunteered for the implementation components "courageous." Through the profiles and study experiences of these participants, this chapter will examine the ability of teachers to survive, thrive, and make a difference by participating in antiracist education efforts. This research may be of value when attempting to encourage teachers to address racism in schools through curriculum and practice.

For the most part, the white teachers and the small sample of Asian teachers did not recognize the racial biases present in schools and how those biases alter the success of students. As we will see in this chapter, however, whites can and do exhibit courage in combating racism through antiracist education. Nonetheless, getting the majority of teachers to realize that if they are not part of the solution, they may be part of the problem is now the ultimate challenge for antiracist educators. How is it possible to help teachers who are insensitive, silent, ignorant, or isolated to realize the importance of recognizing the part they play in keeping racism alive in schools? What type of teacher confronts racism by volunteering for an antiracist study? Do such teachers fit the denial profiles noted earlier?

In this chapter, each of the 11 teachers will be profiled by "telling his or her story" about the antiracist curriculum development and implemention experience. The accounts were given by a number of the cohort members; their names have been changed to protect their anonymity.

THE PROFILES

Do Willing Teachers Fit a Profile?

The teachers who volunteered to go on with the study displayed courageous and outgoing attitudes. Many of the teachers had prior interest in addressing the problem of racism in schools but felt they did not have curriculum guidelines, the knowledge, or the support to do so. Therefore, most were elated about the opportunity to enhance their antiracist approaches for the classroom. These teachers had the tendency to fit a number of profiles, such as (1) being of an oppressed racial group; (2) having had some exchange with diverse groups (e.g., having grown up in a diverse neighborhood, attended a diverse school, had close colleagues and friends from diverse backgrounds, or been in the Peace Corps); (3) growing up in a liberal household; (4) having gained strong human rights views through education and/or involvement in civil rights and human rights causes; and (5) aging and wanted to set things right.

The cohort groups demonstrated awareness and developed implementation strategies more often than the nontreatment (pre and post survey) group. For example, a significant difference was found between the pretest mean scores of the teachers who participated in the intervention versus those who did not participate, with the teachers who participated having the lower mean score (2.87 vs. 3.35). It appears that the intervention group teachers wish to protect children against racism and are proactively fighting it. The same cannot be said for the other group.

A Few Courageous Teachers

Those teachers concerned about antiracism found a number of challenges. Many of the cohort members felt a lack of support by administrators or by fellow teachers. Yet each region, as well as each school's response to this lack, was different. One cohort member commented, "Administrators were either indifferent, not interested, or lacked funding and/or knowledge themselves." In another case, the principal made antiracist education mandatory, and many teachers became antagonistic to this mandate. In this case some individuals were for and some were against the move, and those against felt they could be doing something better with their time than dealing with racial issues and antiracist education development. Another volunteer remarked, "Some teachers frowned upon those who volunteered. I felt I could not trust these fellow teachers in terms of underhandedness by putting obstacles in our paths to sharing ideas and changing policy and curriculum to be more antiracist and multicultural." Thus, taking a public stand against racism and showing an interest in enhancing antiracist education teaching skills was not an admirable thing to do among the masses of teachers. However, formulating cohort groups and creating a team of allies empowered the volunteers.

THE NORTHEASTERN REGION

Facilitation of the workshops and implementation strategies had much to do with the success of teachers beginning antiracist units or engaging ongoing curriculum. With the research team based in the Midwest, on-site investigators in the other regions were often working alone, which at times made it difficult to address ongoing issues at the school or to give additional time, support, and resources. For these investigators, constant contact and resource participation was not available, as it was in the Midwest. This may explain why the study in the Northeast was less successful than that in the Midwest. However, the teachers in the Northeast had numerous ideas to share in the final interviews, as well as various cultural perspectives. Their responses may serve as a model for the northeastern region. The interviews will be presented with the northeastern urban high school teachers first, followed with the northeastern elementary school.

John (identifies as a white male with over 30 years of urban school teaching). *"I think that the kids' overall responses in the high school exhibits a willingness to discuss race. Over the past twenty years the topic has become 'less flammable.' It is easier to discuss."*

I am basically a Caucasian European sort. My grandmother's brothers are from England central, everyone else is from Nova Scotia and then suburban areas in Western Massachusetts. My dad was Scottish; I don't know much about his family or about my own cultural backgrounds.

The student enrollment in the last three years is about the same to me. Not much change in ethnicity or demographics. About 90% are minorities here. Blacks, Hispanics, Asians. Fewer Asians, and of course only about 10% whites. My selection of course materials is affected by the demographics in a sense. I use the materials that the students prefer to an extent. I'm interested in the process of how students learn. I don't rely on a "read this story and tell me what you learned from it" technique. That doesn't mean much to the student. What does make a difference is that they know how to get information from a given source. They can choose the medium. I have a lot of special projects that allow them to choose. In reference to the antiracist study and recent class lessons, we've watched a film (*Prejudice: Answering Children's Questions*) that you provided. A portion of that film was scientific. Why people have different color skin and how, based upon what region one's ancestors came from, cultural backgrounds were determined. It really didn't do much, but it was interesting. The social and cultural bases provide the means for communicating. The "stuff" about the two kids entering a store and one kid being harassed, the kids could relate to that universally; black, white, and Hispanic. Everyone seemed to have some experiences with that.

I think that the kids' overall responses in the high school exhibit a willingness to discuss race. Over the last 20 years or so the topic seems to have become "less flammable." It's not so inflammatory now. It's easier to discuss.

I think that the survey was fairly straightforward. Sometimes I had to answer based on generalizations that I really didn't agree with, but it is hard to say that all students do any one thing. But generally I think you achieved what you wanted to achieve with it. It was fairly open ended and I think you provided enough options.

The workshops with the principal investigator introduced us to some activities that led us to feel what exclusion was like. I remember trying to get into the group and though it wasn't traumatic in that context, I'm sure having to live it would be so. Arthur Ashe's book outlined his daily confrontation with being black and the fact of having to address that everyday with people. I only feel that in certain crowds. I have to face the fact that I am white here at the school. I'm the minority here and I resent that [having to fight it]. So, though the workshop was sort of a little game, it does bring you closer to what other members of society are going through. It makes you very uncomfortable. I've been to so many workshops that I have a general opinion of workshops, conventions; they are a waste. They don't do much for me. I'm not sure why. It has to be germane to what I am doing. I guess it is just my learning style.

I've been accused of excluding people from classroom participation based on race, and I resent that deeply. I try very hard not to exclude anyone due to race. But there are people who are going to use race as a wedge if they can do it. I didn't see in the workshop a place in the classroom that I don't ordinarily provide. Race shouldn't be used as a force to get other people to do something. So that workshop didn't help me do anything that I don't already provide. Could the workshops be beneficial to others? It certainly couldn't hurt. For some people in our society, additional knowledge is not going to change their behaviors. The workshops could benefit some, but some people, black and white, are never going to change.

The curriculum is good. I think of vegetable soup. The more you toss in, the more you can get out. I welcome anything that can help us see more, whether it is health, social, sex, race; any issues. I'll discuss them, and the kids will discuss them. But the [antiracist education instructor's guidebook] handbook, to be frank, I've never looked at it or discussed it with anyone. I don't know that I'd look at a handbook on racism and then impose myself on another teacher, even if I had the time to do that. If there were an occasion in a discussion to say, "I've got some information pertaining to that situation that you may want to look at," maybe I'd do that. But I don't think that I would ever impose something on another teacher. I have had positive effects on other teachers on many issues if someone says something that I disagree with. I don't hold back when that happens. So that would cover race and women's issues and whatever. My interest in the study wasn't the study itself; it was me. When I start something I like to finish it. I like to see if I can learn from it. I don't know why others didn't participate in it [implementation phase]. I chose to fill out the survey because I'm getting older. I've learned that if I rely on old information, then I miss the point. Race at school will only meet with proper understanding if you can keep people together all the time. Politically correct statements won't work alone. You will have to sit down and get to know people as well as possible. That dynamic, that experience, may break down reservations, and a person is what they do, to me. Not even what they say, the bottom line is what they do. As you work with people you get to know their actions and how they do things. To get to racial harmony or any kind of harmony, you have to get through the weeds. You have to deal with people. You have to have understanding and they have to have understanding. You have to do this to build any relationship.

To get all teachers "on board" would take more than an act of Congress. More than an 11th commandment. It's never going to happen. Some people believe their job is just to give information out and race has nothing to do with it. I don't agree, but some teachers will live and die by that rule. A lot of people just want to do what they have been doing. They'll resist change as much as possible. So, you should be selective about what you push to have changed. We have plenty of brains cells, I think, but . . . oh well, we'll see.

Race is a germane part of our daily existence so that we have to find ways to include it in our teaching from time to time. I like projects like "family trees" and discussing cultural things through a more general knowledge approach. Should the study be practiced? I don't think the package is the answer. I think that we need to get people together in the work setting and just do it. I can talk about making a quilt all day, but until I actually sit down and make one, I won't have much more than a clue. You have to deal with each other. You have to face issues. I find that I usually get along better with the students after two to three years. I feel that if I'm going to have to give, they're going to have to give too. We all have to take time and work things out.

Christine (special education teacher, 13 years teaching and of African American and American Indian heritage). *"I've experienced a lot of political racism here. Separate but*

not equal. We're very scrutinized as minority teachers. Is she certified? Is she qualified? If I
was a white person these questions would not be asked."

I'm a special education teacher and I teach accelerated math now. I've been teaching
for 13 years. I'm [American] Indian, African, and I guess some European. I have noticed an increase in variance of enrollment here. There are more Hispanics and West Indian students here now, not just blacks and whites.

I try to get my materials to fit for all students, not just one particular race. I used the
handbook exercises in my classroom, looking at histories and events from this school.
We watched the film (*Prejudice: Answering Children's Questions*) and discussed how it
related to them. I think the majority of students were unaware of their heritage. They
weren't really concerned with that. They didn't seem very sensitive to each other's
needs either. It's like they don't want to be bothered. They're very nonchalant. If it's
not recent and it's not personal to them, then it doesn't matter.

I'm working with the citywide multicultural group. The group started because of
cultural problems. My interest in this study stems from my overall interest. I hoped the
study could help me learn more and also bring some things in for the students to help
them learn some things about themselves.

The survey questions were appropriate. All teachers need to know that racism does
exist regardless of whether they want to or not. All students deserve to have an education. The workshop brought out a lot of issues that teachers avoid because they aren't
comfortable with them, like the fact that everyone is racist to a degree, like it or not. I
wish the workshop was longer, and that the students could have sat in on it, and that
more staff could have been there.

Workshops can help teachers break down racist behaviors if teachers will take the
chance. It's hard to erase things in people's minds, but if we provide them information,
then maybe we can change people. Teachers just don't want to be bothered with anything extra. The kids have so many problems and concerns that you have to go through
the issues to teach your topics sometimes. If you get down to the "Nitty Gritty" then
it's race a lot of times. It doesn't matter that I teach math; the racism issues stop students from learning anything.

I'd like to see the curriculum handbooks across the board in all the schools. I discussed the handbook with other teachers from the citywide rainbow group. I did use
the handbook in class. I think the handbook is even good for businesses. I wouldn't say
that I've had much impact on other teachers here. A lot of them have their minds set on
what they will and will not do, and that's it. I think exposure to more workshops and information is the only way to change them. Right now they only discuss race during
Black History Month. They don't address the racism problem otherwise.

The administration would have to make multicultural education training mandatory for all staff in the public school system to get all teachers involved. It should be
mandatory and across the board. I plan to continue dealing with antiracism. I'm meeting the D.A. to discuss the curriculum this week. There's a lot of unresolved issues at
this school. We need this curriculum. I don't know about packaging the study for other
schools, but it should be dispensed periodically, a little at a time. This school should
support the project monetarily to pursue antiracist education. It should be expanded.
Kids need support groups to work out these issues here now. I've experienced a lot of
political racism here. Separate but not equal. We're highly scrutinized as minority
teachers. Is she certified? Is she qualified? Instead of does she have common sense? If I
was a white person, these questions wouldn't be asked. It's still separate but not equal.

A Brief Comparative Analysis of the Two Northeastern High School Teachers

Both teachers appeared interested in bringing antiracist discussions and activities into the classroom but seemed to part regarding the personal motivation. John felt it was important to stay abreast of student concerns. He felt that he had been accused of excluding students based on race and was therefore interested in broadening his awareness and infusement capabilities (but only from time to time). His main motivation for staying active in the project was that he takes pride in not being a "quitter." John also resented being in the minority as a white male having to fight for respect from the students of color, who were in the majority. In contrast, Christine felt as a minority teacher she experienced political racism, and she did not receive the same privileges and respect as the white teachers did in the school. She saw racism affecting the school at many levels and therefore was drawn to participate in the study. She spoke about the many conflicts students had and that often the problem would boil down to race. She wanted the students to clearly understand issues of racism and the teachers to participate in the reduction of racism more fully. Christine appeared to give much more time to the project than did John. She became a member of a citywide multicultural group because the overall response from the teachers in her school was disinterest. She presented the antiracist guidebook to the citywide group, whereas John never read the curriculum guidebook or had an interest in sharing antiracist concepts with other teachers.

In conclusion, we have at the same high school two teachers whose perceptions of racism at their school were quite different, even down to the racial makeup of the students. For instance, John described the students as 90% minority (black, Hispanic, Asian), without much change in enrollment; Christine described the student enrollment by the changing ethnic composition, which now included more Hispanics and West Indian students. Christine viewed the incoming black students as culturally different than black American students, a viewpoint that seemed to be overlooked by John. Here the difference of culture and experience between the two teachers gives us some indication of the problem teachers have in coming together on these issues even when they reach the point of implementation. Again, as in the ANOVA models presented earlier, white teachers had more difficulty than black teachers in understanding the degree of racial crisis caused in schools by biased curriculum and instruction. This proved especially true for the northeastern high school cohort group. As John suggested, you have to get people to sit down and communicate their different outlooks, and understanding each other may help to build better relationships. In developing such relationships, perhaps understanding will lead to actions to reduce racism.

Northeastern Urban Elementary School

The elementary school implementation practice went a little differently in that the principal investigator conducted two antiracist education workshops with fourth and fifth graders. The administrator chose to have the implementation begin this way to ensure that teachers would participate in the implementation component.

Each teacher was required to attend the student workshops and to co-teach with the presenter, but only two out of six really got involved. In addition, only one of these teachers (an African American) agreed to be interviewed for the implementation. All fourth and fifth grade students took the student pretest before beginning the workshop, but only the one teacher did an additional writing lesson in follow-up of the student workshops. The resulting composition papers, mailed to my office, were outstanding in the students' interpretations of the significance of the workshop and their enjoyment of learning about cultures and racial harmony. However, because of an unexpected emergency, this teacher did not finish out the school year. Therefore, we did not have the opportunity to interview her regarding the implementation process.

The researchers selected three willing elementary educators from the school: one white, Irish female, one black male, and one Latina. The three elementary staff brought forth unique documentation for the study because they did not participate in the guidelines for implementation. Instead, their own antiracist and multicultural strategies were highlighted. In addition, they were chosen because of the lack of volunteers from the implementation group, but ironically they represented each of the cultures of the school's teaching staff. Mary and Anna worked with all grade levels and teachers in curriculum development and enjoyed infusing multicultural concepts into their classes; Preston worked with all students, teachers, and parents regarding sensitive issues such as racism; and each attended at least one antiracist education teacher seminar, therefore the researchers thought they were appropriate candidates for the final/implementation interviews.

Mary (identifies as Caucasian and has taught school for 13 years). *"Teachers need to go the extra mile and let students and parents know you're willing to work with them to learn."*

I teach computers K–6 [Mary tested the antiracist computer software designed by researchers Visani and Donaldson]. I've taught for 13 years, 9 years here. I was in Hartford before. Student enrollment in the last nine years here hasn't changed that much. It's about the same and I'm not even sure about the percentages, but we've got blacks, Hispanics, and Russians. The background of the students does make a difference when selecting books, etc. You want everyone to know that they are all important in society. We use books in several languages. You have to dig deeper to find things in the computer software areas, but we've purchased quite a few new programs. Society as a whole knows that there's a mix of races all over the world now. It's more common. There's a lot more out there now; I think that we've done very well in getting multicultural software for each grade level.

Since the beginning of the study, being a computer teacher, I have tried to address issues of race and gender as they occur. Different cultures interpret the way you say something differently. I've learned that from colleagues. So, I think my multicultural teaching is more informal and deals more with issues as they arise. What types of things come up? Name-calling and things like that. We address feelings and talk things out as much as we can. For student intereactions, the response has been positive. The students know that I am a fair person and they know the society can run a lot smoother if people are fair. There's a lot of mixed messages from school and at home, I'm sure.

For the antiracist study, our whole school decided to participate, since we're inner city [during scheduled staff meetings teachers were mandated to participate in the study]. The teachers wanted to know more about our students. The survey was good. Some places I felt like I wanted to add a few words as qualifiers. It was hard in some places, but it was good.

The workshops; I remember the first one was mostly Afro-American, but a lot of different areas were covered. What's been done, what we don't want to go back to. It's like the Holocaust; we need to bring these things up and not let them happen again. It's like three steps forward and four steps back. I was born in 1960, and my family was not racist. We had few minorities in my school, very few. Anyone I brought home was accepted. I didn't care about what people thought. I finally ran into racism once, so-called friends would say derogatory things about minorities when we were alone. I thought the workshops were helpful. They were worth my time and they were interesting. It was good because I don't have the time to read everything. But I think that the teachers who attend don't need it very much.

One hour is mandatory, but after that you get paid if you stay, so the ones that stayed wanted to get paid or have a real interest. I think that people are interested in antiracist education as professional development, but only certain people. I've missed a couple of things to take care of my children, but that's all.

The handbook and the software; I've looked at parts, but not all yet. I thought that a lot of the kids would prefer it on the computer. You could do a group approach on a television screen and then print the answers out. That would be good. I'd recommend the software and the handbook to teachers.

I haven't formally affected teachers regarding multicultural education and practices. I hope they see the right things in me, but I haven't formally addressed anyone. I just try to act correctly and show in my behaviors what is correct. A psychology and statistical team came through and said that I should lead the way in teaching others. But I don't know how I'd change anyone. It's like trying to change your husband! I do see myself as a role model. I just try to be fair and show that. I talk to people like I'm a friend to them. It's hard to change yourself, but it helps. They listen as I say, "don't think there's no solution to the problem and give up."

To bring teachers together on multicultural issues, the principal investigator should continue with more classes to bring us closer together. To bring us all together would be nice, by talking about a broader base of racism. Like I'm Irish, and when we first got here to the United States we were really stomped on. I know for people of color they couldn't hide or disguise who they were like my family could, so it is different. But those others points must be shared. [She missed the discrimination of the U.S. five major ethnic groups activities and discussion.] A lot of things did happen to my ancestors too. We could also have classes on about why people are different colors [the discussion covered this as well, along with racial identity development], talk about interracial marriages and the mixing of the nationalities. I think there is a lot that we can learn. Our history books should integrate more than the Caucasian experiences and slants. We should stop placing blame on groups or talking about people as groups. Stop generalizing so much. But I don't know how to talk about people.

Are there trends in groups? You can mention group stereotypes but then list individuals who are members of the group but don't fit the stereotype. Show the individual differences. I just dislike generalizations. We need to teach students as much as we can so that they can become better people. Give a kid a ride to school but don't say, "Oh, they're poor, so they can't learn." Teachers need to go the extra mile and let students and parents know you're willing to work with them to learn. To get teachers "on board," we just have to get them to commit to it. I still hear people say that they don't want to stay after school for anything. I don't know how to speak to them to teach them, though. I'm vocal, but I don't know how to make them change. I'm able to give my opinion.

An outside facilitator could help. Outside would be better than inside. Some teachers will look at you like you think you know it all or that you're better than they are. It's good to have outside facilitation. Regarding multicultural education, I plan to bring it up in a lot of different ways. I'd use the handbook examples. I think it would change the classroom environment quite a bit for the better. I would like to teach kids to treat everybody fair. History books should reflect all races in a yearly fashion; that would help. I hated history when I was growing up because it didn't make any sense. It was so isolated. It wasn't global like it is now, where we say "this happened because of that" or "so and so did this and that made so and so do this." Your software will be very nice in the classroom. I think the school should invest in more multicultural education with outside consultants. Not lecturing but facilitating. Helping people get issues and things out.

Anna (identifies as Puerto Rican and has taught bilingual classes for grades 1 through 5). *"I think that the curriculum should be revised* [include more parent participation]. *I involve parents very much in my teaching. They are my friends, and I talk to them about their children. I include their knowledge, and the children are proud."*

As a matter of choice and respect of preference, Anna's interview was conducted fully in Spanish and later transcribed by one of the researchers. Her responses are as follows:

"I have taught grades 1–5; the majority of Hispanic students identify with the language and personalized contact. I have had to intercede for students who are being rejected, especially Hispanics. Inequity and racism are demonstrated at all levels. Students are mistreated if they are Hispanic; Hispanic and black, it is worse. Their rights are not being observed. For example, one Hispanic child was denied breakfast because he was a little late. I had to fight for the child to get breakfast, knowing that other students come late and are allowed breakfast. I have experienced discrimination myself. For instance, I always come early to meetings. One day I was ten minutes late for a staff meeting and I received a letter of reprimand, while other people have been much later without any consequences. Racism is apparent at meetings. There is a blonde white girl who is the topic of conversation because her dad is black and her mother is white, and they don't know where to place her. I think there is too much emphasis on black and white. How many white? How many black? It is a troubling situation. Latinos are discriminated against already; if you are black it is worse. I think there is too much emphasis on race rather than culture [this sentiment may an incomplete understanding of the history of race-based treatment on the mainland United States]. February is Black History Month, but what about the rest of time? The rest of the time is white. I think that the curriculum should be revised [include more parent participation]. I involve parents very much in my teaching. They are my friends, and I talk to them about their children.

I include their knowledge, and the children are proud. But these same parents do not come when there is English spoken. They do not identify; we need to translate for them. Sometimes English does not translate well for them. Sometimes meetings could be held in Spanish with English translation for English-speaking parents. Why not let the English speaking parents feel the same? [Historically, the Spanish settled in the Southwest regions of the United States and intermarried with Indian populations before the coming of the Pilgrims and later, in more recent years, were one of the cultural groups that proved to be the backbone of U.S. labor and military forces. Respecting the Spanish language as part of U.S. history and culture and alternating the language of English and Spanish in Latino- and English-speaking school settings is a reasonable request.] I am assigned to the orientation office, where all the kids are sent when they get in trouble. This is, rather, a punishment office. Punishment is being implemented in ways that are outdated, ways that were used a hundred years ago. For instance, one white teacher broke a finger when she was going to hit a student and missed. She hit her finger on a table instead. The teacher reported it was an accident, but I went and told the truth about what had happened.

I only participated in one workshop. I did not participate in the last workshop because I only learned about it the day of this interview. I have seen progress in the school in general, but I'm still having to defend the Bilingual Program again and again. The curriculum should be the same and should be balanced out. I teach topics about Dr. Martin Luther King, Jr.'s ideas, but I never teach about race. I convey messages like it is good that we are all different like the flowers. It is one world, and like the flowers we have to share it. In Puerto Rico we are all mixed; we can't separate ourselves into races. It is like a food with various spices and vegetables. There is no way that I could take out one ingredient and claim it as the dominant race, and that is how I see us in Puerto Rico.

Preston (identifies as an African American male and has been teaching for 21 years). *"I'm put in a role where I have to dispense information. The kids want to know why the K.K.K. visited Douglas School* [painted racial obscenities on the wall]. *Are white folk really burning down black churches? Is it going to happen here?"*

I've been teaching for 21 years. I'm the adjustment counselor here. I'm certified in special education, guidance counseling, adjustment counseling, as an administrator, and in early childhood education. I've been at this school for eight years.

The system is "browner" where students are concerned but still white where teachers are concerned. We have many more Hispanics with no English capabilities now. There are more Hispanic parents who can't communicate with us now, which makes for more difficulties. I'm very leery of translation, and who's doing the translation. Where the students and parents are coming from is causing big problems in understanding. I've come to rely on only one or two people in the building. Much of the information is too sensitive not to be careful.

For me personally as a school adjustment counselor the background of the student culturally, and ethnically, is a very important factor in the selection of materials. Also whether the family has assimilated into the "American way." I have to create trust and understanding that I'm working for the benefit of the child. I find that the materials do not move fast enough. As a black American I have some issues with much of what we do. I don't appreciate Black History Month or Hispanic History Month. Or any other "month" a year, and I have a problem with that. I feel that children as they walk through this door should be lifted up in their culture. It is my vision that there should be a corridor of flags representing every country. That would help children's identity and belief that there was someone or thing there that at least acknowledged his or her existence.

The average curriculum just does not "get it" fast enough. And there is too much battle to try to get it. What's the problem? The children are here. Why isn't history written as it happens? We talk inclusion . . . marvelous . . . then we forget it. What's the real deal? Are our children not to know the advances of all people? I have children who suffered from AIDS by losing a major person in his life every year since the second grade; brother, mother, and grandmother. We are heavy with interventions here. Interracial issues and society's handling of that. The children handle that well but the adults "trip" and mess with the kids' minds. We predominantly have single-parent families. Education is moving too slow. Our model of education didn't change, our society changed. These kids deal with families that are quite different than what you and I grew up with.

As the adjustment counselor, I sit back and try to pick up the pulse of what the kids go through. And not act negatively to their definitions of family, and so on. Once parental views are placed on the children environmentally then it shows up here. So we have to deal with sexual issues here. We have children who use the words "nigger" and "spic." We sit down with the dictionary and look up terms and discuss origins. We turn on the news and talk about it. I'm put in a role where I have to dispense information. Kids want to know "why the K.K.K. visited the Douglas School? Are white folk really burning black churches? Is it going to happen here?" I will talk to a child where I see them. We discuss our issues.

There's a thirst of knowledge that we have to take on. I really believe that it takes a village to raise a child. We have a partnership with a nearby college; that's just now being viewed as a place where our children can go. Because there is now a black man who's in charge there. Now we have students saying things like "I want to be a therapist, or a counselor; and I want to go to the nearby college." The mostly white students [college enrolled] are now learning to reach out to the urban child.

If we can make these children more aware of their world, then we've done our job. I try to help teachers infuse ways to deal with issues in their classrooms because it almost always comes up. One child raises an issue, then there are fifty more who speak up. The girls are now starting to speak up about how they're treated differently because they are girls. We have girls that don't want to be like their mothers. There is a cultural change that we have to deal with. My curriculum is situational.

My interest in the study comes from my concern for my colleagues. I know that many have problems working with African American and Latino children. They have problems working for an African American woman. These things cost the children. We keep bumping one another. I want to put things on the table and move on. I don't want to put others down. I just want people to understand that the white man cannot walk in my shoes. Part of me came to these shores not by freedom of choice. Part of this society still doesn't let me exercise freedom of choice. Folks aren't dealing with these issues. I want my colleagues to know this. You can't come in from suburbia and know. My colleagues do not understand that their body language speaks louder than their words. I need to find ways to help me help my colleagues or this system is not going to get right. I want people to be up front and deal with these issues.

I thought the survey was useful. There are some people here who are honest enough to discuss these issues. Some people, though, tried to pass it off. Some just stood in the corner. They couldn't even be involved. I experienced racism in 1959 for the first time with my family. In the state of Texas we couldn't find a hotel to sleep in until we found a black-owned [one]. I remember that. We've made some strides forward but we need to help kids deal with this. It's a real struggle.

As far as the antiracist workshops, the discussion has to continue. When the facilitators leave, somehow there has to be a mechanism that keeps the interaction about these gut-level things intact. Continual development in these areas is necessary. It takes outside forces to be a part of this process. We can't do it internally on our own. I think we can work on it, but we can't handle it alone. Like I said, some people are still "tripping" over working for a black woman. She's the administrator who's a black woman, not the administrator.

If the handbook is read, it'll be useful. I don't think it was read. You need to understand that change won't happen unless the change agent (all of us) does not continually interact. The materials are helpful and can be used. The question is will they?

Issues need to be prioritized. Yes, there's times when we're tired, but antiracist education is needed now perhaps more than ever before. Watch the news, and if you don't think we need to respond, then I'm not sure what to think.

We have to find time to help these forming beings [children] form. I will encourage the continuance of interactions of this particular style. I believe it is necessary to keep our ears to the tracks. A lot of black children are frightened, and we need to deal with that. These church burnings, for example, have raised issues. We have to have antiracism as a part of our professional development that is going on. I'm not choosing to say that anyone is more or less racist than I. But if we are going to be true educators, then we are going to have to deal with this.

We need more structured sessions with the study facilitators to force us to talk about this. If we could just stay until we have finished and that we've put it all on the table, we could dispel myths and solve issues. The discussions that the research team facilitated were fabulous. We need to continue, that's what has to happen. How that happens I'm not sure. I believe our administrator is open to this, and we need this. But we need more than an hour and a half. The research team will have to "tangle with the powers that be." The battle has to be won on several fronts. If we're crying at the bottom saying we need it, and you're presenting the case and saying that you can give it, we can overcome.

A Brief Comparative Analysis of Three Northeastern Elementary Teachers

The question is, How do we see ourselves in the United States? Various races, cultures, and mixtures; a pluralistic society contributing to the betterment of education and economics in the United States? The northeastern elementary school perceived the seminars in a gamut of ways. This illustrates the complexity of developing antiracist education curriculum workshops for cross-cultural teaching staff. Yet, the opportunity to obtain this feedback will have assisted in the design of future teacher antiracist education modules.

Mary, the white female, demonstrated a more sincere commitment to addressing racism in schools than did her white counterpart at the high school. Mary talked about going that extra mile for students and standing up as a child against racism. She reviewed the antiracist handbook and software. After attending most of the seminars, she recommended ongoing education for staff.

Mary felt that she had not acquired the skills to reach out to other teachers on issues of racism in schools. She prided herself on role modeling "fairness" to other teachers and students. Yet, she desired to learn more ways in which to outreach more readily. Her idea of implementing antiracist education in the classroom was to include the contributions and experiences of many cultures. This was the same for the other two interviewees.

All three elementary educators believed language to be an issue when looking at racism in their school. Each had a different solution to the problems of racism and linguicism. Celebrating cultures (i.e., Black or Hispanic History Month) periodically, rather than year-round, was also a common concern.

Anna shared a cultural view that we often overlook, namely, the idea that the the practice of racism in the United States differs from that practiced in Puerto Rico and other countries, for often classism is the main form of discrimination and prejudice in countries of color.

Anna and Preston, as with other teachers of color investigated in the study, pointed out the persistent racism against students as well as teachers of color. The white teachers in the northeastern region never identified with students' plight as did teachers of color. Instead, reverse racism or omission of European culture was often the response teachers of color made to these experiences. And although it was Preston's desire to "get through" to his white colleagues on the "problems" he witnessed as they worked with students, teachers, and administrators of color, the reality is that this is not a simple task. Wanting continued sessions in which to dialogue and receive additional antiracist education strategies is a good idea. Just as the t-tests demonstrated positive change in the understanding of the definition of racism for the intervention participants, it is anticipated that more time spent on antiracist development would render even greater positive change; but the majority must want to participate if overall change is going to be made.

WHEN TEACHERS PERSEVERE: THE MIDWESTERN COHORT

This section will focus on one of four teacher (implementation) cohort groups formulated during the study. The purpose of focusing on this particular group is that its members fully completed the study and were the most successful in implementing antiracist education concepts in their classrooms, schools, and school districts when compared to teachers at large. The midwestern cohort group scored higher than all other geographical areas (mean score of 4.98) with regard to acknowledging the existence of racism in schools. A significant effect was also found for this region and question 27, "As a child, your family members promoted racists beliefs." Inspection of the group means indicated that the teachers from the suburban Midwest scored the highest and were less inhibited about sharing family beliefs and personal racist conditioning in order to reduce their own racist beliefs. There may be a correlation here in that the three lowest-scoring schools exhibited the most obvious artifacts of racism during the study. It could be that the individuals in the midwestern suburban cohort group, all of whose members fit the previous liberal profiles mentioned, are simply more aware of what racism is.

This midwestern suburban cohort consisted of six teachers (one secondary, one elementary, and four middle school) and one school administrator. During the project these teachers completed the pre and post race awareness surveys, tested a pilot antiracist curriculum guide, and attended four antiracist education seminars and several material resource sessions. They developed and implemented antiracist education in the classroom and allowed their students to be surveyed before and after their antiracist lessons. In addition, the teachers completed focus group discussions and individual qualitative interviews. The results of this extensive participation and their commitment to antiracist education, as well as their special relationship to one another, have rendered some fine models for other teachers wanting to address issues of racism in schools.

Key outcomes reported by the cohort group included an increased knowledge base. For example, the teachers became more knowledgeable about (1) research on racism in schools, (2) racial identity, (3) their own stereotypical views, (4) ways to address racial issues, (5) how to integrate antiracist education into basic curriculum, and (6) ways to work cooperatively in developing antiracist curriculum and becoming facilitators of learning. In addition, the teachers in this cohort group became empowered to make a difference.

The cohort group felt that the support and encouragement provided by the research team increased their commitment and confidence when producing tactics to address racism in schools. The secondary-level participants helped to organize a Unity Day, in which one day of school was dedicated to over 50 diversity seminars for students to choose from. In addition, with two student leaders the teachers co-established a multicultural support group and a 15-week multicultural course for high school students. The course was taught by the principal investigator; therefore, cohort members attended or reviewed the class videotapes to enhance their own antiracist education teaching skills.

Most of the middle school–level cohort participants had worked together for over 25 years and had been greatly influenced in terms of diversity education by one African American member of the group. This group made its curriculum more multicultural (before the study the team had focused on integrating only African American, and some American Indian contributions and experiences into the curriculum). Members of this group also committed themselves to rotating as facilitators for the Middle School Multicultural Club, which was a support and education club started by the principal investigator one year before the study.

The elementary (fourth grade) member of the group implemented concepts from the study and also invited the Middle School Multicultural Club to speak about and demonstrate the research on multicultural literature using Netscape.

The cohort group worked collectively, sharing ways to integrate antiracist education activities from their antiracist education handbook (study instrument). They followed team planning with implementation in their classrooms. Pre and post student surveys were administered to all the cohort classrooms. Survey results demonstrated that experienced intervention does produce change in the classroom, change that the students noticed. These teachers have become antiracist education facilitators for their school district. Three of the participants now serve on the school district's Multicultural Education Advisory Committee and have helped to find funding sources for multicultural education programs. In addition, five of the cohort members presented at a national multicultural education conference at the close of the study, along with 25 high school students who received antiracist teacher instruction. Four of the five are current school district planning committee members (along with other district teachers, principals, the associate superintendent, state department, and university curriculum and instruction faculty, and chairperson), to establish an antiracist and multicultural "demonstration" school in order to create a prototype for curriculum and implementation throughout the district. More will be presented on this project later in the book.

In Their Own Words

The curriculum and implementation stories following reflect the concern and dedication of teachers interested in addressing racism in schools. During the curriculum and implementation phase of the study, the cohort group added a number of antiracist lessons to the pilot antiracist curriculum instructor's handbook. The midwestern cohort group had the opportunity to experience all the seminars using the antiracist handbook and saw it as a valuable model to assist in the creation of their own lessons for the classroom. They ultimately added to the "Sample Antiracist Lessons" chapter. All the designed antiracist study instruments are copyrighted and currently being published. The midwestern cohort group sees this antiracist kit as a beneficial tool for all educators seeking to increase sensitivity and skill in antiracist education curriculum development and instruction. These experiences were recorded in one-hour individual closing interviews.

George (identifies as a white male with 36 years of teaching experience). *"I look for confirmation that 'yes' what I am doing is okay."*

Social studies exposes one to diverse cultures, but having students from several other cultures forced me to provide a more diverse curriculum when it came to U.S. history. In 1985 I added an immigration unit (from the Gateway Series). I became influenced, quite frankly, by the only African American teacher at our school. I started seeing more and more the need for multicultural experiences in history class, so components were put in here and there. For example, during our Civil War unit, with regard to African Americans, I only presented the slavery issue and, because of the constraints of time, I never looked at the Reconstruction Era until the African American teacher gave me the *Story of the People* tapes, which I would listen to while traveling across country. It did come through to me that I needed to go back and work on Reconstruction, as it leads me into the civil rights movement, which I do work on. I'm retiring so it becomes a moot issue. But there was a gap there that I should have been filling; I recognize that now.

As a U.S. history teacher I felt I needed to, and I had an interest in seeing what kind of contribution I could make to it and to see what kind of contribution it could make to the course I was teaching. I look for confirmation that "yes" what I am doing is okay or what you're doing is right in line with with what you're doing and that is reassuring. The second thing is looking for things that I can plug into the curriculum; it may be an activity, it may be a short unit or long unit, but something I can take to make my activities or units stronger. The one that we did in the first antiracist seminar about creating a racist society, I brought back and plugged that into the immigration unit that I was working on because it was always based in western European experiences. When we finished up the simulation activity, I thought this was the perfect time to demonstrate how most ethnic groups were discriminated against (in various degrees) when they came to America. We took that idea and built on it. For the most part students caught on quickly; the really significant part was: What kind of laws do we create to make sure the dominant group stays on top? It was a natural fit going from immigration to the activity on living in a racist society.

Harry (identifies as a white male with 25 years of teaching experience in the district). *"Teachers need to deal more with transforming content."*

The students have responded very positively to the antiracist-multicultural exercises and generally want to learn even more. They enjoy sharing their own ethnic experiences as well. The students are supportive. I've been interested in your antiracist study to learn more and also to support the notion of in-service in this area. The most beneficial part of the study to me are the activities and just having groups or individuals become more aware of the experiences of minorities in this country. Four or five years ago I was tasked with finding out what was being done in K–12 schools to teach multicultural education. There actually were quite a few teachers introducing multicultural education topics and exercises into the elementary classrooms, but when I went to the higher levels I found that there were not many classes, if any, involved. At the high school, for example, teachers would say, "Well this course has *some of that* in it." They think they're doing something when they're not. They're not really thinking of educating kids for a global atmosphere, which is what we are suppose to be doing. Teachers need to deal more with transforming content. I think it is going to have to come down to guidelines for teachers and just saying, "Here's some things we are going to have to do." I think teachers will become more aware of the issues when they have to get involved; don't give them a choice.

Jennifer (identifies as Jewish American and has been involved in education 34 years). *"Staff members need to be trained to understand where they are themselves before they make decisions."*

Regarding implementation, I'm concerned that anything that is not done during school hours will decrease the opportunity for students who need to be involved. We're talking about gaining lifetime skills, so I don't have a problem with losing one day's worth of class time. That trade-off should be okay. I do think that the board and the administration would all say that they support equity. But in terms of specific commitments of time, then we do not have enough support.

No one wants to be harassed, but to give more time and money so that racism can be stopped is yet to come. Even your reports from this study will probably not help bring support. I think if we don't move forward on this, we will simply stagnate. It is very difficult for people who don't have knowledge in antiracist-multicultural education to make judgments regarding what they do or do not implement or teach in the classroom. Many agree that we need it, but the implementation is the problem. We need money and time commitments to make it work. Staff members need to be trained to understand where they are themselves before they make decisions.

The events that have taken place this year have made a difference. The students support one another now, those who were involved with the Human Relations Forums, etc. I hope that by next year we would have addressed this issue in such a way as to have antiracist education infused within the curriculum from kindergarten through high school, and not just in social studies but also through content areas elsewhere. We should also have elective courses so that students who want to go deeper into topics can. We need more minority staff. This will only come about if there continues to be enough of a crisis and the multicultural community puts pressure on the board and superintendent to make changes. The community members also need to voice their cry.

Bobby (identifies as Lebanese American with 19 years of teaching experience). *"I can't imagine that teachers do not understand the issue of racism in schools."*

I was motivated to become involved with the curriculum implementation aspect primarily due to my background. I'm of Lebanese descent, and there are not a lot of us in this state. The study helped develop a greater breadth of activity for multicultural inclusion. I've dealt with a lot of these topics at different times, but the study has given me many more diverse ideas. The school doesn't have all of the resources available to do all that I want, but I can find and get those resources. I'm interested in finding those classic *one-liners* and pictures that will allow me to make my classroom into such a learning experience-resource that a kid cannot *space off* without learning something. I do feel camaraderie with teachers outside of our cohort group regarding multicultural issues and trying to combat racism. For instance, I've worked with several other teachers in tracing roots of musical styles and history. I'd say that teachers in general are pretty open to multicultural inclusion. The schedule crowding makes it tough to be less serendipitous and more deliberate, but we try hard to work topics of interest in.

I'm sure there will be a snowballing effect where teachers who are aware of multicultural curriculum and issues will share with other teachers and then all teachers will infuse the concepts into their classrooms. I've seen a lot of cooperation from many teachers regarding contributions of women and minorities in several areas. There is an awareness in working to enhance curriculum to be multicultural.

I can't imagine that teachers do not understand the issue of racism in schools even though there's a sort of knee jerk reaction by many people who would say they are not overt racists. We do have to look at what we do and how it is perceived by others.

Wendall (identifies as African American with 30 years of teaching experience). *"When others know that their colleagues are using the materials, then maybe they will use them."*

Since 1968, with the death of Dr. Martin Luther King, Jr., I have infused an African studies portion into my curriculum as well as a women's issues portion. The study was a reassurance that there's a growing need to expose students and staff to these issues. It affirms our need to be in tune to these subtle incidents that take place in our communities. These are the kinds of things that we are in a better position to counsel students [about] when the issues are brought to the front. We need to have something in place to expose our students to a better understanding of antiracist-multicultural education and to combat intolerance. That way we can make this an inclusive society. The study has provided resources for classroom use. It provides an excellent format for this sort of thing.

The faculty would benefit from the antiracist education seminars, but would they implement the materials? That's the big question. That's the issue that needs to be addressed. I guess I don't have much faith on what people will do. I have to base it on my past experiences and I don't think that they'll do it. They don't see the need to infuse new ideas unless a crisis develops.

If we have a schoolwide crisis, then the school will focus on it for a time. The majority of our colleagues give lip service to it. They say it's good, it's needed; then they say don't take my time. We have to get a core of teachers together, develop details, then move in. When others know that their colleagues are using the materials, then maybe they will use them. I've seen improvement made, but it is a very slow process. For example, the textbooks are appalling. They make it seem that the civil rights movement happened and has gone by and is done. Some people think we have to change the ethnic makeup of the staff and that's diversity.

I look for ideas that can be brought into the classroom all the time. How you apply the information is key. We'll look at social issues happening around the area and discuss them. I've had to challenge the way that students think from time to time, to help them understand their own statements from a wider perspective. We need to do that as teachers. We need to bring these things out of our students. The study videotapes on the students' points of view are an excellent start. I've been impressed with the students' understanding. I think we need to get this on the public access channels. We could follow up by having forums that are parallel to the topics. We've covered things like the Japanese internment, and the Jewish Holocaust. We've had parents who have not wanted us to show these things, since they think the material may be too explosive. I'd like to get the videos and interact with them in the classroom. I think that is a good way to interact with the teachers also. Show the video, then ask, "How do you feel about that, or do you agree with that?" I think this is an excellent approach. They could start good discussions. I'm supportive of students taking social action; I think we need more of it.

Richard (identifies as a white male with 20 years of teaching experience). *"I appreciate the type of curriculum that doesn't just follow known facts and affects you personally."*

My interest in the study stems from my experiences. Diversity has always been a big thing with me. I go out of my way to be as inclusive as possible. My students may not be racially diverse, but the students are definitely not mainstream [Richard is a special education teacher]. I want the world to be an inclusive place. I don't want people to feel like they're left out.

The study handbook was really good. It put things on a personal level for students.

I appreciate the type of curriculum that doesn't just follow known facts and affects you personally. You can personalize it, you can role play. You can drive the points home. It's a more processed approach. I've used some of the activities with my classroom. I stole the racial prejudice labeling exercise and others from you blatantly! We do similar adaptive exercises with the special education classes, but we have to be careful. Sometimes the *lines* vanish, and they don't know that we are just pretending.

The awareness seminars gave me a great deal of information. I like being able to talk about myself and my experiences. It made me realize that I have had the same homeroom for four years, but I don't really remember the students' names and I haven't known their experiences. A formal activity like that is a great way to start off the school year.

Marion (identifies as a white female with teaching on and off for 33 years). *"The study helped me become more aware of some existing problems for minority students, especially facing my own racist background due to my upbringing, on a day-to-day basis."*

I started out as an English journalism teacher, then moved on to multimedia specialties. When I look at software, I've become more aware of the racist subtleties that are there. I had both professional and personal interests in the study. I wanted to be sure that we have materials from all sides available in the library, whether we agree with the philosophy or not. I have a professional responsibility to ensure that we have those materials available representing all races, creeds, colors, and positions. Or if they're not, I have to make sure that the door is a least opened. The study helped me to understand some of the mistakes that I might make and some of the material that I might overlook. It also helps me to see that people from other nations who come to the United States need to be understood rather than have them forced into our belief of what we think we are. I don't think that the staff or student body as a whole is aware of how difficult it is for culturally diverse peoples to live in our society. The study helped me become more aware of some existing problems for minority students, especially facing my own racist background due to my upbringing, on a day-to-day basis.

I've been involved with some of the students who are *surfing* the Internet to find information for the middle school multicultural club; mostly as a facilitator. I've been able to order diverse materials and also lead students who are conducting research by leading them with specific questions.

I would like it if there was a problem with an African American student that we didn't all run to Wendall and say, "What do we do now?" That in itself is a racist attitude. Just like I don't have all of the answers for every white female, Wendall doesn't have all of the answers for every African American kid, and he shouldn't be expected to. The study has brought these kinds of issues to the forefront. I think that many teachers think this is too much for them. There have been several instances this year where I've needed to confront individuals for not thinking through what they are saying. It may be sexually offensive, racially [offensive], or gender offensive. I feel more comfortable making a stand like that now that I know there are more teachers involved. I like to have a safety net. It helps to bounce ideas off other individuals so that my actions to events are tempered. It helps to have a network.

I think that the students of color are not having their needs met here at the school. I see them and hear them and I don't think their needs are being met. I know that in some cases we have been successful, but I think that more often we are not. There's a safe cultures project here that all of the teachers are involved with and that's making us more aware. I don't know how far it will go, but it provides guidelines for teachers and students describing what the *lines* are, the point that you do not go past. The study has helped me realize that I can help change things and that bringing change for even one person is worthy and helpful.

Midwestern Teachers' Concluding Words of Wisdom

How can we help more teachers recognize the role they play in keeping racism alive? During the final interviews the midwestern cohort group had many words of wisdom to share. One teacher said, "I think the results of this study should be shared nationwide. We've made strides, but our acceptance is still lacking. The small contingency of students and faculty involved are themselves a minority. I think there is more unconscious racism today than there was 20 years ago. Our nation and our schools are in a very bad way now. Action has to be taken not to lose the progress that we have made." Another teacher echoed the same sentiments, "There hasn't been the network for supporting people who are proactive against racism." Another teacher replied, "There is a need for the entire faculty to be viewed as accessible. I don't believe that will necessarily happen. Some teachers will minimize what happens to students. Teachers don't want to *tack things on*. There's so much to do, so many meetings, three or four initiatives at one time . . . we're inundated. I'm always re-prioritizing. We need to have a rotation where a teacher chairs the antiracist-multicultural implementation goals for the school and then is allowed to get refreshed and renewed."

All the cohort participants agreed that re-education is essential for educators to be able to address the problem of racism in schools. For example, one of the teachers remarked, "We should facilitate dialogues for problems before they become problems. We should foster trust and develop it. We just need more and more forums to voice the issues. We should involve students in the problem solving. To make it all a reality? I'm not sure. We need the initiative to be taken by teachers to approach the board and ask for this." Another teacher gave the following suggestions: "Now, trying to bridge the gap with my colleagues is going to be a challenge, since we try to teach similar units at the same time; but our teachers need to know how important this all is. If we're really going to be making a difference with students, we have to expand our perspectives. Each student has different needs, and if our curriculum isn't addressing these needs, then we aren't helping the students to feel good about themselves and develop. I don't see myself as one with all the answers, but I do hope to be viewed as a mentor to others."

IMPLEMENTATION COHORT GROUPS: SUMMARY ANALYSIS

There is often the fear of putting oneself in danger when accepting the charge to be proactive against racism and other issues of prejudice in schools, but the larger the team of allies, the more respected and safe these positions appear to become (Lawrence and Tatum, 1997). In understanding the adverse effects of racism on student learning and development, all the midwestern (suburban) teachers have accepted the challenge to become antiracist education mentors for members of the total school environment. When comparing the results of this teacher study with that of Tatum, whereby approximately 40 teachers were able to change some of their behaviors regarding race, and Sleeter's antiracist teacher study (1992), which included 30 white female teachers examining their attitudes about race, most of the cohort groups of this geographical study were able to reach an advanced level of confidence to implement antiracist education in the classroom.

The antiracist curriculum and implementation with teachers was successful in that (1) a baseline for how teachers perceive racism in schools was established; (2) teacher cohort groups and allies were established; (3) antiracist curriculum guidelines were tested; (4) the guidelines were further developed and implemented by teachers; (5) the leadership roles empowered teachers, thereby encouraging additional teachers to become interested; and (6) the knowledge base for teacher-participants was increased, thereby allowing growth in self-awareness, student awareness, and confidence to become antiracist education facilitators for other staff members.

The study helped to recognize the vast challenges of getting all teachers to address racism in schools and provide antiracist education concepts in the classroom. However, it also demonstrated that there is promise; with a few much can be done, and these achievements encourage others to eventually join in.

Teachers in the cohort groups suggested the creation of an antiracist education national network for teachers. One of the cohort members is currently establishing a Web site in which teachers from around the nation can voice their concerns and share their classroom strategies, resources, and efforts to reduce racism in schools. In addition, the study contributed to the creation of an experimental antiracist education course designed for in-service teachers. Teachers enrolled in the course are able to fulfill multicultural professional development requirements. This university-based course is taught on interactive television to reach many remote areas in a midwestern state.

"To get all teachers 'on board' would take an act of Congress. More than an 11th commandment. It's never going to happen." The courageous few who have been featured in this section believe that it can happen if we would only come together and try.

5

Successful Re-education for Teachers Makes a Difference for Students

Chapter 5 attempts to bring the teacher study full circle. The teacher study was stirred by the request to re-educate teachers made by students involved in previous antiracist studies. The students' hope was to make teachers aware of how racism negatively affects student learning and development, to address racist conditioning with teachers and others, and to discover ways to develop and implement antiracist education within basic subject areas and special programming. Teachers who completed the implementation process by conducting antiracist education lessons and/or units had their students participate in a pre- and posttest survey entitled Student's Perceptions of Teacher Race/Diversity Awareness. The findings of the pre- and posttest given to the students will be highlighted.

WHAT ABOUT THE CHILDREN?

The Antiracist Education Teacher Study was created because many students wanted to have teachers assessed and re-educated. They wanted teachers to implement antiracist concepts in regular classroom settings (Donaldson, 1996). The researchers took the students' requests one step farther to explore whether teacher-participants' enhanced knowledge of racism in schools, curriculum development, and actual practice would make a difference to schoolchildren; it did.

We succeeded in the journey that would lead us back to the students because we were able to create a baseline of how teachers perceive racism in schools; provide materials, awareness, and curriculum development seminars; and assist in the implementation process. For teachers who participated in the implementation segment of the study, we were able to administer pre and post student surveys in their classrooms.

Using the Likert scale model, the student survey consisted of 10 statements, among them Q2, I feel comfortable around my teacher(s); Q4, My teacher(s) use classroom activities that reflect the history and contributions of my racial group; Q5, I respect my teacher(s); Q6, My teacher(s) won't allow students to make jokes or talk bad about people who are not of the same race; and Q7, My teacher(s) only pay attention to students who are the same color that he/she is (see complete survey with frequency results in Appendix A). The objective of this survey was to measure students' perceptions of teacher race relations and antiracist curriculum implementation in the classroom setting, before and after implementation.

The northeastern urban high and elementary school and the suburban and urban midwestern regions participated in the student surveys. There were six schools totaling 248 students completing the presurvey (northeastern elementary $n = 77$ and high school $n = 32$; midwestern suburban elementary $n = 16$, middle $n = 16$, and high school $n = 42$; and urban high school $n = 12$). The total sample for the post survey was much smaller (87 students) because the northeastern elementary responses were lost in the mail and never arrived at the research homebase. We attempted to have the northeastern school redo the posttest, but it never worked out. In addition, the midwestern high schools did not complete the posttest because the high school student participants consisted of the human relations course students and the Students of Color Support Group (suburban) and the theater group (urban) Voices of Change. Administrators and teachers felt that to track down each student to do the post-test would be too difficult because the students were all in different classes.

STUDENTS' FINAL STATISTICAL REPORT

The students' final statistical report was prepared by the Antiracist Teacher Study project analyst, Anthony Stevens. An annotated version is presented in this section in conjunction with points of view from the author.

There were reliability issues resulting from the imbalance of samples for the pre- and posttests. The interitem correlation method (internal consistency) for scale reliability was conducted on the 10-item scale. The corresponding alpha coefficient was equal to .72. This coefficient is respectable for a preliminary questionnaire, as many well-established questionnaires hold alpha coefficients equal to .80 and are deemed reliable (Anastasi, 1988). Further research should be conducted using this scale with varying samples to better establish its reliability (Stevens, 1996).

An example of research follow-through was the request of a northeastern suburban school in the process of transforming school policy and curriculum to reflect antiracist education integration at all levels. School administrators asked the author to facilitate the teacher preparation process and for permission to use the "Student's Perceptions" survey at the school. With this permission granted, the school is obliged to share the data collected, at which time the investigator will use the same process of analysis to add to the current student research. We anticipate that several schools and school districts will come on board in similar ways, which will ultimately add to the student sample size.

Analyses were conducted using SPSS-X mainframe version 4.1. The frequencies were listed by school in terms of the percentage of student agreement with each question. The breakdown begins with a total sample pretest, total sample posttest, students of color pretest, and students of color posttest.

The responses from the students were separated into two groups for the analyses. Those two categories, children of color and Caucasian children, were necessary in that one motive for this study was to discover the presence of racist behaviors by teachers against students of color. Whereas, it has been found in earlier studies that children of color are often targets of racism (Murray and Clark, 1990; Lee, 1996; Donaldson, 1996; Daniel-Tatum, 1997), we were interested in detecting differences between the responses of the children by race. Consequently, t-tests were conducted to assess differences between the two groups before and immediately following antiracist curriculum intervention by the cohort teachers and the principal and on-site investigators.

Through the pretest we found that students of color did not feel as comfortable around their teachers as their white counterparts did in this study, and they did not feel that their culture's contributions were mentioned enough in the classroom. The results overall suggest that there are strong discrepancies between the satisfaction levels of students of color and Caucasian students in predominantly white scholastic institutions.

Only one test remained significant after the intervention (i.e., Q1, My teacher(s) mention contributions made by people of color in class). The implication here is that proper intervention does produce change in the classroom. Such change may result in increased interest and belongingness for children of color, especially for those who are in predominantly white educational settings. Nationwide, this could serve to reverse many of our nation's downward trends. Surely our assertions remain to be proven; however, wouldn't it be easier to create welcome environments for all our children if doing so would ensure a more stable and productive society?

STUDENT QUALITATIVE REVIEW

As the principal investigator, I had direct contact with 147 student survey respondents through forum lectures, workshops, affinity support group meetings (mediator, educator, and advisor), focus group interviews, contest judging, drama production, and informal frequent discussions. In addition, the on-site investigators and researchers had various contact with the remaining students from the survey. All members of the investigation team were required to keep reflective/observation notebooks to record their observations and reactions. These data revealed the students' satisfaction at having heightened exposure to antiracist and multicultural education concepts.

Overall, these students duplicated the sentiments of students in past student race relation studies (Donaldson, 1996), namely, that they were hopeful and excited about having "real" dialogue in the classroom. Students had great respect for the teachers who participated in the antiracist implementation portion of the study and were convinced that most of these teachers had always implemented aspects of diversity in the classroom. However, many students mentioned that it was fun having new discussions and assignments addressing issues of racism more directly. There were other students, especially white students, who declared that all forms of prejudice need to be addressed simultaneously. We would frequently explain to students that addressing prejudice of any kind is a step-by-step process and that it is important to detach various aspects of discrimination to understand each "ism" in depth. Students as well as teachers realized that standing against racism may entail hardships. I will speak about student awareness, experiences, and concerns in the following section, Part II. The introduction highlights how teachers and students learned from one another, by sharing antiracist education classes and a national conference attended by students and teachers from the study. Chapter 6 of Part II will begin with a recent study that indicated that black students (teens) are not affected by racism, and an informal, but national internet discussion on the detrimental effects of this poll. This discussion ties into the identity issues that surfaced in the study with the secondary students of color enrolled in the midwestern suburban schools.

II

Students Empowered by the Antiracist Teacher Study

Antiracist education is a give-and-take process. As students view their teachers' intolerance of racism and other biases, they become empowered to do likewise. Consider the following example of collaboration that allowed teachers and students of the study to learn antiracist practice from each other.

A student antiracist-multicultural human relations course was conducted simultaneously with the implementation component study. (This course will be fully discussed in the next chapter.) The principal investigator from the Antiracist Education Teacher Study developed and taught the course, which involved students from all cultural backgrounds. Each session was videotaped and passed on to the midwestern cohort members who could not participate directly in the student course. These tapes served to prepare the cohort for the implementation phase of the study. Those teachers who viewed these tapes commented on the "excellent and informative presentations" as well as the "positive interaction between the facilitator and the students" (implementation field notes, March 1996).

The implementation component for the midwestern and northeastern cohort groups encouraged use of the video *Prejudice: Answering Children's Questions,* moderated by television journalist Peter Jennings, as part of their antiracist education units. Teachers and students used this video to open discussions on prejudice and racism. The cohort teachers did not produce any video footage during their antiracist lessons in the classroom, however. The choice not to video the teachers was a conscious decision by the researchers, who found that the prospect of being videotaped made the teachers nervous. However, we did video the suburban midwestern cohort group's Preconference Institute (an all-day session) participation in the annual National Association for Multicultural Education (NAME) Conference (1996).

The five teachers in the midwestern cohort demonstrated the antiracist education lessons they had administered in their own classrooms during the implementation phase. The multimedia teacher, along with the assistance of one of the researchers, put together a Power Point presentation that included the session's agenda, definitions, and video clips. We followed with mainly interactive sections that included "Africa to America," "Slave Auctioneer," "North America's Immigration Periods," "1960s Civil Rights Movement," and "Antiracist-Multicultural Literature Resources" segments. The Institute culminated in an antiracist education student performance by students from the human relations course and "Voices of Change" (urban midwestern cohort: students from the implementation phase). Over 50 people participated in the day's events.

Verbal and written evaluations from the participants were outstanding. During a break, however, one of our student-participants overheard a discussion in the bathroom claiming that "the session thus far was insulting." The student returned in tears to share this experience with the lead facilitator, who with the student's permission in turn shared it in the session. This became a "teachable moment," showing that many people are not ready to understand American experiences from other perspectives. The woman who made the critical remark never returned.

Many of the participants who were educators said they were proud and inspired to see "everyday teachers" presenting antiracist curriculum that could be duplicated in basic subject area classes; these teachers, they felt, were role models for their students. We found that this level of presentation empowered the teachers, gave them the opportunity to work as a presenting team, and demonstrated the vast possibilities of what teachers can do regarding the area of antiracist education. Further, by demonstrating their willingness to take social action in the classroom and/or on a national platform to address racial injustices, teachers were making a reality what had been the hope of many students—to see their teachers active in reducing racism in schools. This experience will be discussed further in chapter 6 from the point of view of the students. In addition, several other student social action initiatives will be documented.

Unlike the poll results we begin with in chapter 6, the teachers and students who participated in the national conference felt strongly about the existence of racism in schools.

Voice of One Who Has Lived It

As I reminisce on my old school days, I ask myself the question, "What teachers did I have who fought against racism, or were civil rights activists?" My answer is, "None that I know of." I recall having several good teachers, two of whom were black and the only teachers of color I had during my elementary and secondary school experience. I had one of the black teachers in second grade (she was a friend of my older sister, who was also a teacher), and the other was my high school art teacher. They both motivated me, more than my other teachers did, to be the best I could be. However, I did not see that as a form of activism then.

My role model for teacher activism was my eldest brother, who was a high school sociology teacher at a white suburban school. I remember our riding an old school bus together, along with many others, to Washington, D.C. We participated in an antiracist march to the Lincoln Memorial. I remember complaining about all the miles we had to walk, and he just simply said something like, "You've got to be strong if you're going to help right the wrongs in our society."

As a high school student I was one of many students who boycotted the poor conditions of our inner-city schools. My school building in particular had been deemed unsafe by the city inspectors, but it wasn't until years later that it was demolished and a new building erected.

The lack of supplies, good teachers, and extracurricular activities led students to go on an attendance strike. We picketed our schools with signs of protest. For a number of days following, we barricaded ourselves in the school auditorium to devise a plan of action. During that time we were visited by black college students who told us that they supported our protest and were trying to help the schools in our community. As an alternative, those of us who were out of school during this time were offered tutoring by local black college students. These college students had formulated a citywide effort to unite the area colleges' black student unions for the purpose of keeping the striking high school students abreast of their studies. The college students were able to secure a building for classes. We had to sign in and stay the full day, just as if we were attending regular school. I felt I had learned more in that three- to four-week period, than I had my entire time in high school.

There were many arrests during that time, as we were considered truant. At the same time, our schools began to acknowledge our demands for better schooling. Greater funding, more equitable hiring practices, and school programs began to surface. For the students who stood up for this legitimate cause, we realized our efforts had made a difference. Yet, I couldn't help tasting the bitter with sweet, as I was compelled to go back to a school that could never match the education I received from the black college students. My only thought was to help to make public school education better and more equal for all students. This thought led me to pursue a career in education. With this feeling of empowerment as a high school student, I gained the confidence to allow my aspirations to come to fruition.

6

A Recent Poll, Student Antiracist Programs, and the Social Action of Students

DISTURBING FINDINGS

Contrary to the recent Time/CNN poll that black teens are not touched by racism (*Des Moines Register*/Associated Press, 11/17/97), school age students of all racial backgrounds are affected by issues of racism in schools. The Time/CNN poll reported that nearly nine out of ten black teenagers said racism has little impact on their daily lives. When asked about racism in their personal lives, 89% of black teenagers said racism is a "small problem" or "not a problem at all." The poll also found that more than half of all teenagers, 62% of blacks (300 respondents) and 58% of whites (301 respondents), believed that racism is a "big problem." The statistical findings of this survey appear to be quite confusing; nonetheless, these polls can be very dangerous to the American public that care to believe that racism is not an issue in schools. The idea that black students are not bothered by racism can easily convince taxpayers, school environments, and government that little to no attention or finances should be invested to reduce the racial injustices committed in our schools and society. The poll also fell short by viewing racism only as a black-and-white issue.

This report is questionable because it lacks full discussion of the students' understanding of racism. As a researcher and antiracist educator in the field for close to two decades, I ask myself from what region, school districts, and so on were these students who were polled? I am reminded of the numerous times I have interviewed, surveyed, and worked with students unable to define racism and unaware of historical racial injustices but able to describe obstacles, incidents, isolation, policies, mistreatment, and ignorance that were purely racist.

Several colleagues in the field have also expressed these sentiments during an antiracist scholars and activists e-mail discussion about the poll. The discussion, prompted by Bakari Chavana, a high school teacher in California and executive committee member of the National Coalition of Education Activists, offered his views. Bakari said, "If the results of this survey have any validity regarding the views of black students, then I think black students are either in denial about the effects of racism, or they are ignorant of how racism exists in this country. Perhaps our youth have been schooled to view racism only in its most overt forms, e.g., racial slurs, church burnings, and stereotypical media images."

Bakari invited the views of others on this subject. Linda Mizell, author of *Think about Racism,* a book designed for secondary students (The Think Series, Walker and Company, 1992), was one who responded. Mizell stated that she was not surprised at the results of the poll. She further added, "I would argue that these kids are BOTH in denial as a survival mechanism, and oblivious (sometimes unconsciously, sometimes willfully so) to the effects of racism. I've listened to numerous panels and discussion groups in which kids of color insisted that there was no racism in their schools, then went on to describe incredibly racist situations. I've been convinced that the emotional survival of many kids (and adults) in minority situations depends on not seeing the daily acts of racism to which they are subjected." Carlene L. (parent; anonymity requested), agreed fully that it was denial and spoke about attending a recent parent meeting where the parents' children are bused out to suburban schools. Carlene mentioned a recent poll of these parents that "showed the parents as being very happy with the suburban schools their children were attending, and having little or no racism in the schools." She went on to say that the parents at this meeting confirmed their satisfaction with the suburban schools, "and then went on to describe 'incidents' which they handled directly with their teachers. These racist incidents (name calling, not calling on their child in class, etc.) were looked at as separate, individual events . . . not connected to any larger climate or systemic racism . . . and easy handled on a 'one to one' basis with a 'very receptive' teacher." Carlene made an interesting point: "If systemic analysis about racism is part of the conversation for kids, teachers, administrators, and parents, we can see beyond 'incidents' to actual change." But Carlene felt there was too much at risk for the students and the parents and suggested that "it is up to the antiracist education activists [and, I add, researchers] to create a space on the margin where there is support for this and folks like the parents that can join in without being quite so vulnerable."

Living in a predominantly white community with four children enrolled in the school system, I am inclined to agree with Carlene in terms of families becoming targets when parents take a vocal stand against racism. I've had it happen to my family and to other families I am close to in my community. I found myself on many occasions having to sacrifice work time to visit my children's schools to "straighten out a situation" with teachers or administrators. I have one child who because of her unusual African name is seldom called on in particular classes because of the slight difficulty of the pronunciation or is called "Miss Donaldson" when all the other students are addressed by their first names. My child often feels embarrassed and left out because of her name and her cultural affiliation.

Therefore, it is important to have activists, scholars, and researchers take a leading role to provide a safe haven of support for teachers, other school personnel, parents, and children. One underlying concept in our antiracist education research is to involve the total school environment, working simultaneously on all levels. As we concentrated on teachers as facilitators of knowledge for students, we understood that students can themselves be facilitators of knowledge for other students and for the entire school community.

Past studies have revealed the positive influence older generations of students have on the younger generations in terms of mentoring on various subjects. Secondary students involved with antiracist education projects have often been the heavy hitters in conveying the ills of prejudice to other students (Donaldson, 1996). In acknowledgment of this finding, one goal of the antiracist study was to allow secondary students to participate in antiracist curriculum development and practice within the project.

STUDENTS OF THE MIDWESTERN SUBURBAN COHORT

As principal investigator for the antiracist teacher study, I maintained regular contact with the local participating school district and the cohort group of teachers at the elementary school, middle school, and high school. At each school we set up antiracist support programs with the cohort teachers based upon where they felt they needed assistance. The fourth grade elementary school teacher was involved with teaching ongoing multicultural and antiracist literature for his language arts unit and wanted his students to be exposed to the vast world of multicultural literature. In order to demonstrate how primary and secondary teachers can pool their resources, keep a connected progression of antiracist education work, and involve students in a mentor teaching situation, we had the middle school's Multicultural Club students enroll in a multicultural literature technology project designed by one of the technology-based researchers. The project was under the direction of the middle school technology cohort group member and the technology researcher. The Middle School Multicultural Club students met in the media lab each Wednesday to prepare Power Point multicultural literature presentations, games, and research for the fourth graders at the elementary school. Once this process was completed, the Middle School Multicultural Club was allowed to visit and conduct a multicultural literature-technology demonstration class for the fourth graders at the elementary school. This Multicultural Club had done several such visiting projects, as well as presentations for their own school peers, since its inception in 1994. In addition, the fourth grade teacher and a number of the cohort middle school members each year provide an MLK (Martin Luther King Jr.) educational and student presentation day. All the student participants were exceptional, and there was a noticeable flair of presentational style and scholarship with the cohort teachers' students. I was given the opportunity to judge the Power Point presentations of the seventh grade entries, which featured the Jewish Holocaust experience, worldwide child labor injustices, and the 1960s civil rights movement, to name a few. The presentations were professional and about 99.5% accurate. It was evident that these students had put in numerous hours of researching and developing the technology and group verbal presentations. I voted them all outstanding.

ANTIRACIST EDUCATION HIGH SCHOOL EFFORTS

The two midwestern suburban high school cohort members, one an associate principal and the other a special education teacher, had been very active in addressing multicultural issues at the high school. The special education teacher had served as the faculty sponsor for the Student Human Relations Committee for several years, and the associate principal had become an administrator sponsor for a students of color affinity support group. The associate principal gained, by struggle, permission for the students to meet during school hours. This time was granted because of a number of racial incidents and a continuing dropout rate of students of color at the school. Both the associate principal and the teacher had also served as advisors for the "Diversity Day Event" held every two to three years for students at the school.

The Students of Color Affinity Group (1995–96), conceptually, was a follow-up of the support and at-risk group evening meetings held by a previous high school employee, who was a counselor and coordinator of the at-risk program. During her tenure at the school she administered minority student, parent, female, and male support groups and often recorded the discussions and concerns in a focus group interview format. These sessions during 1990–91 were developed into a report format and submitted to the school district office for review. The comments shared by the participants in this report were some of the same concerns shared by the Students of Color Affinity Group in 1996, thus indicating that not much change has taken place.

During the 1990–91 interviews the students were asked to describe their experiences and share concerns related to their being a minority in the school district. Areas of concern were placed into five categories: (1) socialization, (2) discrimination and/or insensitivity, (3) achievement, (4) discipline, and (5) comments and suggestions. The study indicated that students of color, especially black and Hispanic students, were experiencing racial prejudice regularly. For example, students said they were often ignored in the classroom, were placed into lower-track classes, unjustly received detention and suspension for perceived misbehavior, often had their names mispronounced, heard stereo-typical comments made by teachers and peers in class about their race, faced social events that were white oriented, were often directed to pursue voca-tional or community colleges after graduation, and were never given the op-portunities to discuss applications and entrance into black colleges.

Excerpts from student interviews show common themes mentioned fre-quently by five or more students from the sessions: In the area of academic achievement students remarked that "teachers have never put personal em-phasis on learning in the classroom. Most of them really didn't care and do not care if we learn or not. They just let us sit there." "Most of the teachers in this district do not expect us to do well. When we do a good job, they never say 'good job.' I've been in other classes and teachers have told other students they have done a good job. I also did very well and they totally ignored my work." "Many teachers feel that we cannot make A's. I have compared my pa-pers with other students in some of my classes and my answers were also cor-rect. I, however, received a B or C while other students made As." "When I was in junior high school, a teacher told me there was no reason for me to take the Algebra Aptitude Test. He said, 'You won't make a high enough score to make a difference anyway.'" Comments about discrimination and insensitivity were numerous also: "Teachers, administrators, and students stereotype quite a bit. They only think we are good in sports and dancing. The only time they seek us out is when athletics are involved." "In history class, students stare at you when slavery is discussed. The teacher also looks directly at you. I've never had a history teacher teach or mention the achievements minorities have made and/or are now making in this country." "On several occasions, I have raised my hand to answer or ask a question and it was conveniently ignored. This has happened in elementary, junior high, and high school." "Teachers inquire about our home and personal lives." "Teachers and students are always ques-tioning us about our hair." Some of the students stated that staff members make insensitive remarks such as "Why don't you go downstairs with your own kind," "Please do not bring your ghetto boxes [radio, tape, or CD players] to this room," "They only relate to how sharply we dress" and/or "You did well in the game last night." In the area of discipline, some students felt that "if a student is punished for using profanity, then students should be punished for calling a person a 'nigger.' " "I detest being yelled at when called into the disci-pline office. I am a person and I can be talked to like anyone else. As soon as I object to being yelled at or question something, I usually get additional days in restricted study hall or [I am] suspended." And, "When questioning the ad-ministration about an event, they always say we are too sensitive." Just as the students in the more recent group, these students wanted more and adminis-trators of color: "We suggest more minority teachers and administrators." "I have not had a black teacher since I've been here and I started in elementary school." "Some of us were lucky enough to have Mr. C. ["Wendall," profiled in the teacher study, chapter 4], and that was it." And, "We would like to have an elective course in history on contributions minorities have made and are now making to this society" (Jackson, 1991).

Throughout the school year 1995–96 the high school's students of color affinity group and the Human Relations Committee were given the opportunity to assist in devising curriculum, presentations, and panel discussions. I will concentrate on their efforts now as they relate to the Antiracist Teacher Study and share both the victories and the pitfalls of including high school students in the process of antiracist education curriculum development.

A HIGH SCHOOL HUMAN RELATIONS PILOT COURSE

During the year that the Antiracist Education Study became involved with assisting the high school cohort members (1995–96), seven African American males left the school for various reasons (i.e., expulsion, inability to cope with perceived discrimination, and moving out of the state [university affiliated families are often quite transient]). It was also reported by the former at-risk coordinator, now at-risk district coordinator, that over the past several years black male and female students had been leaving the high school before graduation and that student demographics had shifted, with increased minority enrollment in elementary and middle school, but decreased enrollment at the high school level.

As an antiracist education educator, I was invited to one of the students of color affinity support group meetings. At the meeting, students asked me to share my national data and experiences with working with students on these issues. They were interested in learning more about individual racism and institutional racism and how they affect students' equal access to education. (This inquiry confirmed Bakari Chavana's assertion that many students are unfamiliar with how racism exists in this country). They specifically wanted at least one African American teacher hired at the high school. They also wanted an African American studies and/or multicultural studies course taught at the school. To oblige the students' request, I offered to submit a proposal to teach a pilot multicultural studies course at the school. My goal at the time was to give immediate help to the students, have some interested high school teachers and our school district cohort group sit in on the course, and have the participating teachers keep the course ongoing.

I submitted two names of African American preservice teachers ready to graduate and looking for teaching positions in the area. Both had outstanding academic records and superb references, but they were not hired by the district in a timely fashion. As a result, both accepted jobs in nearby cities. One of these teachers became teacher of the year in her school district and will receive sabbatical leave to speak to schools throughout the state. This experience reflects a not infrequent problem in predominantly white school districts: They share the difficulty of recruiting teachers of color but procrastinate when opportunities arise. Nonetheless, students wanted immediate responses to their requests because they were aware that responses to these requests had been put off for many years.

Both the Human Relations Committee and the Students of Color Support Group requested that a human relations forum be offered at the high school to address the need to strengthen diversity awareness and appreciation at the school. The objective was to pilot these forums in hope of developing a permanent human relations course for the high school students. The goal of the forums was to develop sensitivity to, knowledge of, recognition of, and techniques for dealing with human relations problems relative to selected microcultures (i.e., issues of prejudice, racism, discrimination, sexism, stereotypes, myths, and misconceptions). Congruent with the Multicultural Nonsexist Education (MCNSE) course objectives taught at the local university, this objective was thought to have influence with the State Board of Education to ultimately grant curriculum and course approval.

I was asked to present the course proposal to the school board, which unanimously accepted it. Making the pilot course an ongoing course was discussed. The associate principal (cohort member) suggested applying to the state curriculum board to make the program an independent course; another suggestion was to go through the school's social studies department. Since the pilot course ended, neither avenue has been followed.

MIDWESTERN SUBURBAN HIGH SCHOOL HUMAN RELATIONS: A 15-WEEK FORUM

The midwestern suburban high school "Human Relations Forum" provided a series of multicultural topics for interested high school students. Although the principal investigator and research team presented three announcement forum seminars and provided newsletter advertisment to the larger student body (approximately 1,600 students), the students who signed up for the course were mainly members of the Human Relations Committee and the Multicultural Support Group (the Students of Color Affinity Group). These students were of many ethnic backgrounds and mixed heritages such as East Indian, Arab, African, Korean, Columbian, Puerto Rican, Thai, Panamanian, African American, European American, Jamaican, Peruvian, and Russian Jewish; also included was an exchange student from Germany. Attendance at sessions fluctuated because of students' school commitments. Yet, over the 15-week period 26 students attended some portion of the course.

The forums included the use of several mediums, such as the arts and multimedia, to broaden student awareness of diverse groups and issues in the United States. The forums provided a basic introduction to multicultural education and examined from theoretical perspectives and experiential exercises the nature of pluralism and intergroup relations in U.S. society. The intent was to expose the basic causes and complex dynamics of racism, sexism, and other forms of discrimination and intergroup conflict. Furthermore, the forums explored the historical and contemporary experiences and contributions of people of color, white ethnic groups, and women in U.S. society and also reexamined U.S. history, culture, and institutions from the perspective of these groups. This course description was adapted from Dr. Sonia Nieto's (University of Massachusetts, at Amherst) "Introduction to Multicultural Education" for college students.

The course, which began with a class oath of respect, covered a range of topics: *What Is So Important about Developing Good Human Relations?; Oral Traditions: Telling Our Stories; Prejudice: Answering Children's Questions; Prejudice/Discrimination Based on Age, SES [Socioeconomic Status], Religion, Exceptionality, Race, Gender, Language, and Ethnicity; The Five Major Ethnic Groups in the United States; Defining Racism in the United States; Examining Sexism in the United States;* and *Understanding Classism in the United States.* The last two sessions focused on developing solutions to create better human relations at the school, within the community, and worldwide. The course was implemented in a lecture and experiential format. Originally, the course was to center on student-facilitator discussions, but because in many instances the material was new to the students, the lecture format prevailed during sessions. One observation made during the review of the videotaped sessions is that two European American students dominated speaking time. Both appeared eager to discuss their family histories and lineages. They did not react as if the only people with issues were people of color. They too seemed to feel that their respective European cultures are lost in America. The one European American female often monopolized the speaking time, and other students spoke most often only after she had responded, since she usually responded first when questions were asked. This was a dynamic that may be noteworthy, especially with regard to what would happen later in the student input curriculum development and the antiracist projects that followed.

The course began February 21, 1996, and concluded May 29, 1996. Following the conclusion of the course, the students were invited to participate in the Midwest urban (study site) community's "Race Unity Day." Drama students of one of the midwestern urban cohort members were also invited to participate in this event. During preparation for this event, scheduled June 9, 1996, a renowned social change theater director was in the area working on another project associated with the principal investigator. The investigator invited the director to visit both sites and to work with the students to generate ideas for the event. This director had the students begin with writing fictious letters to a racist. The letters produced were very thought provoking. In almost every letter the students asked the racist to try to understand the pain and divisiveness racism engendered and to make time to speak with them to find solutions to the problem. One white student wrote that the racist's views caused problems with his becoming friends with people of color because most people of color are convinced that all whites are racist. The students invited the racist to become open-minded and assured the individual that being racist was a matter of choice, not dictate. Some said that the racist was putting the world in a bad situation. In essence, the students wrote that if the door were opened for positive discussion, the racist would never regret it.

Following return of the letters, students discussed what they had written and why. These discussions helped the students to develop short vignettes for the "Race Unity Day" event. Some presentations dealt with institutional racism, such as applying for a bank loan and being denied, shopping at the mall and being forced to show an I.D., visiting a clinic and being encouraged to take birth control pills because of ethnicity, and being the victim in a case of mistaken identity and arrested. The other component of the performance focused on racial prejudice—a white girl is accused of trying to be black, and the black sell-out. Both groups were well received during these performances. It was apparent that they felt pride and achievement. I decided at that point to invite the students to participate in two upcoming events (fall 1996): a panel discussion for the teachers state social studies conference and a national conference. Excited by the invitations, the students looked forward to the fall events.

As the events approached, both schools contributed to bringing the social change theater director to the Midwest to work on the preparation for the panel discussion and the national production on antiracist education. The director worked with each student in preparing remarks for the panel discussion. The students discussed diversity issues and experiences in schools. Each had a particular area of emphasis such as gender, class, race, or language issues. The teacher-audience asked students numerous questions about what they would like to see in the social studies curriculum development and what suggestions they might have for more sensitive approaches for the classroom. The students were very articulate and received very high ratings in the conference evaluations.

Knowing they were being listened to by teachers empowered the students greatly. Yet, along with that confidence came challenges to the artistic director. The director attempted to prepare the students for the national multicultural education conference in which the primary objective was to deliver a presentation dealing with antiracist education. The students were told on several occasions that this presentation would deal with racism issues because it was being slotted into an antiracist education seminar and presentation. The suburban students agreed to the focus initially, but later they resisted the director's ideas for the presentation because they preferred to do a presentation that would be inclusive of all the issues. This preference came especially from a few of the white students in leadership roles who had convinced a number of the students of color to fight for this change in focus. They argued that there was no racism in their school and, therefore, they could not share stories or experiences about racism in school. At this point some students made disrespectful comments to the director, who then refused to return to coach the group. When it appeared that the students' presentation would be canceled, the students involved came to apologize. Although the apology was accepted, the director felt it best not to return. Instead, she focused on the urban drama group. As principal investigator and producer of the presentation, I took over the last rehearsals, which combined the suburban and urban groups. Despite the challenges, students learned lessons in respect. The students performed to full audiences, and in both the workshop performances and the evening performances the students received standing ovations for their creative work. In addition, during the all-day workshop the students were able to work alongside the antiracist teacher cohort group as they presented their sections.

The suburban overall production, entitled *We Wear the Mask,* consisted of a number of vignettes featuring students' actual experiences of racism. How could this be if there was no racism in their school? The point is made once again that denial runs deep even at the student level. This group used a bell timer to go from one presentation to the other. Some of the subtitles were "I Colored Myself Brown"; "Advised to Take Less Complicated Classes"; "Making Jokes about Jews"; "Stereotyped as a Gang Member"; "Fed up with Racial Epithets between Friends in the Lunch Room"; "A National Achievement Finalist Not Recognized"; and "Standing up against a One-sided Curriculum." As proven with many earlier projects with students, using art mediums greatly assisted students and their audiences in opening the door for discussing deeply ingrained issues of racism.

STUDENTS EMPOWERED BY THE ANTIRACIST TEACHER (CURRICULUM DEVELOPMENT AND IMPLEMENTATION) STUDY OPPORTUNITIES

The observation field notes, reflective journal, focus group rehearsal interviews, presentation discussions, class participation, and video analysis data rendered the same results from the quantitative student pre and post survey, namely, that intervention (antiracist curriculum development and implementation) facilitates positive change and empowerment for students.

As we acknowledge that misleading studies on students' perceptions of racism are a danger to the American public, and as we produce findings that numerous educational institutions and communities verify, we assist in addressing and reducing racism in this country. Through the antiracist study we are able to recognize that racism exists throughout the United States and is negatively affecting our citizens, either directly or indirectly. Some students as well as many teachers in the study were in denial, but the students who became active in the antiracist education projects broadened their understanding that denial makes them vulnerable to pain through racial injustice and puts their health at risk of the ill effects of this social disease. In addition, students realized that being uninformed disempowered them to make change. This student shattering of denial seemed to address denial as a survival mechanism that makes one oblivious (unconsciously, sometimes willfully) to the effects of racism as mentioned by Linda Mizell, author of *Think about Racism,* in the internet dialogue.

Students involved in the project learned to develop positive coping skills such as standing up to racist jokes from peers, becoming multiculturally literate and able to share that knowledge in their classrooms and in other public arenas, and becoming more aware of institutional and individual racism and how acts of racism hurt others. Not all students were close associates or even knew each other before the programs; but during the implementation and social action process, they became friends and antiracist allies. As young citizens, they experienced what standing together can do. The five areas of inquiry—socialization, discrimination and/or insensitivity, achievement, discipline, and suggestions–students' input—established through Jackson's interviews were addressed in the implementation component. Student-participants said the program's boost in students' self-esteem had a positive effect on their academic achievement, intercultural socialization, behavioral attitudes, and antiracist education problem-solving techniques, especially during the high school students' presentations.

Having their teachers (cohort participants) as antiracist education role models made a positive impact as well. Students realized that they could go to these teachers for advice and support regarding these issues. At the NAME Conference, the students reported that they learned about courage and standing up for what is right from the cohort teachers. Furthermore, they spoke highly of the lessons the teachers presented at the conference. Many said they learned new things about the history of racism in this country and more details about segregation and the civil rights activism of the 1960s. They realized that people from all walks of life and backgrounds fought for civil rights for all, and that this struggle helped to change oppressive laws and give racially oppressed groups greater opportunity. They nonetheless acknowledged that the struggle has not ended; that inequality still exists. This acknowledgment aided them in discussing their role in dismantling racism. Joint efforts of students and teachers helped to demonstrate to them and to the public that they are not alone in the struggle to reduce racism in schools.

Twenty-five student-participants were involved in the national conference. Parents encouraged their efforts. Many students involved their parents in fundraising, driving, chaperoning, and so on. All the parents showed a commitment to standing against racism and were proud of their children's dedication in this effort. Parents and students were conversing at home about these issues. Many of the parents let their children know how proud they were of them; this additional encouragement from home empowered the students even more.

Later some parents noted that exposing their children to antiracist education professionals prepared them to be future leaders in this area. A number of the parents had read some of my antiracist education publications and knew of Askew's involvement in coordinating the 1998–99 "Interfaith Pilgrimage of the

Middle Passage" (her advisory committee consisted of Tom Feelings, David DuBois, the Most Reverend Desmond Tutu, Cornell West, and a host of other scholars and activists).

Showing their growing leadership, a number of the students had started their involvement as members of the Multicultural Club (established fall 1994) at the middle school. Many of these students were top candidates during the high school's Human Relations Committee recruitment of incoming first-year students. Many of these students also participated in the ongoing annual districtwide MLK Forum (started in 1992 by two suburban cohort members). This continued participation in multicultural-antiracist education programs and events has progressively elevated students' leadership qualities.

The implementation phase of the study made a difference; it "touched" the total school environment and beyond. Although the involved teachers and students were not formally recognized by their schools and school district (no publicity, no honorable mentions, etc.), negotiations to maintain the program's momentum were initiated. A research report of the findings was distributed to district administrators, some of whom are members of the Multicultural Nonsexist Education (MCNSE) School District Committee. Through the MCNSE Committee, the antiracist teacher cohort group is currently seeking funding for continued programs and recognition to serve as antiracist education facilitators for the school district. The implementation phase demonstrated to the school district the fruitful potential of teachers, students, and local university researchers collaborating on such efforts. This has assisted the antiracist education movement in the school community in its effort to gain permission to administer a multicultural experimental school longitudinal research study.

Teachers' and students' suggestions on ways to continue to educate teachers on awareness, curriculum development, and implementation led to the offer of an antiracist education curriculum development course by way of interactive television. The experimental in-service teacher outreach course was made possible by the local university through their continuing education and extension program. Both study sites in the midwestern region agreed to allocate professional development funds to the teachers who registered. Part III will discuss this pilot course and focus on the midwestern region's additional university and school district(s) antiracist education collaboration(s). It will highlight efforts made at the university level to further prepare preservice teachers in the area of international and domestic antiracist-multicultural education and enhance race relations on the college campus. This section will also feature the creation of an experimental multicultural school research project endorsed by a university and the school district. These endeavors will demonstrate the importance of collaboration at all levels in addressing racism in school communities and share proactive ideas for antiracist education development and implementation in the classroom and beyond.

III

Protocols for the Classroom and Beyond

Part III discusses higher education and primary school studies and projects as they relate to antiracist education. As Part I focused on in-service teacher re-education, and Part II on secondary-level student empowerment experiences, Part III seeks to highlight other levels of education, making clear that awareness of racism must be addressed at all levels in a continuing dialogue if we are to drastically reduce its poisonous venom. The three main ideas of this book remain evident in Part III: (1) how in-service and preservice teachers and others in education think about race, (2) what strategies work to develop their thinking and ability to implement antiracist education teaching, and (3) the impact antiracist education has on students.

This section, "Protocols for the Classroom and Beyond," attempts to demonstrate the vast possibilities of creating and implementing antiracist education curricula to combat racism in schools. Through a case study approach, each of its chapters exhibits research on innovative concepts and actual projects that have successfully integrated these ideas. The higher education antiracist course, the preservice teacher study abroad program, and the multicultural-antiracist experimental elementary school project further demonstrate strategies and research that develop consciousness and abilities to live, think, breathe, and teach from an antiracist-multicultural perspective. Part III focuses on issues educators ponder about multicultural teacher education, distance education and computer-mediated communication, and the impact antiracist-multicultural education has on student learning and development. This section will, in short, bring together all the antiracist education studies and projects presented in this book. It will reflect on the lessons learned and make suggestions for continuing to "shatter the denial" that racism exists and negatively hinders the educational success of students.

Voice of an Activist and Scholar

I was born in 1954, the same year as *Brown v. Board of Education of Topeka*. This landmark Supreme Court decision repudiated *Plessy v. Ferguson* (1896), which had required railroad companies to provide separate but equal accommodations for blacks and whites. The *Brown* decision declared that separate facilities are inherently unequal and that "separate but equal has no place in public education" (Allen-Sommerville and McCormick, 1998, p. 3). As fate would have it, from the start of my life I was groomed to be a civil and human rights activist.

My father was born in 1909, and his mother in 1868 (and her mother was an enslaved African woman who escaped and married an American Indian, so the story goes). My father was a family, churchgoing man, and through his daily living I learned that the average human being can have a tremendous impact regarding change. It was no surprise to me that he stood up against the second-class citizenship he was forced to receive because of his race. For as a young child, I would overhear the stories of my father. Often with his friends he would recall his experiences of being a southern-born black man. He would talk about black lynchings, capturing of black men for the chain gangs, his black porter—"yes-um"—job, being a man yet called a boy, having to duck the head of my light-skinned mother down in the car while getting gas at a southern gas station for fear that they would think she was white and he would be lynched. I once heard a friend of his call him a mathematical genius who never got a chance to further those abilities in a college or a profession.

My father worked three jobs until his death at age 54, as waiter and chef. Yet, in those last years he picked me to accompany him on freedom marches, church rallies, boycotts and protests, for reasons still unknown to me. I used to think it was because I was the lightest of my siblings and he didn't want me confused as to who I was or what responsibilities I had. I was taught about the great sacrifices my parents, grandparents, and great-grandparents made for me to be free and able to get an education. Not to leave my mother out, because her children's education was a vital importance to her also. In her generation, she had received her high school diploma, and that was something to be proud. But she wanted more for her children.

My mother was a hardworking woman at home. She cooked, washed, ironed, scrubbed, and made sure we didn't miss a day of school. She was beyond cleanliness, dusting or wiping every little spot we children would accumulate. I learned that she acquired this habit for excessive cleaning from her foster mother. Yes, racism hit home too with my mother, but she hardly spoke about it in those terms. She was one of eight children born to a Cape Verdean (African and Portuguese) father and an Italian mother. When her mother became ill and was hospitalized, the state removed the children from the home, feeling that my grandfather could not care for them. Relatives from my grandmother's side of the family refused to take the children because they were considered black; therefore, they all were separated and placed in various foster homes, losing touch with one another for many years. Although my mother loved my father dearly, I often felt she married young to become independent. Once married, she had many children and was unable to fulfill her dream of attending college to become a commercial artist. Again, the idea of her children graduating from college was very important to her.

I never dreamed of going beyond four years of college. However, fate would have it again that I would receive not only a master's degree in education but also a doctorate of education in cultural diversity and curriculum reform. Matching scholarship to activism has become a natural phenomenon in my life. As I've worked with educators and people in so many parts of the world, often discussing our experiences regarding racism and other biases, I've witnessed those who were not necessarily activists become so. It takes willingness to learn to take a stand for justice to reduce racism in our schools and society.

The next section of this book takes activism beyond secondary-level institutions to other learning communities here and abroad, expanding antiracist education scholarship through action and adding to the discourse from a global perspective.

7

Curriculum 520X: Antiracist Education Curriculum Development and Research via Interactive Television

NEXT STEPS: FOLLOWING THE ANTIRACIST EDUCATION CURRICULUM DEVELOPMENT AND IMPLEMENTATION TEACHER STUDY

With the completion of the teacher curriculum development and implementation study and with evidence of antiracist education having a positive effect on student learning and development, we concentrated our efforts on what seemed the next logical step, connecting the resources of the local university to teachers statewide.

One finding of the geographical teacher study was the need to provide in-depth antiracist education professional development courses for in-service teachers at large. Understanding that incentives had to be created for in-service teachers to participate, the idea of offering an outreach course that fulfilled the human relations and civility requirement for the teachers throughout the state developed. Initially both midwestern (study sites) school district offices stated that professional development funding and grants were available to cover the cost of the course for teachers. Being based at a well-established science and technology university made it possible to offer the course in remote areas throughout the state. In addition, the state had invested in creating remote interactive television sites in numerous urban, suburban, and rural areas. In fact, the state is considered one of the nation's leaders in distance education. Furthermore, the state had had a multicultural nonsexist education mandate in place for all public schools since 1977 (however, during my research many teachers did not know that this law or these state multicultural guidelines existed.)

Announcements of the interactive television course were made in local and leading newspapers within the state. For example, some of the following excerpts from one of the major newspapers reflected positive reasons why educators should become involved. The title of the announcement article was "Professor/Author Takes Antiracist Education Course State-wide to Educators." The reporter integrated quotes from our interview.

"Teachers and educators across the state could use this course to take a proactive step in terms of ensuring non-racist education in our classrooms," noted Donaldson. "In the past we've basically used a bandaid approach to racial difficulties in our schools," she said. In other words, when tensions flare, people gather to address the current problem.

Her new class and the university's involvement in helping to develop non-racist education curricula and teaching methods puts the university on the leading edge of efforts to research race problems in the K–12 as well as college levels and bring educational direction in step with those findings. "Our findings are that teachers in this state and across the nation are not sensing and are not aware that racism exists in our schools. They do not see a problem. Yet when we interviewed and studied students, we found they see it much differently," Donaldson said. . . . Through teacher interviews, she explained, "We've really been able to understand the attitudes and needs of educators." (*Des Moines Register*, 1997)

The promotional article did a fine job with identifying the attributes of a university and K–12 antiracist education partnership. It then concluded with the deadline to register and the registration information.

The course was designed to develop awareness of the nature of antiracist education and the need for it in professional education. Within that framework, participants would discuss issues of racial identity and conditioning, the historical context of racism in U.S. society, and contemporary views and experiences. They would develop specific curriculum and/or research projects for their major assignment. Understanding the time constraints of in-service teachers, who would be the main participants, I organized a half-semester schedule. We would meet one day a week for interactive television lectures and discussions. We would also do individual "in-practice" labs, the labs would be their own classrooms. Teachers would integrate and test antiracist concepts in their given subject areas. The classroom lab would allow them to do teacher action research. For the remaining credit hours they would discuss case studies given and the process of their stages of development through the class "listserv" (a computer message system designed to reach only the computer addresses of people named on a particular list).

A technology approach using various aspects of computer-mediated communication (CMC) would provide greater outreach as well as enable us to experiment with merging antiracist-multicultural education with instructional technology. CMC can be defined as a variety of systems that allow people to communicate with other people by means of computers and networks. Some examples of CMC include computer conferencing, electronic mail, discussion lists, and bulletin boards (Romiszowski and Mason, 1996). In the case of this course, telecommunication that includes interactive television and distance education modalities also served as a characteristic of CMC, as this form of technology can also be used to address and integrate concepts of pluralism.

MERGING ANTIRACIST-MULTICULTURAL EDUCATION AND CMC

The efforts of integrating antiracist-multicultural education with CMC have been limited to date (Donaldson and Carter, 2000). Various views exist on the use of CMC as a liberating technology geared to assist the goals of multicultural-antiracist education. Some scholars assert that use of CMC has emerged as a Eurocentric and male-oriented discipline and therefore cannot meet the needs of multicultural societies (Appelbaum and Enomoto, 1995; *AAUW Report 2000*, Washington/CNN). Furthermore, numerous scholars and educators agree that harsh economic realities and racial inequalities exist regarding access and representation in CMC (Leigh, 1999; Hoffman and Novak, 1998; Damarin, 1998; Appelbaum and Enomoto, 1995; Doctor, 1992). The skepticism surrounding the convergence of CMC and multicultural education is valid when we consider the concerns mentioned above. However, an increasingly popular perspective is that the goals of multicultural-antiracist education can be served by CMC because of its ability to foster access to previously unavailable, dynamic, self-sustaining learning communities such as those represented by the graduate courses presented in this chapter (Leach, 1997; Appelbaum and Enomoto, 1995; Cummins and Sayers, 1995).

Although some scholars believe that CMC has great potential for fostering the goals of multiculturalism, and although widespread popular belief holds that CMC can contribute significantly to the cause of multiculturalism, little research has been done to support this claim. Little is known about the links between CMC and antiracist-multicultural education communities. CMC research calls attention to its potential to create dialogue on multicultural issues and practices while simultaneously allowing multicultural experiences to occur. The results of this course case study can contribute to the research on the alliance of multicultural education and CMC and distance education. Furthermore, the participation of upcoming academics and educators of varied ethnicities will demonstrate the assertion of Broholm and Aust (1994) that diverse backgrounds and concepts help to reduce the social inbreeding of ideas within an institutional culture.

A COURSE CASE STUDY APPROACH

The "Antiracist Education Curriculum Development and Research via Interactive Television" course, which as implied by the title, used interactive television to enhance student antiracist and multicultural awareness, curriculum development, and implementation skills. This was done through human interaction including image, voice, and data, between an origination point and remote sites. As an outreach extension and experimental course, its primary objective was to develop an awareness of the nature of antiracist studies and the need for it in professional education. In addition, it sought to exhibit and empower student-participants to understand the role technology can play in this introduction to the historical, sociological, philosophical, and pedagogical foundations of antiracist education. Furthermore, as an experimental course fusing antiracist-multicultural education and CMC and distance education, the course used other technological mediums of instruction such as internet discussions, electronic journaling, video, and Power Point presentations. Data from the use of these mediums were also collected and analyzed for the purpose of evaluating the course.

Table 7.1 outlines the general course and may be helpful for readers wanting to design and teach similar courses.

The required reading included *Deculturalization and the Struggle for Equality* (Spring, 1997) and *Antiracism in the U.S. History* (Aptheker, 1993). The latter focused on the first 200 years in the United States and the antiracist efforts made especially by blacks and whites (often whites do not feel that many of their foreparents fought against a racist system). I was encouraged to order these two books by Professor Hudson at Lesley College in Massachusetts, who is teaching one of the very few education-based college courses on racism. Her course is entitled "Racism in Education: Post Perspectives and Correct Realities" and is taught through the Intercultural Relations Program at her college. Students were also required to read *Through Students' Eyes: Combating Racism in United States Schools* (Donaldson, 1996) for a better understanding of K–12 students' views.

The school districts did their share in publicizing the course, and I expected that we would get a good number of participants, but teachers were not registering, reflecting the comment made by "John," the northeastern teacher profiled in chapter 4, that "to get all teachers on board would take more than an act of Congress. More than an 11th commandment." Certainly that became true in the teacher study and in this case with the course. Yet all was not lost; I was able to influence the State Board of Education elected officials to rank antiracist education in the state as a priority for its schools and educators, and the State Department of Education to suggest the course offering the following spring (1999) in conjunction with the university's continuing education and extension program and the State Department's Area Educational Agencies (AEA) program. The AEA provides required professional development seminars and courses for recertification of teachers statewide.

In addition, graduate students began registering for the 520X antiracist education course. This gave me the opportunity to test the benefits, if any, of an antiracist course taught on interactive television before the in-service course

Table 7.1
Antiracist Education Curriculum Development and Research

Prerequisites:	(1) Basic Use of Technology, (2) Social Foundations of Education, and (3) Introduction to Multicultural Education
Introduction	• Course expectations (goals and objectives), required reading and assignments. • Equipment overview • Rationale for linking antiracist-multicultural education & Distance Education • Working definitions of the disciplines (a) historical, philosophical, theoretical, sociological, and pedagogical underpinnings of antiracist-multicultural education, antiracist studies, and Distance Education
Research	(review of antiracist-multicultural education, antiracist studies, and Distance Education educational issues) • Instructor's lectures & materials/handouts/references • Student readings & investigation

Awareness	• Self-examination
	• Pluralism/various ethnicities: understanding cultural contributions and experiences
	• Mediums for enhancing awareness:
	• Interactive Television: lectures, guest panel of educators, and interactive class discussions
	  (a) Electronic Communication: listserv dialogues
	  (b) Personal reflective journaling: e-mail posted to instructor only
	  (c) Support resources: films, literature, stages of development models and other antiracist-multicultural education/ Distance Education frameworks, guest educators

Antiracist Education: Methods	• Interdisciplinary approaches (antiracist-multicultural education/Distance Education concepts integrated with other subject areas, i.e., communications, sociology, education administration, teacher education)
	  (a) Interdisciplinary model used (every subject area can be integrated with antiracist-multicultural education concepts),
	  (b) levels of integration model
	  (c) antiracist-multicultural education effective curriculum model

Application	• Curriculum unit assignments completed • Piloting of units through implementation: testing at "lab" sites (action research model used) • Class presentations of unit (including development process & pilot implementation results)—class (supportive) critique and recommendations, student self-evaluation and future goals in areas of antiracist-multicultural education and Distance Education

Source: Teaching Strategies in Ethnic Studies (Banks, 1998)

offering. I decided to continue to make this course a teacher action research study and announced my interest to the students as they registered. All the students permitted the collection of data from class discussions and assignments.

Each class was scheduled to be videotaped and later transcribed for the teacher action research project I would be modeling to the class, which consisted of collecting participation data to enable the building of empirical evidence to address the void of knowledge on merging multicultural education, antiracist studies, and CMC.

Graduate students of color, mainly from the College of Education, registered. However, one student from the area of communications, another from sociology, and another from higher education and educational leadership took the course. In addition, two European American females, one an in-service teacher, registered and attended two different remote sites. In total, nine people registered, along with one audit and one teaching and research assistant (from the teacher study research team; with an emphasis in technology and diversity education).

Few antiracist courses are being taught at this time. This reflects the nation's attitude about using the term *antiracist education*. Those college courses that are being taught and researched, for example, Dr. B. Daniel-Tatum's (Mount Holyoke College, Massachusetts) and Dr. J. Hudson's antiracist education courses, generally have a white majority student enrollment. As indicated by Tatum (winter, 1992), white students often hesitate to discuss race or do not recognize their position of privilege and the differences between whites and people of color regarding stages of racial development.

Contrary to the traditional silence that reportedly greets the topic of racism in white majority classrooms, our first class began vocally with the students of color (as the majority group) very open with their opinions. Students of color often demonstrate that they have much to offer in this area: however, they should not be expected to have the responsibility of stimulating discussion.

STUDENTS' STORIES

Interactive television focus group interviews began on day 1 (Videotape I, January 1997; transcription) with the facilitator (African American female) noting that the course was highly publicized, but that just a small number of people enrolled. All participants at the origination site (on campus; a predominantly white university) were students of color, and the students at the satellite sites were European American females. "What does that tell you about this course?" the facilitator asked. All students responded with similar observations, such as the majority doesn't feel that this course is important or that the issues are essential. One student of color mentioned, "Because minorities have experienced racism, we know the impact of it and the importance, and that's why we're here." One of the white females expressed that it was interesting that "the European male, who really needs to be here, is not here. I think it has a lot to do with fear and resistance." Students talked about the European male's not understanding how much suffering has really resulted from racism and how using the word *racism* may make him feel uncomfortable and that's why European males weren't there. Students talked about resistance, saying that people who possess the power to resist do not give it up freely. One student remarked, "Ignorance is a big part of it too. I taught a class and the papers seemed to show that students didn't think racism was anything but calling someone else an outright name."

Essentially, students were saying that antiracism-multicultural courses are resisted by those people who possess the power to make change. Believing that white males have power can most certainly disempower underrepresented groups to take social action to inspire change. However, in this case, it did not. White male power was associated simply with economic advantages to make change; here it was important to have white males present to experience the empathy necessary to help with overall reform.

Given the influences of racial identity and the motives for taking antiracist education courses, we believe the students' ethnic backgrounds and geographical upbringing was of significance. Although we were missing white male participants, other cultural representations, and in-service teacher participation, our students came from a variety of backgrounds and had many different experiences with racism. These differences made for eye-opening discussions of how each handled living in a racist society and what projects they would eventually devise to add to antiracist curriculum development, implementation, and research.

Studies of teachers of color and their reactions to race issues in schools (Foster, 1993; Ladson-Billings, 1994) have revealed that many teachers of color (mainly African American) feel alienated, ignored, belittled, and passed over in their schools. These sentiments have a direct correlation with the decline in the number of people of color who seek positions in education. Graduate students of color in education also experience institutional and individual racism. Antiracist education courses give such students a forum to critically analyze their situations and prepare them better for the pervasively racist educational institutions in which they may ultimately be employed. Little discussion materialized about students of color taking antiracist education courses or about how these students may contribute to antiracist education development. As we consider increasing antiracist education courses and ways to better recruit and retain educators of color, this information may prove useful.

As in 520X, students anxiously pressed their microphones to speak and often began at the same time, but they were thoughtful in giving the floor to those most eager to speak. They cought on quickly to the use of interactive television. As students attuned themselves to each other, the dialogue flowed naturally. Excitement about the medium for discourse grew noticeably. A brief ethnic and geographical profile of each of the students, for the purpose of understanding the dynamics of an antiracist course with black students in the majority, took place (see Table 7.2).

Students discoursed openly about race issues using CMC and distance education. Examples of these discussions on students' racial identity and racism experiences are presented in this section. (The students' names are fictitious to provide anonymity.) We begin with Antonio.

Antonio. We lived in an all-white neighborhood, and when we moved in the local newspaper came out to interview our white neighbors. My dad is a doctor, so our socioeconomic status allowed us to live in that area. Well, someone said, "What do 'niggers' need with four bathrooms?" (The man who built the house put bathrooms everywhere because his wife was in a wheelchair.) At that time, I was born in the '60s, being black meant being willing to die for the cause. That actually caused me trouble later on in life, that "I'm never going to back down" attitude. I thought that life centered on fighting your way through, being black. Later on I learned about faith in God and perseverance. In the '60s people were giving their lives to give us what we have today. I think that we're going to have to give our lives too, in some sense, for those who follow us.

Table 7.2
Student Demographics

Name	Major	Ethnicity	Birth place
Antonio	Curriculum & Instruction: Educational Testing	African American	California
Jennifer	Professional Development	German American	Iowa
Carol	Curriculum & Instructional Technology	African American	Mississippi
Grace	Communications	Puerto Rican	Puerto Rico
Tamara	Curriculum & Instructional Technology	African American & Seminole Indian	Philadelphia
Deanna	Curriculum & Instructional Technology	White American	Iowa
Lorriane	Curriculum & Instructional Technology	African American	North Carolina
Terrance	Sociology	Biracial (African & European American)	Iowa
Christian	Professional Studies (Educational Leadership)	African American	New Jersey

Jennifer. I grew up in small town Iowa with no or few minorities. My grandparents were first- or second-generation German immigrants. My grandfather disowned one of my cousins when I was in high school because she married someone who was black. So that had a really big impact on me. Later on in my life, my husband and I befriended a minority couple, and when we went together to a drive-in movie, they felt uncomfortable being with us in public. That made me feel bad.

Carol. I was born in Mississippi; my parents were field workers with no education. They told us to get educated. I was educated in Waterloo, Iowa. I went to Mississippi each summer. I saw my parents address younger [white] people as "Yes, sir," or "Yes, Ma'am." We had to use segregated facilities. I worked with adults that made $2.50 an hour chopping cotton. It was so hot, I lasted about three hours. It got so hot I remember being just sick. My mom did it so that I would learn to get an education. Getting my education was hard because blacks in the area discounted me for doing so well in school. As a teacher [now full time Ph.D. student] I often had white male students try me. People think you're uppity because you speak well. I hope this course helps me become calmer and to help people who don't understand the pain of racism. Sometimes it just seems like it's been so long.

Grace. I've always been aware of my heritage. As Puerto Rican we are Indian, Spanish, and African. I never thought of myself as Latina. That's American. I am and will always be Puerto Rican. My strong Catholic background taught me that everybody is equal. But in my childhood I saw prejudice even in my own family. Everyone is dark on my mom's side. We can't say we were racist, that word is taboo; but we were racist. One of my brothers wasn't accepted by the other side of the family because he was dark. My slap in the face was coming to the U.S.; here they say you are Latina, not Puerto Rican. Or they'll say you're mixed. I thought it was about money, but it wasn't—it's racism. And here in the Midwest they say, "you talk Mexican"; I just laugh. I don't talk Mexican; I speak Spanish. I want to teach through the media. I want to teach and give back. We are different, but we can live together."

Tamara. I used to always hear my mother crying. She cried tears of anger. As I got older (I was the youngest of five), I realized she had to fight for everything, being a black woman in America. I used to ask her what was wrong? She was a social worker, and she had a lot of tears for how she and black families were treated in the system. I didn't want to have to fight that way. She had to fight to keep us out of the public school system. I had to study harder. I went to a predominantly white high school, but there were enough blacks in the city to keep in touch with my heritage. I get bothered when I feel people are resisting racial issues. When it isn't comfortable to address issues, say, in class, then people want to change the subject and ignore the problem.

Deanna. My dad grew up in the depression era in Virginia. My uncles were the Archie Bunker types. They'd spout off some bigoted things. I'm not sure they meant half of it, y'know, but they said some things. Some of that may have had to do with economics. I'm not making excuses, but in that situation I think white people will look down on others. Fortunately, my dad didn't share their views. They raised us to believe that racism was wrong, but they also pretended that everything was just, y'know, okay. They didn't want us to discuss race issues. I went to a white school, mostly, and I befriended an African American in the fourth grade. This friend would ask us if we were proud of our race. We didn't get it. I don't know that whites think like that. During the 1970s there was a lot of racial tension. My friend wouldn't even talk to whites anymore. My sister married a Jew, and my father made the comment that he was concerned that she would be a victim of racism due to her husband. I hope that in my teaching that I don't show any biases. That's sort of why I'm here. I hope that racism someday doesn't exist. I'm afraid that my daughter will learn racism.

Lorriane. I've always been aware of my culture. I'm first-generation in college for my family. Racism was smacking me in the face early on—way too early! We lived in the South. My mother wanted the best for us, so that put us into situations where we were the only blacks. That exposed us to a lot of ignorance. I remember even in kindergarten going to the store with the teacher and the other kids and the lady in the checkout said, "Oh, Shelton, I didn't know you had spots or darkies"—or whatever she called me. I as a little kid took it upon myself to keep my teacher from being embarrassed. I just acted like I didn't hear what the lady said. The teacher stood up for me and tried to hide me, but I could not believe that an adult, someone with responsibility, said that. People would say, "Hey, you, the black girl," or "You, the black one." Because I'm a darker African American, I'd even get abuse from other African Americans. Right there I realized that I wanted to implement equality and somehow cast racism out. Antiracism should be a way of life. There should be no more perpetuating of the ignorance.

Terrance. I was adopted into an all-white family. I'm mixed. I really experienced a lot of social and psychological torment. I lived in an all-white community, went to an all-white school until I got to the university. I was immediately pegged in grade school as "the nigger," "the black sambo," and whatever. I didn't understand until I saw the movie *Roots*, and then I remember beating my fists into my pillow and crying, crying a lot. I knew what they meant when they were calling me "nigger" and that they were getting it from their ancestors and parents. My adopted parents gave me facts to help me understand the differences, biologically. I was separated in first grade and put in special education until second or third grade. I used to fight everyday. I saw the school psychologist and he got me a "big bro." It was a very good move. I believe in the oneness of humanity and I caught heat from the black culture. A black administrator said, "Terrance, I see two sides of the road. I see whites on one side and blacks on the other. Which side are you going to be on?"

I left the country and lived in Israel a couple of years. I got more in touch with the spiritual. I went to Africa too. I am a builder of peace who fights for racial equality.

Christian. My friends on the block recognized that my mother's mother was white. I probably spent at least the first twenty-five years of my life trying to deny that my grandmother was white because I didn't see her as a white person. Most of my friends on the block, because of my hair and complexion, saw me as American Indian. This reminded me of that movie *Bingo Long and the All Stars*, where Richard Pryor pretended to be Indian to get into the Majors (being Indian was more acceptable than being black). In my case, American Indian was more acceptable than having my friends think that I was part white. I'm taking the course hoping that it will allow me to face some fears and maybe help me to expose some skeletons in the closet. From a professional standpoint, working in a student support services environment I realize that you have to be aware of your own cultural identity and the cultural identity of others.

Telling these personal stories indicated that many students have had great struggles with racism. Their stories also subtly reveal why they possibly have an interest in antiracist education and/or becoming educators. For the students of color, these were ongoing incidents from childhood to adulthood, and their graduate student status made no difference regarding racist treatment. All the stories needed to be heard in order to recognize the pervasiveness of racism and its damaging effects. At the graduate level the students could articulate well on these experiences. Relief in having others hear these stories in a class environment, each learning from the other, would later add to the impact of creating curriculum reform projects to outreach to all students suffering from a racist or biased curriculum. Including personal stories at this stage drew students together early on; it also built trust.

These stories shared by the students assisted in setting up the racial identity development component of class. At the push a of button, video clips of *The Chamber* (about an ex-Ku Klux Klan member given the death penalty) and *A Family Thing* (about a racist white male finding out he had a black mother) were shown on the monitors and used for discussions about identity. Using "Elmo" (interactive television overhead projector), students viewed transparencies that indicated that whites and people of color go through very different stages of racial identity development. For the most part, people of color are forced to recognized at young ages that they are looked upon and treated differently by the majority group because of skin color; whereas members of the dominant group seldom recognize their racial identity. Instead, they live in a society that enables them simply to say, "I'm normal" when asked how they identify.

INTERNET DISCUSSIONS

The internet discussions complemented the personal and theoretical identity experiences previously mentioned. For the most part, students agreed with the Stages of Racial/Ethnic Identity Development in the United States model developed by Tatum; this model incorporated previous models taken from the works of William Cross (1991) and Janet Helms (1990). For example, Tatum's Immersion Stage for People of Color concluded that with visible symbols of one's racial identity, one could reject white symbols and glorify one's own group, thereby affirming one's sense of self. However, there were some exceptions; a number of the students of color felt they did not experience the stages as presented in the model. For instance, Christian stated, "As I was reviewing Dr. Tatum's stages of identity, especially the Immersion part, I reflected on my youth. My father was a Black Panther; we owned black cultural stores; he was an African drummer. He's probably been to Africa a hundred times. I started to develop an aversion because I began to be ridiculed by my own people for wearing cultural wear. It caused me to go away from wearing those things because of the overzealousness of my father at the time. I mean, I'm proud to be called an African American and I still own lots of cultural wear, but I wear it because I want to, not because I want to prove my blackness." Tamara also talked about her dad owning an African art gallery and how clothes, crafts, and other ornaments were a way of life for her family. Furthermore, Grace felt that the People of Color Racial Identity model did not accurately describe her identity stages as a Puerto Rican female. That we are not just dealing with race issues in black and white is very important to note. However, all the students expressed satisfaction at learning that there are stages of racial identity people undergo during their lifelong development. In understanding this, students noted their own growth in racial understanding and coping skills.

Frequently, internet correspondence would get hot and heavy. This happened especially with the historical case study assignment from Herbert Aptheker's work on the first 200 years of antiracism in United States. Lorriane suggested, "We need to give our own [black] perspective. We can speak for ourselves as individuals and as a group. In this historical case study someone else is speaking for 'us.'" This set off a barrage of critical responses, which the students viewed as part of the learning process. For example, Christian remarked, "The oath of respect which the class took is near and dear to my heart, and I hope I did not disrespect or offend anyone. I have some definite, strong views concerning the second-class treatment of people of color and the ways in which to combat this disease. Overall, I think the class is the vehicle by which we start the transformation process, and I look forward to the rest of our meetings." Carol added, "I'm certainly glad we're all in the same class and trying to do what we can individually to help. This is the first step—dialogue to try to understand each other."

As Jennifer reflected on the historical case study and everyone's input, she replied, "It's almost discouraging to think that this many learned people of both races had so little impact on the direction that racism was to take. I hope the involvement of people nowadays will be more effective and longer lasting. This class and others like it, dialogue on the internet and this listserv, and community projects that have all groups of people working together should be helpful."

Often the students would use the e-mail discussion times to announce antiracist events, identify antiracist literature, and tell about personal experiences. Deanna responded in this way to an antiracist workshop listed by Carol: "Even though I can relate to discrimination on a gender basis, I do not pretend to be able to truly understand what racial discrimination would feel like if it were directed at me. The workshop that Carol described sounds like it would give whites a better idea of what racism feels like. But, as she pointed out, I would be able to leave the workshop at the end of the day and the racist 'treatment' would stop. I've come to realize through our readings and class discussions that people of color face racism more often than I had realized. Thanks for opening my eyes." Other students made comments such as "This kind of exchange is excellent. I enjoyed seeing some similarities in many of your thoughts and mine. Hopefully the listserv will last all semester!" (Jennifer). Students almost always signed off with "looking forward to seeing all of you in class."

AN IN-CLASS FAVORITE

The students all agreed that the highlight of the interactive television experience was the midwestern suburban cohort panel discussion. During the origination site visit and discussion the teachers in the midwestern cohort group shared their experiences with racism and their antiracist curriculum development and implementation efforts. Students were able to ask many questions of the group. The cohort group answered all questions at ease and with true conviction that they would forever be steadfast on the road to helping to reduce racism in schools and in society at large. This panel presentation gave the 520X students that needed push to get on track with their projects. The projects included curriculum development and practical applications.

FINAL PROJECTS USING DISTANCE EDUCATION STRATEGIES

We followed this discourse with a review of the timeline legacy activity in which students were asked to share why they had taken the course, focusing on their antiracist education interests, and to create a personal timeline chart beginning with their first recognition of race or ethnicity then indicating subsequent encounters with racism, and finally noting their commitments to addressing racism. Last, they wrote their legacy, that is, what they would want to be remembered for regarding their antiracist education contributions. These legacy timelines also helped to frame their projects as they started envisioning their long-term goals.

Most of the students, including the auditing student (African American) and the research assistant (biracial, first-generation Italian and Trinidadian American), had majors in curriculum and instructional technology. This is important to note as we assess the interest level of technology graduate students registering for interactive television and CMC courses and the increase in students of color majoring in instructional technology with an emphasis in diversity.

Not much has been mentioned about these two additional students because they spent the majority of their time in the operational booth learning the technical procedures for the distance education studio. However, they managed to "convert" the white male student operator and would often interject their opinions from the booth. After each class the operator would ask me for all the reading materials that were handed out to the students. With their technology backgrounds, most of the students created projects centered around technology.

These projects were variously titled: (1) Multicultural and Antiracist Materials in the _____ High School (Media) Library; (2) A Compilation of Media Stereotypes about Puerto Ricans; (3) Technology Equity; (4) Internet Resources for Antiracist Curriculum; (5) Cultural Differences in IQ Testing; (6) Lessons in Antiracist Communication; (7) Structuring Antiracist Workshops Using Antiracist Literature; (8) Diversity Technology Curriculum Development: A Practical Application Case Study; and (9) Antiracist Education and Its Implications for Higher Education Majors.

The final projects helped to make significant additions in the students' areas of employment and research. In addition, the students gave outstanding presentations using the interactive television medium. By the end of class, students were very aware of interactive television techniques, such as knowing not to turn their backs to the audience. Students used video, Power Point presentations, interactive television transparencies, and so on. The students wrote quite moving evaluations; they spoke about the course reaching beyond their initial expectations. A few shared personal revelations, and all highly recommended that others take the course in the future.

Not only did the facilitator have the opportunity to test the curriculum, but the open group dynamics demonstrated the depth that antiracist education courses can reach in developing reduction strategies for educators and educational institution. As the facilitator, I believe this demonstration was made possible through the majority participation of students of color, but I also believe that all students, regardless of race, can reach such depths. The students showed that though we are all different in our thinking and experiences, there is common ground for discussion and growth as human beings. If we choose to take the time to find that middle ground and meet there with an open mind, work can be done and victory can be "one."

LIMITATIONS

Overall course limitations were slight, but worth mentioning. In our case the remote sites were truly remote, with one person per site (both European American). The field researchers were isolated physically from everyone, and during times that a gentle touch would have meant a lot, it could not happen given the logistics. This limitation supports somewhat the contention that participants in antiracist courses need a certain degree of face-to-face, physical contact when confronting hard-hitting issues. However, the benefits of telecommunication programs and CMC far outweigh this limitation. Another limitation was the issue of affording computers. Not all students had computers at home and were disappointed that they were unable to keep up with what turned into daily internet dialogue. Still other limitations included the absence of other ethnicities, such as European males, Asians, and American Indians. Students also felt restricted by having to stay in their seats during class. Small-group work and kinesthetic experiential activities could address these issues, however.

WHAT THE STUDENTS ARE TELLING US

Despite the issue of access for internet dialogue, using CMC and distance education to help meet multicultural course objectives still surfaced as an initial concern. For instance, students acknowledged how the electronic environment broadened perspectives, challenged the ideology of social inbreeding and individualism. The idea that CMC is counteractive to the goals of multicultural-antiracist education was dispelled as students enrolled in both courses proclaimed the opposite phenomenon. Students concurred that "storytelling," questions of experienced teachers regarding reform strategies, in-practice opportunities, self-inventory, and projects that enhanced skills in merging antiracist-multicultural education with CMC concepts were vital for the demonstration of curriculum development and reform in this area.

Students in the course also help to identify why using CMC for antiracist-multicultural education should not be ignored—namely, because it has far-reaching possibilities in addressing social ills within our educational institutions and society. As it pertained to doing research, students reflected that technology is heavily based in quantitative approaches only, thereby omitting qualitative aspects such as the opinions and "voices" of the subjects. Furthermore, students said that antiracist-multicultural education should not be offered only behind the closed door of technology but also through the open doors of innovative approaches exemplified by the course. Students felt that their experiences and views on linking CMC or distance education with antiracist-multicultural education should further encourage transformation in these fields.

Overall, participating students were able to use their projects in practical ways, most demonstrating the exciting fusion of antiracist-multicultural education and CMC. Furthermore, being able to communicate with the midwestern antiracist cohort teachers through an interactive television panel discussion exhibited what collaboration is possible among antiracist cohort teachers, university courses, and students. Keeping the cohort group active in presenting the antiracist education work continued to provide participants with positive experiences, as they were able to deduce the importance of their contribution in this area. In most cases teachers do not receive positive reinforcement for antiracist-multicultural efforts.

The experimental antiracist interactive television course also helped to prepare undergraduate (who viewed 520X class videotapes) and graduate students participating in a half-semester course entitled "International Field Trips in Antiracist and Multicultural Education." During this study abroad program, we were based in South Africa. Students did student teaching and research with an emphasis on antiracist education. Three of the students from the 520X course became participants in the study abroad program. Having the experience with CMC and telecommunication programming, we collaborated on an interactive television project that gave professional development seminars for in-service teachers in the rural areas of the Northern Province. This study abroad project will be discussed further in the next chapter as we continue to look at protocols for the classroom and beyond.

8

International Field Trips in Antiracist and Multicultural Education: South Africa Study Abroad Program

I have learned a lot that I do not think can be expressed in words, mostly about myself. This has been a life-changing experience for me and I will never forget it. (U.S. student teacher, UP Teacher Education Project: Final Evaluation, 1997)

INTRODUCTION

This chapter focuses on an international field trip in multicultural-antiracist education designed for preservice teachers to experience their student teaching requirements in a foreign country. In particular the student teachers and graduate students who participated did their practice and research with an antiracist education theme. Selecting South Africa as the site for exchange was of particular benefit because the United States and South Africa have had similar systems of segregation and apartheid. Experiencing and exploring a postapartheid system, and examining the deracialization parallels between these countries, exhibited the height of what a multicultural teacher education program can offer through a field practicum.

Much discourse has surrounded the question of how teacher preparation programs can prepare competent, culturally sensitive teachers who are able to provide leadership that promotes cultural sensitivity in their schools. Many teacher education programs respond by requiring preservice teachers to take courses in multicultural education. Often, this is a one-course requirement that must condense critical studies of diversity awareness; historical and theoretical, sociological, philosophical, and pedagogical contexts; and methods into the single course offered, with no room for field experiences and/or practice. Emerging studies indicate that little ideological movement occurs with enrolled students, presumably because of the minimal importance placed on multicultural education in teacher education programs.

This chapter asserts that quality expansion of multicultural education courses, including field experiences, and in-depth critical exploration in areas such as race must take place to realistically prepare preservice teachers to create successful and equitable classrooms. It examines efforts to establish effective multicultural teacher education programs through an international case study field experience. Furthermore, it analyzes the information presented for the purpose of elucidating the need to create viable multicultural teacher education programs, thereby enabling researchers to study more accurately how multicultural education can enhance awareness, teaching skills, and leadership of preservice teachers.

The following national overview contains a review of studies reviewed by the author and Ph.D. student James McShay (Donaldson and McShay, forthcoming).

NATIONAL OVERVIEW

Teacher education programs have been under a tremendous pressure to prepare competent, culturally sensitive teachers for our nation's schools. Some studies (Boyle-Baise, 1998; McCall, 1995; Tran, Young, and Dilella, 1994) support the notion that teacher education programs as they are currently structured will continue to receive low ratings for their inability to prepare teachers who are ready and willing to teach from a multicultural perspective. Many teacher education programs require preservice teachers to take a singular course in multicultural education to prepare them for their work in multicultural schools. Some studies (Leavell, Cowart, and Wilhelm, 1999; McCormick and McShay, 1996) indicate that multicultural education courses do have a positive impact on preparing preservice teachers to teach from a multicultural perspective; however, there is still much debate as to whether these courses are doing enough to prepare dedicated guardians of equity and social justice. Other research (Gallavan, 1998; McCall, 1995; Phuntsog, 1995) shows that preservice teachers often view the goals and practices of multicultural education as being insignificant, cursory, and a low priority for preparing them to be effective teachers.

Leavell, Cowart, and Wilhelm (1999) studied the effects of the Professional Development Institute (PDI), a program they created in an effort to increase the multicultural awareness of preservice teachers. The PDI enables preservice teachers to participate in an intensive four-week combination of coursework and multicultural-based field experience in a school setting. Additional experiences of these prospective teachers included reading multicultural literature, exploring and making critical observations about different communities, taking multicultural-based field trips, and participating in diversity seminars. Leavell and colleagues (1999) concluded that these experiences enabled prospective teachers to challenge their previously held beliefs about various cultural groups and think critically about the instructional decisions they will make in their future multicultural classrooms.

In another study, conducted by Boyle-Baise (1998), 65 preservice teachers participated in a community service learning (CSL) project specifically developed to work in conjunction with a multicultural teacher education course. This CSL project was a field experience designed to enable preservice teachers to learn about the pressures of parenthood, the realities of poverty, and the social inequities that exist within various communities. Boyle-Baise found that preservice teachers use what she refers to as a "middle-class lens" to interpret the living situations of their students. Preservice teachers were more likely to intercede on the behalf of parents with low incomes. Boyle-Baise's observations support Zeichner and Gore's (1989) findings that claim prospective teachers in lower-class schools feel more compelled to act as representatives of their students and families than do prospective teachers in wealthier schools. Boyle-Baise concluded that CSL motivated students to want to learn more about the intricacies of cultural and social diversity. However, students were still not inclined to critically question the various factors that contribute to social inequalities as they relate to conditions of poverty.

In another study, McCormick presents the results of a program developed to prepare teachers to work in ethnically and racially diverse settings. The Co-operative Urban Teacher Education Program (CUTE) located in Kansas City, Kansas, enabled preservice teachers to participate in a 17-week field experience. Preservice teachers worked with both in-service teachers and administrators throughout a semester-long internship. The goals of this program were to enable preservice teachers to learn about other microcultural groups, to learn how to live with people different from themselves, and to deepen their understanding of how race, class, and gender play an important role in shaping their students' lives. McCormick concluded that the preservice teachers had a stronger, more positive understanding of racially and ethnically diverse students at the end of the experience.

In order to address the concerns documented by researchers within teacher education, multicultural educators have called for their programs to be restructured. This restructuring would enable teacher educators to be more flexible, innovative, and resourceful in developing multicultural education programs. Furthermore, the integration of these expanded multicultural education programs would have tremendous effects within teacher education. The quality expansion of multicultural education courses would foster an environment in which faculty would feel supported in developing new pedagogical approaches and transforming their respective curriculum in order to support the goals of multicultural education.

Teacher education programs throughout the nation have already begun to take new initiatives that support the quality expansion of multicultural education courses and field experience. In a study conducted at Jersey City State College (Heinmann, 1992), preservice teachers participated in a six-week field experience in an urban setting. They examined pedagogical, social, and political issues inherent in elementary and secondary urban schools. The preservice teachers were required to keep journals and they attended seminars where they reflected on their teaching and learning experiences and critically examined what had been observed. Results of the study showed that these early field experiences in urban schools diminished stereotypes and fear while energizing and challenging students with new insights about themselves.

Cooper, Beare, and Thorman (1990) studied the effects of different field experiences on two predominately white groups of Moorhead State University (Minnesota) student-teachers after they had taken three multicultural courses that addressed the values inherent in a pluralistic society. One group ($n = 85$) was given a field placement in a culturally different classroom in Minnesota; the second group of student teachers ($n = 18$) lived in a Mexican American community in Texas. Results from the study, based upon self-assessment questionnaires, showed that the students in both locations demonstrated increased multicultural competencies; however, the group that had Mexican American experience showed greater gains in cultural competency. The researchers reported, "The opportunity to student teach in Texas, with its attendant exposure to another culture, appears to generate among participants an articulated willingness to demonstrate multicultural competencies" (1990, p. 3).

Another researcher (Mahan, 1984) provided his students with multicultural knowledge and understanding through course content and community field experiences in Navajo and Hopi communities. During this semester, the preservice teachers did after-school volunteer work with these two communities. Mahan found that young teachers who are immersed in the local culture do make culturally oriented adjustment in their teaching strategies and styles.

At Texas A&M, preservice teachers tutored students of color as their field experience in addition to their training. The students had a one-hour, five-semester multicultural course in conjunction with their tutoring. After pre- and posttesting, the researchers found that this experience did change attitudes and perceptions of the preservice teachers toward African American and Mexican American children (Larke, Wisemann, and Bradley, 1990).

In summary, our national outlook on teacher education affirms Carl Grant's (1994) assertion that all advocates of preparing teachers to work in racially and ethnically diverse settings believe, as we do, that extended quality experiences in culturally different schools are essential.

SOCIAL CONTEXT: INTERNATIONAL FIELD EXPERIENCE

The case study international field trip experience originated in the Midwest at a predominantly white institution. The undergraduate enrollment consisted of about 25,000 students. In 1975 a state mandate for all schools to integrate multicultural education in all subject areas was instituted. Over the next 10 years professional development education and human relations requirements were required of in-service teachers. The state's department of education created an equity office where resource materials such as guidebooks for multicultural education were provided at no cost for schools and educators. Equity officers were also employed to assist in professional development training and school enforcement regarding the mandate. In compliance with the state mandate the Midwest university incorporated a required multicultural education course for all preservice teachers within its teacher education program. Because students at this university took an active step to have the university increase diversity education as a whole, in 1997 two diversity course requirements (one for domestic study and one for international study) for all undergraduate students was instituted. Preservice teachers must now take the required multicultural education awareness and methods course, as well as the additional six-credit diversity requirement. With this requirement numerous diversity cross-listed courses can be selected, and international courses and study abroad programs are encouraged.

COURSES IN MULTICULTURAL EDUCATION: A REQUIREMENT FOR PRESERVICE TEACHERS

Currently, undergraduate students enrolled in the Teacher Preparation Program case study highlighted in this chapter have the opportunity to minor (unofficially) in multicultural studies. All students are required to complete the "Introduction to Multicultural Education" course. However, "Ethnicity and Learning" and the international student teaching courses help to fulfill the minor in multicultural education. Students who have taken the additional courses have said that they feel better prepared and more confident to teach in our diverse world (student evaluations, 1997). Understanding that it is just as important to work with preservice teachers as with in-service teachers, this chapter will focus on multicultural initiatives for preparing future teachers for the multicultural classroom.

During the early 1970s, scholars such as James A. Banks, Geneva Gay, Carl Grant, Bob Suzuki, and Asa Hilliard began to develop conceptual curriculum frameworks for multicultural education. Models such as these were further developed for primary, secondary, and higher education students. As this curriculum reform movement expanded, the American Association of Colleges for Teacher Education recommended that all preservice teachers become educated and prepared to teach in multicultural classroom environments

(Howsam, 1976). Many states and universities began exploring how to institute such courses and curricula.

In recognition of this mandate, the ISU Teacher Education Program developed a required course in multicultural nonsexist education in 1981. Before receiving licensure to teach in state schools, the teacher education program requires completion of the multicultural course. In compliance with the state's Multicultural Nonsexist Education Guidelines, the course is designed to broaden preservice teachers' awareness and methods for the classroom.

The course covers the historical, philosophical, and theoretical contexts of multicultural education, multicultural terms, and discrimination based on race, class, gender, age, ability, language, and religion. Furthermore, it highlights the experiences of major ethnic groups in the United States and gives cross-discipline infusement strategies for the classroom. Students are assigned to complete "Contact Activities" (interviews and/or observations with cultures different from their own) and multicultural curriculum units or projects. These field-based and cooperative experiences assist the students in developing confidence to teach multiculturally. Research has demonstrated that introductory courses without field-based experiences in multicultural education merely provide a baseline of information (Boyle-Baise and Sleeter, 1996; Goodwin, 1994). In Goodwin's investigation of "What do preservice teachers really think about multicultural education," 67% of 127 students completed questionnaires. The preservice teaching respondents were graduate education students along with 20 undergraduate students visiting from southern black colleges. The study results demonstrated that teacher education programs must do a better job with multicultural education (Goodwin, 1994).

Similar studies were conducted in the college. In 1986 a pre- and posttest instrument to measure the effectiveness of the multicultural education courses taught was designed. In the late 1980s a revised and restructured final version was created, but not until 1994 with doctoral candidate Jean Ju Lui did actual data analysis take place. The study found that many students are hesitant to broaden their views and to step out of their comfort zones even after taking the course, and therefore they were not likely to infuse multicultural education as classroom teachers.

In more recent years the instrument has been modified by several graduate students interested in testing field-based enhancement. The student-respondents (field-based treatment group) experiencing additional practice teaching indicated greater acceptance of multicultural education values and concepts. For instance, James McShay (graduate student) compared survey responses of two groups (control and experimental). The control group (fall semester, 1994) and the experimental group (fall semester, 1995) were taught by the same instructor. Both groups were required to use the same syllabus and text for the course, but the experimental group received one additional credit for a multicultural education semester practicum arranged within an urban school setting. These students received the opportunity to practice implementing the multicultural lessons and units they had developed within diverse K–12 class-room settings. This added practicum did, in fact, make a difference for students. The results from the 81-question instrument that was designed to measure students' attitudes toward a range of diversity issues using a five-point Likert scale showed that 14 out of 63 of the survey questions were significantly different between the 1994 and the 1995 courses. Students enrolled in the 1995 course showed significant growth in attitudes compared with the students enrolled in the 1994 course concerning feelings toward teaching from a multicultural, nonsexist perspective (McShay, 1996).

COORDINATING THE INTERNATIONAL FIELD TRIPS IN ANTIRACIST AND MULTICULTURAL EDUCATION: SOUTH AFRICA STUDY ABROAD PROGRAM

The McShay findings, along with acknowledging concerns of minority students and diversity efforts of the university, influenced my decision to coordinate an antiracist education study abroad program for university students. Students of color had long been advocates of diversity on campus and helped to convince the university to make diversity a priority goal.

The idea of an Africa study abroad program began with two African American students coming to my office to inquire whether or not there was an international student teaching program available in Africa. I immediately checked with our international student teaching field experience office and was told that we did not have an exchange student teaching program in Africa. Aware of the prioritized "internationalization" and "diversity" strategical goals of the college and the university, I approached my department chairperson about the possibilities of creating such a program. I stressed the positive results of students' experiencing multicultural education in practice, with the opportunities to further prepare our students for the world's diverse classrooms. This further preparation would also meet the new university requirements to have all undergraduate students fulfill at least six credits in international and domestic diversity studies. The chair permitted me to pursue the possibilities. I contacted administrators of the Study Abroad Program on campus. They were very interested in giving me assistance because at that time there were no Africa study abroad programs originating from that office. I submitted proposals to the College of Education International Studies Committee, Office of International Students and Scholars, Study Abroad Program, Student Affairs, and the President's Office.

As the program coordinator, I arranged to make a site visit to construct the program. My first choice was to have the program in West Africa. I had been there several times, and there was a colleague interested in collaborating on a research project in Nigeria. I felt that I could participate in the research project, along with some of my graduate students, and establish the student teaching component of my study abroad program while there. The Study Abroad

Program director suggested adding a second site exploration during my initial site visit to West Africa. I chose South Africa because I had recently developed internet communication with a professor at the University of Pretoria (UP), Dr. Thea de Kock, who was interested in a collaborative distance education project with ISU. The suggestion of the Study Abroad Program director proved to be useful because Nigerian university professors had gone on strike to protest insufficient salaries and lack of support from the government. The government, in turn, enforced the closing of all universities. Following my stay in Nigeria, I went directly to South Africa, where an exchange study abroad program was forged.

In August 1996 I visited the Northern Province (Pretoria, Johannesburg, and some rural areas such as Siyabuswa) and the eastern region (Durban). The University of Pretoria became the most likely candidate for the project. Educators there were interested in blending their pilot project, "To Facilitate Lifelong Learning Supported by Interactive Television and Multimedia Technology" (a rural in-service professional development course), with our student teaching program. The idea was that our student-teachers, with an emphasis on antiracist and multicultural education, would partner with theirs to student teach while in-service teachers were released to attend remote interactive television sites for professional seminars. This project was directed at serving black teachers who were traditionally denied access to professional development courses. While in Pretoria I visited schools in the designated rural site and school sites in the Pretoria city limits. In addition, I investigated accommodations, transportation, and other resources available to successfully base the study abroad program at the University of Pretoria.

Returning to the states, I presented the plan to the interested parties at the university level and to the College of Education. Both College of Education (UP and ISU) deans signed an agreement to collaborate on this pilot student teaching study abroad program; this was the first venture of its type in the history of both institutions. I was given permission to begin advertisement and interviews with interested students.

The International Field Trips in Antiracist and Multicultural Education: South Africa Study Abroad Program was scheduled as an eight-week program (March 2–May 2, 1997). As a new international program, this endeavor required an exorbitant amount of preparation. The suggestion from Study Abroad Program administrators, to allow eight months to a year in planning was sound advice. Dr. Thea de Kock became the UP exchange coordinator, and together we worked on housing, transportation, school site assignments, an internet "buddy" system between participating students, visa permits, school permits, field trip excursions, and so on. At this same time I pursued financial assistance for the program. Partial scholarships were provided for students through the Study Abroad Program and the Office of Student Affairs; tuition fees were waived, and students' financial assistance for the term was credited to their university bill to help with Study Abroad Program fees. The

College of Education contributed funds for special activities and excursions. However, because the agreed-upon exchange housing arrangements—namely, that accommodations would be free for students in exchange for free accommodation for UP students arriving in the United States—fell through at the last minute before departure, funds from the program fees and the College of Education had to be used to pay the UP student housing bill. This sudden change would later cause a breakdown in communication with the students.

The Coming On Board of Students

The project was advertised as having two components: a student teaching component and an antiracist education research component. Knowing the research interests of some of my graduate students, I was inspired to add the latter, and I saw a natural fit in not only inviting them to participate in the 520X antiracist education course on interactive television but also giving them an opportunity to become more eligible for the study abroad program if they desired to apply.

I received 21 applications; this impressed the International Student Teaching Field Experience Office and the Study Abroad Program, which generally witness fewer applicants for study abroad programs. However, my agreement with the University of Pretoria was to limit our participant registration to ten students. Therefore, ten students were accepted; six student-teachers and four researchers. The prerequisites for the study abroad course included the multicultural education course, in addition to the 520X antiracist education course for graduate students.

One of the student-teachers accepted into the program completed her local eight weeks of student teaching with one of the antiracist education cohort group members. This proved to be very rewarding for her while in Africa. She established a pen pal project between her fourth graders from the United States and her third graders from South Africa. This student and the three graduate students from the 520X class were able to prepare well-developed prospectus outlines for teaching and research based upon their additional exposure to antiracist education strategies.

An added criteria for the study abroad program was to balance the participation of students of color and white students. The rationale for doing this was to address "underdeveloped" student race relations on campus. During the program, students would be assigned to room with a student of a racial background different than their own, and upon returning to the university, student-participants would share their diversity experiences in panel discussions and class presentations.

The students were required to attend three orientation seminars held before their departure and three during their stay in South Africa. The predeparture orientations included (1) state of affairs in South Africa: a (multicultural) historical view of South Africa (with a special focus on apartheid and postapartheid) presented by ISU history professor Modupe Labode; (2) South African cultures, schooling, student teaching requirements, school and research placements; and (3) Part I: Transportation, housing, banking, international information, e-mailing and other correspondence, travel opportunities, immunization requirements, etc.; and Part II: Travel rules and regulations and expectations. Preparation for the program also included a pot luck dinner at the coordinator's home, the viewing of the Mandela and de Klerk Home Box Office film and discussion of the similarities and differences of apartheid and segregation.

Current Conditions and Schools in South Africa

South Africa has 11 official languages, but standardized tests and textbooks are all written in English. Generally black teachers have been limited because for financial reasons they are forced to attend two-year teacher education colleges. In major South African cities racial stratification is very apparent. For instance, whites (English, Afrikaners, Germans, etc.) remain on top regarding wealth, education, and power. Following whites are Indians, coloures (a mixture of various cultures, i.e., black, Asian, white), and blacks. With the new government having many racial and ethnic representatives, racial and economic stratification is changing, but very slowly. Schools remain unequal with regard to resources, and racism is blatant in many parts of South Africa (Soudien, 1994).

Curriculum 2005 (1997) speaks to a need for change, namely, that all South Africans want a prosperous, democratic country free of discrimination and violence and with the ability to compete internationally. The curriculum proposes moving from fostering passive and exam-driven learners to promoting active learners assessed on an ongoing basis. In addition, The goal is to move from rote-learning to critical thinking, reasoning, reflection, and action. The curriculum is to be planned by parents, teachers, and education authorities as well as learners to make the curriculum flexible and relevant. Although antiracist and multicultural education is not clearly defined, it is evident that the *Curriculum 2005* objectives are attempting to transform the curriculum so it is antiracist. Meeting these reform objectives will be a challenge in the next few years, expecially because of the meager funds available for education.

Our Arrival

We were greeted at the airport by the UP coordinator, another professor involved with the interactive project, and our transportation service. Because there were no UP vans were available for the program, we were forced to hire a somewhat expensive "Combi" (van) service. When we arrived at the international dormitory, students were quite surprised by the satisfactory condition of the rooms and that the rooms had been decorated with welcome signs and there were fruits and snacks left by their student "buddies." Students spent the weekend adjusting to the new environment. The "buddies" came out to welcome the students and to show them around town. With the start of the new week, we were given a reception by the UP dean, who was amazed that we had accomplished our goal in getting the project started. Students quickly learned that there would be difficulties in getting on line (internet) and that prices for incidentals were higher than we had been told. Nonetheless, students were experiencing the "honeymoon" stage and everything was wonderful. The actual cycle as delineated by the Rotary International involves eight stages: (1) application anxiety, (2) selection/arrival fascination, (3) surface adjustments, (4) mental isolation, (5) integration/acceptance, (6) return anxiety (preparation for departure), and (7) shock/reintegration (Rotary International Guideline, 1998).

The Siyabuswa Experience

One week after arrival students packed their gear for a week-long stay in Siyabuswa. UP and ISU students were paired with host families in the Siyabuswa community. Because of a death in her family, the UP coordinator was unable to attend the week-long event as scheduled. This caused confusion with placement. Furthermore, our late arrival as a result of insufficient transportation prevented the student-teachers from meeting the classroom teachers for whom they were scheduled to student teach. However, we did make it in time for the king's reception. The king ruled over approximately 1.5 million people belonging to the Ndebele culture. In order to be welcomed into the king's kraal, we had to offer a gift through his counsel (I had made the king a silk pillow). The gift was accepted and we proceeded into the kraal. We were not told that males should sit on one side and females on the other; therefore our entire group sat on the same side. Only later did we discover that the males of our group had sat on the wrong side of the room. During the reception students were introduced to their host families, and directly following the reception students were carted off to the host family houses. In most cases these houses were impoverished, without bathrooms, running water, and other amenities many of the students were used to. This was the first time UP students had ever participated in a student-teaching assignment in a rural black community, and they were therefore as ignorant of the Siyabuswa lifestyle as our own students.

The week-long project in Siyabuswa emotionally and physically exhausted students. The project coordinators therefore felt it important to have a short debriefing for the students to allow participants to share any frustration, illumination, and so on, before transporting them to their homes or hostels for the weekend. Therefore students were taken to the University of Pretoria for the processing seminar, whose purpose was to document the opinions and experiences of the student-teachers involved in the project. This documentation would assist evaluators in assessing the success of this portion of the program. Success would be measured by the students' growth in understanding different conditions and a different culture. For example, the antiracist education processing and analytical skills students used to connect the effects of apartheid in rural black communities (school, housing, and employment) were explored.

The debriefing sessions directly explain students' points of view. Some key responses are summarized below. The students will not be identified by name to protect their anonymity. However, college affiliations are mentioned (ISU—Iowa State University/USA and UP—University of Pretoria/RSA). The ethnic makeup of the students was mixed. Two UP students were black and seven were white. Five ISU students were black and five were white. This session was videotaped, but the reactions below were taken from the discussion notes. From time to time the ethnicity of the respondent will be mentioned to give an idea of the difference in perception and experience.

Question 1 explored personal perspectives and project experiences. Students replied that the project was "very eye-opening [ISU]," "a challenge being there [UP]," and a "wonderful experience, absolutely nothing I imagined [UP]." One of the white ISU students remarked, "I come away feeling responsible, sad, feeling powerless. We have so much." Other students made comments such as "The project had a lot of potential [UP]" and it was "a life-changing experience [UP]." One of the black UP students sadly replied, "I should never forget; I forgot because of living in Pretoria."

Question 2 asked, from a student-teacher and/or researcher (professional) point of view, what were the student's project experiences? One student shared that the "problems of education in South Africa were limitations regarding language/English [ISU]; and a UP student also said that the "language was difficult. A practice session for U.S. students would have helped." An ISU student listed three items: (1) outstanding students, (2) extremely dedicated teachers (or else it was just a job), and (3) need for a training program in the administrative portion of the schools; this student said that "the administrators didn't offer leadership to the teachers." One of the black ISU students wanted to know, "Why are cultural and education kept separated? It shot the theory of formal education, there is cultural and there is education." Students said that they "couldn't use the materials; I had to think quickly on the spot." Another UP student echoed the same sentiments: "If I had been at a facility, I would have grabbed technology. We had to do programs and classes with nothing." A white ISU student admitted, "I had a hard time with this experience. I had high expectations and none of that happened. We were just there to keep them busy. We didn't talk about education strategies [with administrators or teachers]." Other students had similar responses, such as "having to hold back from interacting with teachers and not wanting to insult the classroom teachers by sharing new ideas."

Question 3 asked about the host family experience. A black ISU student answered immediately: "Rough! Outhouse bathrooms—unsanitary. I couldn't bathe properly, and this affected my demeanor in class. People who had beautiful homes were either teachers or policemen; professionals." A UP student replied with an opposite view: "It was very comfortable, I did not expect much. I spent hours discussing education and sharing ideas; very frank. My host was one of the teachers participating in the [professional development interactive television] workshops." An ISU student responded by saying, "People were all very different and real. As a teacher we must have an understanding of different people. It opened my eyes." The same black student who mentioned the unsanitary conditions further remarked that it was "a good idea to use the host families. It was the opposite of what I was used to. There was no running water or electricity. This experience was important to understand the children." Another black ISU student did research at a teachers college and had this to say: "At the Teacher College, I had the opportunity to interact with future teachers; exchanging USA and RSA (Republic of South Africa) stories. I have a better understanding of the teachers now in Siyabuswa. The teachers and students in rural areas get a bad rap. This project was needed to get the teachers and students' point of view. The Teacher College folks had their children in the schools where the project was being conducted, therefore their information was useful." A UP student commented, "After a week I was just getting accustomed to the setting. I needed an extra week."

Question 4 asked the students about their impressions of the king's reception. One white ISU student said, "It shocked me that he was in a suit and making jokes; it didn't seem real." Another ISU student stated, "I didn't connect it until I got to the school and we talked about Ndebele culture. The teacher asked, 'Who is your King?' " There were other students who felt that the king was a focal point of that culture; still others said, "He was no way near to that culture. They [Siyabuswa students] could not feel the presence of the king in the classroom. Being down to earth is an important role [this student felt the king was too far removed from the people]."

Question 5 enquired about the students in the classroom and the student-teachers' impressions and perceptions of the students. A UP student remarked, "They are the heroes." Another UP student commented, "There were times that I would walk into class and students wouldn't respond, I spent the whole day taking photos with them. It cost 7.50 Rand per photo and students were paying for it [a lot of money for a Siyabuswa student to afford]." Student-teachers were lost as to what to do. One said, "Monday I was not sure what to do in the standard four classroom [grade-level description]. I asked the principal, 'What work are they doing?' He said, 'Have no idea, just keep them busy.' The kids could not tell me what they were doing. I asked myself if I was teaching them the right thing? The teachers said they are just terrible and deserve the stick." A UP student replied, "The Government no longer allows corporal punishment." An ISU black student shared a question asked of her by one of the school administrators: "The principal asked me if we whip the children in the United States 'Because of Bantu [one of the larger black macrocultures within South Africa; Ndebele is a subgroup within the Bantu culture] education and no discipline or motivation we whip the children. It is the only motivation that students understand.' " A UP student said that the "students and staff were interested in having me stay, except for some of the male teachers. The students often say yes, but do they really understand? I don't have a clue." An ISU student said, "The principal and teachers said that the students really liked me and responded well. I was concerned with giving the students a voice; students asked, '*Do we get to?*' " Another ISU student responded with this experience: "In one of the classrooms students said, '*You are white, we are black—why would you want to teach us? Why are you here?*' I said, 'What you look like doesn't matter; what is in your heart matters. They all clapped.' " Students shared more strategies, such as "Students were very respectful and wanted to know a lot about America. I spoke their language and gave a sheet of paper in their language. The students were very excited." Another replied, "None of the children asked any questions, but the class was excited. The principal commented that teachers would come and watch the students raising their hands from outside the window. I noticed a man would walk around with a whip. I asked who he was, but no one would answer [he was the school disciplinarian]." One of the white ISU students said, "I felt I was a circus side-show; something to watch." And a white female UP student said, "I must teach at a boys high [school] because boys responded but girls did not."

We concluded the debriefing by asking students if they had recommendations for the project. Students gave a list of responses: "We should have been well prepared as student teachers." "We stayed a long way away from the schools; better to stay closer." "Get one class. Useless going into so many classes." "More warning about how students would react; we were not prepared for age group [some of the students were older than the student-teachers because many would stay in class until they passed to the next standard or grade level, and sometimes this would take years, because they received late opportunities to participate in schools]." "We must take along more creative activities." "Host families should be interviewed, so we know what type of people they are [the Siyabuswa coordinator was given only a week's notice from UP coordinators to set up host family situations and there was no time to match students appropriately to host families]." "Know the responsibility of hosting/living arrangements." "Prepare them on our diets." "I was not comfortable with host family; two males drinking—poor automobile, group unity would be good." "People need to have reliable transportation." "Make it longer than a week." "Have direct contact with supervisors." "Talk to principals prior to attending the schools; look at the textbooks prior." "Teachers should interact with us and share professional experiences." "Regarding host families, know who lives in the house; men were walking in and out." "Needs a lot more coordination. Would assume more controllability if students stayed together." "Better communication and coordination."; "Lacked a visible coordinator." "Observe classroom with teachers prior." "No women should be alone." "Get on a personal level with the students; establish a bond to enable better out-reach." "One strategy to enable better teaching was that I identified the class leaders and encouraged them by allowing them to assist." "Better preparation all the way around." "Know where your classmates are staying." "See others more often. Sit and chat with others and hosts (not informal)." "Language is important; learn a few words."

At this early juncture and given the students' fatigue, it was not surprising to see most students focus on the immediate difficulties and not on why things were the way they were. But certain issues did surface, such as classism and the high level of rural black poverty of South Africans and the connection to rac-ism. Recall, for example, that a UP student commented, "I forgot because of living in Pretoria," and an ISU student indicated that the only professional jobs for blacks were as teachers or policeman, tips to the differences that ex-isted as a result of classism and racism. Language and gender issues and cultural differences were also acknowledged by the students, which clearly demon-strated the inescapable intersections of race, class, language, and gender.

In reviewing this debriefing, some additional items are made evident. The UP students appeared to be more accepting of the poor housing conditions of the host families and the overall project. All the students displayed antiracist concepts in their teaching styles while in Siyabuswa. Yet many of the American students were not cognizant of the lessons to be learned because they were fo-cused on the "dissatisfactory" conditions of living and education. The ISU students had viewed pictures of the school sites before departing from the United States. We had talked about the poor living conditions, but not until we reached Siyabuswa did these things begin to really register.

Students were correct about the organization of the project. With one co-ordinator unable to attend, I was split between visiting the students' school sites, the host homes, and the interactive television program for in-service teachers. Students were placed great distances apart, and in some instances I was unable to get to their host family dwellings because I was dependent on rides as they were made available. I did, however, visit all the school sites. As was mentioned, in most cases the schools had no electricity, no toilets, no run-ning water, and no textbooks or other school materials. Generally there were about 60 to 80 students per classroom. Building structures were falling apart, with old desks cemented to the floor (approximately 20–25 in a classroom). The native language was not English, but English was the language in which subjects were taught. It was a rough experience for the visiting student-teach-ers, but I believed that in the long run this experience would add to the stu-dents' character and make for better teaching in their future classrooms.

The project made a big impact on the Siyabuswa community. The Siyabuswa project liaison made the following remarks: "I thought we were lucky to be a part of the whole thing, good for me and the community—for example, social interaction in community and with international students, which could not happen if we did not accept the invitation to participate in the project. This will forever remain a mark in Siyabuswa. This was something unthinkable, to see white students staying in Siyabuswa. It is generally not done in South Africa. We have white colleges, but they have never attempted to send their students to black rural areas to teach necessary social action, which leads to social interaction. All involved were able to go to a different level of thinking. This was quite a different experience that we wish to see continued." These students were a part of making historical firsts all along the way.

Pretoria

As we visited Durban and Capetown the question was always "Why Pretoria?" Pretoria was very much stigmatized because it was once the seat of apartheid. My answer was always "It is a good place for U.S. preservice teachers to receive a sampling of what the beginning process and transition stages of integrating schools were like in the United States." Most of the preservice teachers were in their early twenties and not old enough to remember the U.S. transition period of school desegregation. One of the program goals was to add to their characters an understanding of discrimination based on race, since especially for white students it is often difficult to notice the covert changes of insitutional and individual racism in the states.

The University of Pretoria began to integrate its institution approximately a decade ago, but blacks remain very much in the minority as instructors and students. As one U.S. student put it, "Pretoria was like walking into a time warp, reliving my parents' stories of segregation and racial oppression in the United States." Blacks were pretty much in domestic roles, wearing domestic uniforms each day to work, or they were cheap construction laborers in the city of Pretoria. My students often experienced the blatant racism of not being served appropriately in restaurants or being stared down if they were traveling blacks and whites together.

Student teaching within the city limits of Pretoria gave perfect lessons in how racism is manifested in schools. There were segregated classrooms, with white students on one side of the classroom and blacks students on the other. This was similar to classrooms I have visited in the United States, except students in the United States were choosing to sit with their own racial groups, whereas Pretoria students were being separated according to language differences. The black students could usually speak at least several different languages, such as their native tongue, Afrikaans (Afrikaner was the ethnic group name established by the Dutch and Netherlands people who immigrated to South Africa a few centuries before; Afrikaans is the language), and English; in contrast, the Afrikaner students spoke mainly Afrikaans. The teachers, almost all Afrikaners, would teach in Afrikaans to the Afrikaner students and in English to the black students (rather than in their native language). Black students received second-class treatment in most of the classrooms: They were disproportionately suspended and disciplined (as in the United States). Ability grouping dominated the classroom setting, so visually it looked like racial segregation. Teachers would outright label the groups "clever," "not so clever," "slow to learn," and/or "behavioral problems." Cooperating teachers would ask the white student teachers how "kafers" were treated in America. When one student didn't understand the question, the teacher changed the term to "niggers." During this time white teachers were very dismayed by the incoming affirmative action policies. Many were enticed to sign early teacher retirement contracts as the populations of schools were becoming more integrated and the government was seeking to balance the teaching force with more teachers of color. Throughout the student experience in South Africa, both the student-teachers and I, as student-teacher supervisor, experienced daily racist comments, attitudes, and treatment.

As this daily racist assault mounted, tensions grew between the white students and the black students within the group. For instance, students were discovering the many cultural differences among them. The students presented panel discussions for college classrooms, and it was there that the differences in experiences became apparent. Many times the white, Iowa-born students were politely corrected by the black southern or East Coast students. Why? Because their experiences were not the same as those of the white, Iowa-born students, so they painted a broader picture of Americans and American life. In addition, blame was concentrated on the University of Pretoria for poor program organization (schools were frequently closed down for holidays, cooperating teachers were not cooperative, more money than had been agreed upon was being charged for school site transportation, and access to e-mail and computers was stifled). Often I became the object of blame with regard to money issues (as mentioned previously, the change in housing arrangements put a strain on our overall budget). Through all of this frustration and dispute I saw that the students, especially the white students, were in denial. They were embarrassed by the blatant racism of white teachers in the schools and their lack of exposure to other cultures, and as the African American students voiced their anger about their blatant racist experiences in South Arica, all the students were at a loss as to what to do to change the situation. Therefore, they focused their energies elsewhere, finding fault at every turn with the program. Although the students shared integrated rooms, they began to travel in segregated groups, with the exception of two white students. As we hit our all-time crisis of communication breakdown, I arranged to have a "Racism 101" seminar.

We talked about the issues at hand, and about racial identity development and international travel cycles. Most of the students were grateful for the session and expressed this verbally or through notes. One other later shared that he was racist and sexist and had been brought up this way all his life. He said, "This diversity thing is new to me and it is taking me some time to adjust." Although students were interviewed with regard to their commitment to taking a stand against racism and diversity interest, none of this came out until we were confronted with these situations staring us right in the face. Being an antiracist educator is a difficult job, but I could recognize the progress being made in our group.

Final Evaluation

The University of Pretoria Teacher Education Project prepared four questions for the final evaluation. Those questions consisted of the following: (1) Give as many statements as possible reflecting your views on South African students, teachers, principals, and education in general. (2) Taking on the role of an enquiring researcher, reflect your experience of South African education in the form of questions. (3) Through introspection try to establish what you have personally learned from the total experience up to this point in time (upsetting, frame of mind, insight, personal identification, personal growth, etc.). (4) Would you recommend the continuation of this pilot project in future? (Circle your choice: yes or no.) Give the most important reason for your choice. Students' answer sheets were anonymous. The following are excerpts from the final student evaluation of the program. Answers that reflect the general opinion of the group have been selected.

Responses to Question 1

"S.A. student-teachers welcomed us into their natural environment with great enthusiasm and open arms. I wish we could have kept more contact with them after Siyabuswa. We really had a good time getting to know them; they were key players in our initial feelings, attitudes, and impressions of RSA. They also helped in educating us right away in S.A. [mainly Afrikaans] cultural norms."

"S.A. in-service teachers I found a drastic difference between teachers here in Pretoria, teachers in Siyabuswa, and teachers in the USA. I can only speak from a limited perspective because I have only visited briefly each school, but my initial impression is that the teachers in Pretoria are more equipped to teach (from the standpoint of being more informed and educated) than the teachers in Siyabuswa. Overall I see the standard of education being lower here than in the United States. I also see punishment as being a way to keep students on task; instead of rewarding good behavior, the focus is on catching the negative behavior after it has happened."

"From what I have observed, the South African system of education including student teachers, principals, teachers, and other educators in general, are faced with several challenges. The system has been left with the responsibility of righting the wrongs of past political agendas while simultaneously stimulating development and growth for the country's future."

"I find S.A. educators to be in a progressing and changing time in their careers. They are needing to change their curriculum, attitudes, and their beliefs to fit the new concepts of multiculturalism."

"Education in rural areas is very lacking due to the effects of oppression. There is a cycle of recurring events. Teachers are denied education and are not capable of using effective teaching methods. In turn, the education that the students are receiving is lacking, which will cause them to remain at their current social and economic status. Education in the city public schools is more well rounded and provides better opportunity for the students, yet I feel that it is still biased. At a 'multicultural school' [many South African educators refer to integrated schools as multicultural schools purely based on student population and not multicultural education concepts] that I taught in, a bulletin board had all-white family members. A black student in that class may question why a black family is not used for an example."

Responses to Question 2

"What is the meaning of diversity?"

"Do teachers have any idea what multicultural education is?"

"What measures are taken to ensure equal education for all South Africans?"

"Why does it seem that the most ignorant have the most power in schools?"

"How do teachers combat racist attitudes in a 'multicultural school'?"

"Why do principals in the townships tend to be powerless in terms of leadership ability?"

"Will the education reform really work?"

Responses to Question 3

"I have learned that principals can be incompetent and teachers might not care."

"I have learned to appreciate cultural differences, and that I can survive without close friends and family in a different environment."

"Total immersion in a foreign culture is more powerful than reading about it or hearing about it secondhand."

"Professionally, the whole experience enhanced my research skills."

"This experience has reinforced my belief that there are only two types of people in this world, good and bad."

"I have also found some personal identification, where I have learned a lot about who I am."

"It has opened my eyes to the diverse world around me, and has made me a stronger more independent person, and it has given me the opportunity to build some nice, long-lasting relationships."

"I have learned that ignorance and racism is everywhere."

"Personally, I have learned what oppression can do to a group of people. I have taken note of who in South Africa is fulfilling domestic roles, who is patronizing restaurants, and who is filling business roles. I have seen the power of education and what denying people of education can result in. As a future teacher, I will be even more dedicated to providing my students with an equal education, and encouraging them to work up to their potential."

Responses to Question 4

(All the students said yes, they would recommend this program to other students.)

"This project gave both South African and American students the opportunity to learn from one another about different cultures."

"This program offered the students of Iowa State an opportunity to step out of their comfort zones to learn through direct experience about another culture. The program in South African is particularly effective to the students aspiring to be educators because it offers a look at the effects of racism in a more blatant way than that in the United States."

"I think this was an eye-opening experience for me. I have learned a lot, despite the obstacles. I think the next time University of Pretoria should be more prepared in accommodating students as far as transportation, computer setup, and what to expect."

"Because it truly is an educational, multicultural experience, this experience has taught me more than any textbook or lecture ever could. It has benefited me in ways of learning about different cultures and revealing a lot of feelings, attitudes, and beliefs I have inside."

"To live the experience is far better than to read it."

"It is a program that will lend itself to further learning, speculation, and self-discovery. The trip may end, but the learning and experiences we gained from the trip will not."

Students articulated well and demonstrated signs of growth in areas of antiracist education. This international field-based experience went a step farther than some of the local experiences that were highlighted in the chapter. The 10 students who participated in this trip made an impact on many other people's lives in Siyabuswa and Pretoria, as well as back home with their families, peers, and university. Acquaintances throughout the eight-week experience, students made e-mail entries to a news reporter with the *Iowa Stater*. One student's research, entitled "Utilizing the Internet to Create Multicultural and Global Awareness," connected two ISU multicultural education classes (406), Pretoria secondary students, and the University of Pretoria in continuous discussions about race and education issues (Visani, 1997). Upon return, students were featured in many news articles, and they presented their educational experiences on panel discussions at the university. Most of the students have remained in touch with one another since the trip and continue to be involved with antiracist education projects.

The Exchange

On September 2, 1997, nine UP students and one faculty sponsor came to Iowa State University. Five of the nine students were "buddies" of the ISU study abroad group and had participated in the Siyabuswa project. Much was learned from the first exchange, and therefore student teaching assignments, multicutural and antiracist education orientations, accommodations, transportation, and other items were all securely in place for their arrival. Eight students of the ISU group were available throughout the stay of the UP students. Extensive coordination went into arranging host families. The ISU coordinator invited community and university residents to become host families. We interviewed and matched the students and faculty member to host families who had common interests.

The University of Pretoria was unable to offer scholarships to their students. Therefore, only students who could afford to finance their trip were able to participate. This had a direct effect on who participated. The agreement was to have 50% white and 50% black students enroll. But to the surprise of the ISU College of Education, and the host families, only one black student was able to participate. I decided not to mention the race of the students. Knowing at least five of these students, I knew there would still be benefits for all involved.

Beyond their busy schedules in student teaching, multicultural seminars, and host family activities, the students spoke in at least 12 ISU classes and two community churches. Letters came in from many community members who were touched by their presentations and teaching. The students spoke to issues of racism as young South Africans with open minds and hearts. The dean of education received this letter from a parent (only the first paragraph is presented because of length):

I'm actually writing to you as an Ames High School parent whose daughter had the privilege of reaping the benefits of the South African student exchange. My daughter, Emily, is a senior at Ames High and had two of the South African students as teachers these last several weeks—one in English and the other in American Government. Emily has come home repeatedly and told me how much fun and how interesting these two students were. They bonded well with the high school students and were so willing to talk to the students about their culture, their school system, and life in general in South Africa.

Of the host families consisting of ISU faculty and community, three are planning to visit the South African students in their homeland in the near future.

At an exit dinner for UP students and host families, sponsored by the Department of Curriculum and Instruction faculty, UP students said they had learned an immense amount about midwestern American life. These students were fascinated that we lived without gates and bars around our houses, as many upper- and middle-class South Africans, mainly whites, do in fear of burglaries and/or retaliation from poor black South Africans. They commented on how they enjoyed this freedom. They were very grateful to their host families, and both the South African students and their host families shared positive stories of cultural and international exchange.

The students shared that they were excited about returning home to implement multicultural concepts and other strategies in South African classrooms. There were many "firsts" for the students. They attended a black church service, the Kuumba Multicultural Experimental School Research Project (teachers and students are of many ethnic backgrounds), and antiracist education seminars, and they were assisted by several graduate students of color during the program. A few of the students attended my Theatre for Social Change class and a university lecture by Jane Elliot on prejudice. The students were amazed by the outwardness to reduce racism and spoke about becoming leaders in their country to fight against racism.

Since this was the second exchange (ISU to UP was the first), we were able to avoid some of the organization problems we had had in South Africa. The UP students repeatedly expressed their satisfaction with the overall program setup. Also pleased, the faculty sponsor is currently working on a faculty teaching exchange with the Department of Curriculum and Instruction. However, it was my observation that the organization of the student teaching experience could have been better.

High school teachers were told that the exchange students would be coming to observe in their classrooms and not that they would be student teaching (the administration was fearful that teachers would not respond well). This caused initial confusion, but all the teachers adjusted their programs to allow the international students to student teach. Once the school administration realized that their teachers were open to international student-teachers, they offered to have the exchange students for a more formal student teaching experience. A further suggestion would be to add teaching orientation to prepare international students for teaching in U.S. classrooms.

Because of their temporary status, UP students also had difficulty in receiving e-mail addresses, student flat rate bus fares, and university library cards. Since this exchange was part of the year-long feasibility study, these glitches were noted and measures have since been taken to allow greater access for the next exchange group.

Both colleges deemed the International Field Trips in Antiracist and Multicultural Education: South Africa Study Abroad Program feasible and consented for the international exchange to be an ongoing program. The exchange program is now in its third year (2000). The South African educational partnerships have grown to include teacher and faculty exchanges, national and international studies in antiracist education, and so on.

CONCLUDING REMARKS

The purpose of this chapter was to demonstrate the rewards of developing innovative field experiences for students. The research indicates that one-shot courses in multicultural education are not enough to make a solid impact on antiracist-multicultural teaching. The idea of connecting issues from a global perspective is very important as we recognize how technology and travel make our world an accessible global village.

This chapter has shared a bird's eye view of how preservice teachers think about race and highlighted the conflicts that they go through discovering their own identity and biases. Seeing blatant racist practices in schools and having to relate those instances to similar attitudes in U.S. schools made a lasting impression on the preservice teachers. Most vowed not repeat such ignorance in their own classes.

Strategies of having mixed backgrounds of students participate in the exchange and having them experience a microview of racial and cultural differences within their own exchange groups also built appreciation. The students related this to actual teaching in the workplace, and that all staff must find ways of understanding varied racial outlooks if they are to be productive as a whole. As American and South African students worked together, their global awareness was enhanced. American students and white South African students were also able to realize their privilege within their own societies as they worked in rural areas that were quite impoverished.

The preservice and graduate student participants made a tremendous impact on the elementary and secondary students they taught. As I return to visit some of those schools today, the students will often ask me to carry letters back to the very first student-teachers of the exchange program. These letters speak of the fun ways the student-teachers taught and how the teachers encouraged them to continue in school and someday go on to college. These young people enjoyed the openness to discuss diversity issues and to watch our future teachers work together in harmony despite difference of race. In-service teachers both in the United States and in South Africa should strive for such harmony because it demonstrates to the students racial appreciation.

Most of the exchange students are teaching at inner-city schools now, and all seem to have a strong emphasis in antiracist-multicultural education in their teaching. For the most part they have kept in touch, just as the second and third groups from both countries have. They often share their multicultural experiences or ask about multicultural resources and program ideas; sometimes they have me visit their classrooms.

The findings of this chapter support the contention that additional and concentrated antiracist-multicultural courses and field experiences make more of an impact on preservice teachers going into the field of education. The strategy to create additional antiracist-multicultural studies, such as the international field experience featured in this chapter, worked to develop the preservice teachers' critical thinking and abilities to implement antiracist teaching. These preservice teachers also had the opportunity to witness firsthand how this form of teaching positively affected the students with whom they worked. I attribute these additional experiences to their later choices to teach in diverse settings and/or to emphasize multicultural concepts at their permanent job sites. One of the preservice teachers, who is now a sixth grade teacher, has, two years in a row, brought all the sixth grade classrooms in her predominantly white school to my university for the "Africa to America" workshop. Her fellow teachers have remarked how much they have integrated multicultural concepts into the curriculum since she came on board. This example shows how these now in-service teachers are getting others on board—contrary to the usual comments I hear from my regular course preservice teachers now out in the field: They generally say that they give up because they are so isolated with their ideas and most often lack support from other teachers. The more exposure to antiracist-multicultural education strategies, the more likely confidence builds, whereby teachers so trained will do the integration in their classes, and colleagues will often take notice and perhaps become curious enough to ask questions or to experiment themselves.

9

Kuumba Multicultural Experimental School (KMES) Research Project

"He's made a couple of comments to me that I know don't come from Matthew [five-year-old participant]," she said. "One day he said something to me like 'I'm special.' I'm paraphrasing, but I know that didn't come from Matthew. It came from Kuumba." (parent excerpt news article interview, "Working Together" *Tribune*, October 20, 1997, p. B1)

INTRODUCTION

The Kuumba Multicultural Experimental School Research Project (KMES Research Project) began as an official pilot study in August 1997. It was based at the ISU Black Cultural Center and has received approval for research by both the local school district and the ISU Human Subjects Committee. The project is a five-year longitudinal study to measure the academic and cultural impact of an antiracist multicultural curriculum on kindergarten through sixth grade students. The elementary students enrolled represent over 10 various cultural backgrounds. The theme of the one-year pilot study is that all inhabitants of the world are part of the human family. This acknowledgment lends itself to the development of strong intercultural relationships.

The KMES Research Project ties in to all the featured studies and protocols for the classroom presented thus far in this book. The antiracist teacher study influenced the making of this research project because of the hesitancy of teachers at large to address the issues of racism in schools. The KMES Research Project seeks to create an antiracist education curriculum and implementation prototype and to add to the research of the local school district, state, and beyond. Video excerpts from the KMES experimental classroom are scheduled to be used in the next interactive television 520X antiracist education curriculum development course for teachers.

During the International Field Trips in Multicultural Education: South Africa Study Abroad Program (1997), four elementary students enrolled in the Kuumba School traveled abroad and were tutored by preservice student-teachers. By tutoring the Kuumba students, the student-teachers were able to compensate for teaching hours missed because of South Africa school breaks. The students talked about "being fortunate to be able to participate in an American [multicultural] school which was brought with us from home [student research paper, 1997]." Furthermore, the Kuumba students, as one student teacher put it, "had a classroom without walls," integrating South Africa into their daily lessons, and having nature reserves, and so on, to stimulate higher level thinking skills. Four of the preservice teachers who participated in the South Africa Study Abroad Program taught or researched for the KMES Research Project. In addition, preparations for the creation of a sister pilot study in South Africa are currently underway, funded for 2000–01.

Last, five of the (suburban) midwestern antiracist education ccohort group members are currently serving on the KMES Planning Committee, which consists of teachers, school administrators, university administrators and faculty, parents, and state education representatives, to raise funds to incorporate the project into the local school system. They are also scheduled to do guest teaching and implementation workshops at the school as demonstration for other public school teachers.

This chapter is written with the assistance of co-principal investigator Dr. Carlie C. Tartakov. We will begin with background information of the project.

BACKGROUND INFORMATION

The notion of the Kuumba (Swahili word meaning creativity) Multicultural School stemmed from the need to create an educational alternative for the multicultural community in Ames, Iowa, by fostering diversity through the arts. Originally this idea was implemented through the Ames Few (meaning the "few" African American families in Ames) Dance and Theatre Co., established in 1995 by Dee Abdullah, theater producer and director, and me. Having an emphasis in African-centered dance, the program was supported in part by the local university and housed in the university's dance department.

The Ames Few Dance and Theatre Co. offered Saturday classes to all age groups. It was able to bring together residents of the Ames community and local university students and staff. The classes lead to discovering many talented performers of all ages, and two performing companies were formulated. These consisted of a youth company and an adult company. These companies performed for schools and community and university organizations and also produced many professional productions independently. The program also brought in national and international artists to do guest teaching, give performances, put on exhibits, and direct.

Our goal for the program was to reinforce and teach about multicultural heritages through the arts; parents and ISU students along with some faculty were the backbone of this organization. Over two years numerous parents stated that the program helped to build confidence for their children in the regular school setting. In addition, many ISU students remarked that the program gave them the cultural and community support they needed to stay enrolled in school. As the program grew, we began to make it more structured. We offered a tots program (dance, storytelling, and arts and crafts), a junior program (dance and drumming, voice, and drama), and an adult program (dance and drumming, drama, and Tai Chi). I directed the educational component, and Dee Abdullah directed production.

Our work for this program was voluntary, since it was difficult to generate steady funding. Yet, theater was also a professional career for Dee Abdullah. When she became unable to continue volunteering in 1996, the production portion of the program ended. The Saturday school served as the educational component; although limited formal research was done during the first two years of the program, the benefits of such a school were obvious to all involved. Seeing the positive results of the program and understanding the national need for multicultural transformation in education, we began to conduct further research. Simultaneously a curriculum framework was designed to develop an ongoing experimental multicultural school. To reflect this change in concept and curriculum, the name Kuumba Multicultural School was adopted. At that time (spring 1997) the school consisted of the Saturday cultural arts program and a diversity technology class for children held in the Technology Center of the Department of Curriculum and Instruction at Iowa State University.

It was at that time that I approached Dr. Carlie Tartakov, who had been a member and advisor of the program since its inception, to consider partnering with me to explore the possibilities of creating a formal research-based multicultural experimental school. Dr. Tartakov had been an elementary school teacher for 23 years and later became a professor of curriculum and instruction with an emphasis in multicultural education.

We were interested in exploring the impact of a multicultural-antiracist school curriculum on student learning and development K–6 and beyond. We envisioned creating a five-year longitudinal study multicultural school. The central investigation would be based upon a small sample population of elementary students of diverse ethnic backgrounds. Attempting to discover if research of this nature had been done in recent times, we began with a literature search for research-based multicultural schools with a concentration in antiracist education. None were identified; however, we did locate schools with multicultural and international themes, such as the Hans Christian Andersen (concentration: gender-fair) school complex in Minnesota and the International School of Minnesota, both private schools.

We also became familiar with the Thomas Jefferson Middle School and the Magnet Arts (Eugene, Oregon) antiracist education school effort. The faculty standing committees include Discipline, Social, Grantwriting, and Racism Free Zone. The curriculum, behavioral expectations, and teacher attitudes reflect the commitment to educational and social equity (Jefferson Middle School Profile, 1995–96). To date these multicultural and antiracist schools are without formal research data to document the impact on academic achievement.

Mount Holyoke College (principal investigators: Beverly Daniel-Tatum and Phyllis C. Brown) in collaboration with the Northampton School District (western Massachusetts) conducted a two-year antiracist education study project entitled Improving Interethnic Relations among Youth: A School-based Project Involving Teachers, Parents, and Children. The project is investigating the combined effect on young people's intergroup relations of interventions involving teachers, students, parents, and the school district (Daniel-Tatum, October 31, 1997). Furthermore, an antiracist education project was conducted in schools at Wards 11 and 12 of the Toronto Board of Education and administered to (1) 213 parents of students in grades 3 through 8 in 1994–95; (2) 155 teachers in 1992 and 71 in 1994–95; (3) 625 students in grades 3 through 8; (4) 1,169 elementary school students in 1991–92. The results suggest that teachers have succeeded in validating racial and ethnic backgrounds of students and that curriculum materials have become more reflective of the student population (Cheng et al., 1996). Given this exploration of antiracist education school studies, it is gratifying to know that more research is being conducted in the areas of antiracist curriculum development and implementation within the schools, but we recognize that there remains a void in measuring the influence of antiracist education on academic achievement. With this in mind, we continued to proceed in the development of such a research project.

African-centered (Afrocentric) and other cultural schools have long proven the benefit of culture-centered schools on academic achievement (Ruenzel, 1994). As a student-teacher and parent during the early 1970s, I was associated with experimental, Afrocentric, and "freestyle" (parent-operated) schools in the Boston community. In the beginning 17 such schools existed; all have now disappeared. But for many students who attended these schools, success has followed. These schools are nonetheless rooted in the culture of the student-participants and do not generally use the multicultural and antiracist frameworks described in this book. As public school populations are becoming more diverse, the impact of antiracist-multicultural curriculum and implementation on student learning and development needs to be assessed.

One such school did exist in the 1970s. We have used its 1976 curriculum framework, designed by Dr. Sonia Nieto, University of Massachusetts, Amherst, as a guide for developing our multicultural experimental school research project. The following excerpt, taken from the *Des Moines Register* (October 26, 1997), highlights the efforts of Dr. Carlie C. Tartakov to explore benefits to students attending a multicultural school over 20 years ago.

The Che Lumumba School in Amherst, Massachusetts, had a multicultural student body and did embrace some multicultural concepts. Tartakov, who lived in the town of Amherst during the school's tenure and participated in many of their activities, is in the process of interviewing the students, parents, and teachers who were involved in the school. The youngest student in the school, who graduated in 1981, is now 27. The preliminary interviews suggest positive reactions to their experiences. When asked would they recommend this type of school to other students, without exception, the answer was a definite "yes." The benefits they report included social awareness and citizen action skills, positive self-esteem, and parental involvement, naming a few.

REMINISCING A MULTICULTURAL SCHOOL FROM THE 1970s BY DR. CARLIE TARTAKOV

Transition

The transition in the late 1990s from the Ames Few Saturday school to the Kuumba Multicultural Experimental School is for me reminiscent of the transition of the New Africa House Afrocentric Saturday School in Amherst, Massachusetts, that my daughter attended (in the 1970s) to the full-time Che Lumumba School. In both cases, programs were started by concerned African American parents and community members, having an afrocentric focus, and for the most part with student bodies of African American children. In examining the process and direction that multiculturalism education has taken in this nation over these same years, similar comparisons can be made.

Multicultural Schools

First concerns centered around self-esteem and self-interest aspects of those families: "Black is beautiful," and then moving on to socially and economically empowering interests and activities with "We are young, gifted, and black." There seemed then (and for some now) an urgent need by educators and parents to not only raise their children's self-esteem and capitalize on their self interests, but also to prepare their children for the changing world that lay ahead. One that would connect them to understanding and appreciating the diversity of the human family. And one that would give them the skills and experiences to be socially, academically, and culturally literate enough to function well among the diversity.

The Che Lumumba School, as the name suggests, was what we called Radical School [*Che* Guevera, Argentine by birth, world freedom fighter; Patrice *Lumumba* (1960s, assassinated), leader of the former Belgium Congo, where

Mubuto ruled in the 1970s]. The school stressed political empowerment as a way to reach their goals. In the case of the "Ames Few," the focus was on cultural awareness, and the transition to a more encompassing and multicultural focus was more clearly articulated. In the 1970s, as with New Africa House, there were many other schools that were emerging all over the United States and other interests asserted themselves: ethnicity, linguistics, religion, and so on. All these organizations and activities were attempting to give their communities and families what they thought or, in fact, could not get from the mainstream institutions available to them. Alternative schools of the 1990s are also trying to enhance, augment, or replace the standard school setting.

My involvement with this process has spanned many years. And I have moved through those very stages myself. As an elementary school teacher for over 23 years in the public schools of California and Massachusetts, and as a college teacher for an additional 12, my experiences and interests have always placed me in the middle of the process and as a participant in those changes. In the school systems, the best (and maybe then only) avenue for change that was open to teachers like me was through policy and curricula committee work. So we took advantage of those doors that were cracked open for us—though as some of us look back, we may now realize that the potential for major change can only be realized if you were allowed into rooms with the real decision makers.

The problem for me was that unless real changes could occur in the policies and the curriculum of the district, we as teachers would be confined to fine lines. It was as if someone gave you a coloring book and told you to create a new picture. What was already in place guided the direction. That is why developing our own curriculum and then measuring its effects is so rewarding. We are given a clear slate to create the environment and are not constricted to stay within lines. When I was asked to consider the possibility of developing and studying the effects of a multicultural school on children's academic, social, and emotional well-being, I felt that in a sense I was coming full circle. What better way to move the agenda of multiculturalism forward than through finding out what difference it makes.

Having an acquaintance with the founders of Che Lumumba for over 25 years, I have always had a sense that these children have been successful in their lives, due to many factors of course, but an important element in their success had been their involvement with the school. Is this true? I ask, as we embark on this project. I have begun an investigation into the lives of past students, parents, and teachers in this program, and the results so far are encouraging.

So far, interviews of students, parents, teachers, and resource people have suggested that the students' school experiences were of benefit to the students. When responding to interview questions, it is found that the participants, now the youngest, at 27 years old, are doing well in their lives. All interviewed so far graduated from high school and most sought degrees of higher learning. One of the youngest members is finishing up her Ph.D. in sociology next year.

One of the parents reported that his child is now comfortable in ethnically rich environments, and that most of her friends are either of mixed heritage, Latinos, or African Americans. This, he feels, can be attributed to her earlier years in the Che School. She seemed to develop more self-confidence and acceptance of herself during her time at Che, and he feels that this has helped her as an adult.

Most of the respondents talked about parental involvement as being central to the program's development. For example, one of the students interviewed said, "We learned about slavery, people you only hear briefly about. Field trips and demonstrations, social action activities, parents were involved. We were more aware of social issues, even though throughout high school I was embarrassed about having background that was different, and at the same time proud. The experience raised my consciousness and helped form my career as a teacher, it instilled in me the desire to help other people."

Though at the same time the main problem was also burnout of the parents with so many meetings and trying to accommodate the academic curriculum (diverse ages). And there is the issue of money to run the program. But on the other side of that was a spirited, interesting community that enriched all of their lives. That would include people like me, who were part of the community that supported the school. This spirit was in fact passed on to the students who attended the school. For instance, one student responded to the leadership qualities that were instilled through the school: "I am more political as compared to other friends; and liberal. Lolita La Brun was my pen pal, and my hero. [I am] open minded, and nonjudgmental, it made me think independently. I wish it were still around!"

THE DESIGNING OF THE KMES RESEARCH PROJECT

Dr. Tartakov's tracking of Che Lumumba students was helpful to the KMES Research Project in getting started. It gave samples of the effectiveness of a multicultural school in creating nonbiased citizens. The interviews also gave an indication that the concepts of multicultural education must concentrate on academic achievement within all the basic subject areas. During the Che Lumumba school, achievement was not cultivated in areas such as the sciences and math. Consequently, some of the students commented that they were weaker in those disciplines when entering high school.

This early exploration of schools, past and present, enabled the development of a sound proposal for research. Furthermore, the understanding that little empirical research has been done in the area of antiracist-multicultural education schools and achievement encouraged us as principal investigators to make such a contribution to the multicultural education field and to national scholarship in general. The leading motivation was to develop a model that could be tested and utilized in the public schools. In preparing the initial proposal, Dr. Tartakov and I decided to split our efforts into two areas: curriculum development and research methodology preparation. Although Dr. Tartakov leads in curriculum development and I in research, our duties often overlap. Such was the case in developing a proposal that would suggest a collaborative venture between our university, the local school district, and the state education department.

CURRICULUM DEVELOPMENT

Our goal is to study the impact of a multicultural curriculum on young children. We want to show evidence of what we think to be true, namely, that children do learn better and develop higher self-esteem when exposed to a multicultural educational setting. The curriculum should accurately reflect the cultural diversity within the United States, to respond to these realties within the nation and the world, and it should help students to develop decision-making and social action skills (Banks, 1997).

Both the written and unwritten curriculum—that is, the content of the materials and the methods used, as well as the policies and procedures, personnel, teachers, and student body—reflects multicultural considerations and approaches. It is curriculum developed and carried out by those who hold to the principles of multicultural education. Included in that is the input and involvement of the community, that is, parents and their children.

The project combines academic guidelines set by the state, multicultural and nonsexist curriculum guidelines all preservice teachers are required to follow, and the Ames Community School's guidelines. For instance, the academic concepts we are following in science are those covered in the Ames School's science curriculum. We have also incorporated concepts proposed by multicultural experts in the field of education, including James Banks (*Teaching Strategies for Ethnic Studies*), Sonia Nieto (*Affirming Diversity*), Carl Grant and Christine Sleeter (*Turning on Learning*), Christine Bennett (*Comprehensive Multicultural Education: Theory and Practice*), and Phillip Chinn and Donna Gollnick (*Multicultural Education in a Pluralistic Society*).

The curriculum frameworks include the Integration model, the Interdisciplinary model, and the Effective Curriculum model of James Banks (1997), as well as the Characteristics Multicultural Education model of Sonia Nieto (1992). In addition, we use the Racial Identity model of Beverly Daniel-Tatum (1997) and the Affinity Group model of Phyllis C. Brown (Brown, 1995).

The co-principal investigators serve as lead administrators of the KMES Research Project, and at least one certified head teacher is with the students at all times. In addition, there is an immersion Spanish teacher and graduate and undergraduate students on the curriculum and instruction team. The KMES Research Project affords local university students diversity practice, student teaching, independent research projects, and cross-cultural and international community and university research. Since the study focus is on antiracist education this form of networking helps to break down prohibitive structures for all involved.

The pilot study project has an open door policy to parents and is an antiracist education practice ground for local community schools and university teachers, administrators, students, and other interested programs. Through regularly scheduled parent meetings and focused interviews with the students, parents and students have direct input into the curriculum design.

Curriculum for the experimental school project was designed to begin with a part-time pull-out program. Students enrolled in the project would be released from their respective schools during "school specials" to attend the research site school. Three subject areas were designed for this initial part-time school project; these included science and technology, interdisciplinary studies, and affinity exchange. An overview of each subject will now follow.

Science and Technology

Research suggests that many students in our nation's elementary schools have an inadequate grounding in science and technology and are therefore unable to develop the necessary skills and understanding they will need in the next century (NAEP, 1983; Harding, 1993; Tartakov, 1995). In spite of recent improvements, achievement scores are low in science and technology compared to those of students in many nation states around the world. In addition, white females, children of color, and the physically challenged fall below other groups (Tartakov, 1995). With this in mind, our program will attempt to address factors that enhance learning in science and technology. Such factors include teaching and learning styles, stereotyping, the self-fulfilling prophecy, and ethnicity and learning.

The unit is geared to motivate science inquiry through exploring our environment through culture (3–6)—for example, recognizing differences and likenesses through observations, practicing recording skills, understanding how science and technology fit into our lives, and becoming aware of contributions that diverse cultures have made to science and technology. The rationale for stressing science and technology is that these disciplines are on the cutting edge for productivity in the new millennium, the local university is noted for its science and technology emphasis, and many critics do not believe that antiracist-multicultural education concepts can be infused into these subject areas.

Interdisciplinary Studies

The Interdisciplinary model (Banks, 1997) was used as a framework for this course. Antiracist education was added to the center entitled "Culture." Within predominantly white educational institutions minority students are easy targets for racial and ethnic prejudice (Murray and Clark, 1990; Pollard, 1989; Donaldson, 1996; Daniel-Tatum, 1997). In addition, when minorities are omitted from the "American experience," majority students perceive that minority experiences and culture are abnormal and noncontributing to the mainstream culture. This introductory unit seeks to expose students to a variety of cultural contributions and experiences, thereby assisting students to develop a positive identity and take steps to address racial and ethnic prejudice. For example, one of the first lessons emphasizes the science of skin color by having students mix color paints to match their complexions. Students discover that race has a function and that though we may look different on the outside (our genetic inheritance), for good reasons we are more alike in significant ways. Issues of adaptation are discussed. Students are also scheduled to bring in homework from multiple disciplines, and with their academic mentors—cross-discipline ISU students—they complete home assignments that integrate multicultural concepts into the learning process.

Likewise, in immersion Spanish (models from Dr. Marcia Rosenbusch, Foreign Language Program, Department of Curriculum and Instruction, Iowa State University), dance, theater, photography, and storytelling through exposure to a variety of cultural contributions and experiences, students will be assisted in developing a positive identity and taking steps to address racial and ethnic prejudice.

Affinity Exchange

All students come together in a multi-aged cohort to explore relevant issues and to be architects in their own learning. This group activity is based on "multicultural affinity" or blended exchanges, the final stage of the cultural affinity group model co-founded by Phyllis Brown, the Fort River Elementary School, and the University of Massachusetts (1994–95). From Brown's paradigm, students are traditionally placed into same-race support groups and eventually move into blended group discussions. Because our students are a small multicultural sample group, our approach is to have blended group class discussions from the beginning to the end of the project, thus creating a micro pluralistic society working out issues of prejudice and awareness collectively.

The students set goals and programs that help them take control of their own lives. For instance, if they identify for themselves a social need, they may wish to become involved in a social action project such as raising money or providing other needed resources or writing letters to senators, thus developing citizen action skills. An entrepreneurial piece comes in at this point. The students conduct fundraising, such as bake sales, for hands-on multicultural education field trips.

RESEARCH METHODOLOGY

The suburban midwestern site provided an atmosphere feasible to conduct multicultural research because of the influence of the local university. Furthermore, the community's public schools have been involved with antiracist education research since 1995 (Donaldson, 1996). Such commitments demonstrate a sustained interest to support the KMES longitudinal study. Beginning research has been designed and administered using the qualitative and quantitative skills of the research team (12 members).

The methods of research are quantitative, qualitative, and action-based. When students first become part of the project, they submit their previous academic files with work folders. These materials assist researchers in comparing student academic progress and multicultural awareness development.

Following file submissions, KMES Research Project qualitative approaches were done; these included (1) one-to-one interviews, (2) focus group interviews with drawings and video analysis, (3) storytelling, (4) process and progress portfolios, and (5) teacher and mentor observations recorded by code in reflection journals. These qualitative methods, which will continue throughout the duration of the project, were used to measure students' ideological movement and academic growth. The research team assisted in the collection of data throughout the project, using QSR NUD-IST (qualitative) software as a database to enter and categorize the information. All the data from the first-year pilot study will be presented in group norms, to protect the confidentiality of the participants, and documented into an evaluation project report. The theoretical basis for process and product evaluation is provided in the work of Egon G. Guba and Yvonna S. Lincoln in *Fourth Generation Evaluation* (1989); David F. Lancy in *Qualitative Research in Education* (1993); and I. E. Seidman in *Interviewing as Qualitative Research* (1991). See also *Focus Group Interview Procedures* (Sorenson and Sweeney, 1994: Research Institute for Studies in Education) and *Teachers Are Researchers* (International Reading Assn., 1993).

Quantitative measures are designed mainly for year 2 through year 5 of full-time school. They will involve pre- and posttest surveys administered to a treatment group (KMES students) and to nontreatment groups (local community school students, districtwide). The treatment and nontreatment approach will render data for quantitative comparative analyses. In addition to this component of research, a battery of tests will be given throughout the program. The purpose of these tests is to explore the contention of multicultural education research that standardized tests and curricula are culturally biased and set many students up to fail academically (Medina and Neill, 1990; Nieto, 2000). Students of color have been noted to have lower test scores than whites (Educational Equity Data Summary, 1995–96). Research indicates that lower achievement for students of color is partly attributable to culturally biased curricula and testing, school attitudes regarding race, and lack of antiracist educational professional development for educators (Ford, 1996; Donaldson, 1996).

Furthermore, the testing is intended to enable researchers to understand the learning styles and multicultural awareness of K–6 students and to apply those discoveries to revising standardized tests and curricula. Once the tests are culturally adapted, we will retest to examine if students have more success with the culturally inclusive version and to see how the KMES students with this cultural intervention fare on the adapted tests. For example, the Iowa Test of Basic Skills will be modified for use in the KMES Research Project; the test will be tailored to the specific needs and learning styles of our students. Doing so is expected to eliminate much of the variance in test scores attributable to systematic error or bias. Likewise, we have adopted a battery of tests and research procedures that will allow us to determine the learning styles, aptitudes, and progress of each KMES student. The test battery for the first-year pilot study will consist of (1) Student Attitude Assessment (Multicultural Education Project): Assessing Children's Awareness about Diversity (designed by Clark County School District Compensatory Education Division, Las Vegas, Nevada); (2) Multiethnic Identity Measure (Phinney); (3) Teele Inventory for Multiple Intelligence.

A yearly progress research report will be documented and used as a guide to continue ongoing data collection and analyses. These evaluation summaries will include common themes and concerns evident in the data. Recommendations will be made based on these common responses. In addition, external evaluators are regularly called in to critique the design and the success of the project, their report will be added in its entirety to the final research report.

CHALLENGES OF GETTING STARTED

There were many. The challenge of working through the bureaucracy was the most difficult for us. We underestimated the time it would take and the resistance we would encounter, as well as the lack of support we would have in the beginning, but we learned some good lessons, one of which is that until all stakeholders come to a common meetingplace and take ownership of the project, we will always be struggling against unknown forces. Touching upon this finding is the national debate that questions whether multiculturalism is a legitimate discipline. Indeed, there are no guides for this venture. The curriculum and research teams have spent numerous hours developing the project every step of the way.

In the beginning, most of the support for the project came from parents who wanted an alternative for their children. It was, in fact, those parents who convinced us to start with a half-day school while we waited for approval from the local community school district to become a full-time experimental school research project under the auspices of the public schools. It was really the parents who, in many ways, gave us the emotional supportive backbone to hang in. Also, volunteers gave of their time and energies freely just for the love of children and the vision of the school.

A school district planning committee was established following the approval of the district's research committee. The planning committee, representing all the collaborating constituencies, came forth to push this agenda forward and will have the greatest influence on whether our experimental project will proceed in the fall. This body is made up of teachers, principals, an assistant superintendent, parents of children of the KMES, a curriculum and instruction department head, the director of the Minority Student Affairs Office, a member of the State Department, and the co-principal investigators. After voting to put the project into one of the elementary schools, the current task of the planning committee is to raise funds through local, state, and national grant opportunities.

The planning committee has proposed that the project enter an elementary school (August 1998) and remain an experimental classroom for the first year in the school. The experimental classroom would consist of the multi-aged students now enrolled in the pilot study. It has also been proposed that the head teachers, university mentors, and research team, as well as the three-part curriculum design (science and technology, interdisciplinary studies, and affinity group), stay intact during this time. During the course of this first year, all other teachers in the elementary school will rotate to do practice teaching and professional development within the experimental classroom. The experimental students will integrate with other school students for their other basic subject areas. KMES teachers, mentors, and researchers will give multicultural reinforcement assistance to the general classrooms at this time.

It is the goal of the planning committee that the elementary school will become full partners with the KMES Research Project. In essence, the school will become the multicultural experimental school in the district. During this transformation the school will be assisted by the KMES curriculum and research teams throughout the remaining three years. The KMES courses will be made available to all students, and the KMES original sample population will enter into their respective grade levels by the third year of the project. However, the KMES original sample population will continue to be tracked and studied for the purpose of completing the investigation of academic achievement of a multicultural-antiracist education cohort group. In addition, the entire school will be studied and compared to nontreatment schools in the district. It is the goal of the school district planning committee to have this experimental elementary school become a prototype for the school district at large; the school district intends to infuse this prototype curriculum within all its schools by 2007.

FIRST-YEAR SUMMARY

The KMES Research Project pilot study follows the calendar year of the local university. Generally, there are 16 weeks in a semester or session. The pilot study met once a week for three-hour sessions. Students the first-year sessions have demonstrated advancement in both academic work and multicultural awareness. For example, pre- and posttest drawings for immersion Spanish were given to the "Goodness Gorillas," a named coined by the kindergarten–second-grade group); the students were unable to draw the Spanish words spoken during the pretest. However, during the posttest all the students were able to draw the words given—for example, *la casa* (house), and *la familia* (family). In the case of multicultural awareness, 17 out of 20 students scored higher in the posttest. Regarding academic achievement, KMES participants' regular teachers said that they felt the program made a positive impact on the students. Increased self-esteem, problem solving, and other academic enhancements were noted by the students' regular teachers as well as by parents.

More academic achievement testing was emphasized in the second session. We tested and analyzed learning styles to help us create curriculum that could better reach all student-participants, conducted one-to-one interviews and parent conferences, reviewed (public) school academic profiles, and made observation profiles of students. Curriculum during this session was designed more succinctly to fit the profiles of our students. During the first class of the second session, teachers disseminated pretests in their subject areas; posttests were given the last day of the second session. We used the preliminary findings from these tests to further enhance the curriculum and testing for the next year's experimental classroom.

The KMES Research Project is an exciting experiment even during its infant stages, where growth of the students is visible. Furthermore, coping skills to address racism and prejudice (especially for the students of color while in mainstream classrooms) have become evident through the affinity class discussions. As a parent of three of the students who attended the KMES Research Project pilot study, I am grateful to all the people who worked hard to make the project materialize. I can clearly see how the project reinforced cultural pride and confidence to achieve—what we try very much to instill at home.

Thus far the project has reached hundreds of people directly, among them KMES students, teachers, academic mentors, parents, researchers, planners, and college classrooms. Numerous articles have been written on the project, and recently the State Board of Education awarded the project the Educational Equity Recognition Award (October 1999). The president of the cooperating university has often cited the project's endeavors of the project in presentations on diversity initiatives that affect the state. As the project moved into the experimental (public school) classroom, sister-study planning began in Cape Town, South Africa (August 1998). In-service and preservice teachers, faculty, and multicultural scholars and researchers participated in the 1999 KMES Research Project exchange program to South Africa. Cape Town was funded to duplicate the U.S. KMES Research Project, with some adaptations, in 2000. All these efforts have created an antiracist-multicultural experimental school and prototype for others interested in transforming their current schools. The project promoted the human family and the building of solid cross-cultural relationships. What a wonderful way to model to the young that antiracist-multicultural education has a place in our schools, communities, and nation.

IN CONCLUSION: SOME EARLY FINDINGS

The KMES Research Project pilot study explored the impact of an antiracist-multicultural curriculum on the learning and development of elementary school-aged children. It examined the relationship of cultural literacy and student success, gave implications for curriculum practice, and added to the needed literature on the effectiveness of multicultural teaching. The intent here was to demonstrate to regular classroom teachers that antiracist-multicultural teaching does make a difference for all students.

Twenty K–6 students of diverse backgrounds experienced an interdisciplinary antiracist curriculum and a variety of pre- and posttest assessments. NUD-IST software assisted in coding eight sets of data, some of which included student pre- and posttests, one-on-one interviews, and focus group interviews; teacher and mentor action research journals; parent pre- and posttests and one-on-one interviews; in-class audio- and videotaping; researchers' observation field notes; and teacher pre- and posttest interviews. To accomplish the goal of matching common responses, we keyed into six items explored by the co-principal investigators, quantitative project analyst, and consultant school psychologist; those items included (1) what the students were saying about the curriculum, (2) student growth in understanding antiracism-multiculturalism, (3) student reaction to curriculum implementation, (4) student learning and behavioral development, (5) student sensitivity toward peers and others, and (6) student ability to understand class assignments.

The following are significant findings of the pilot study: (1) Students were able to grasp the contents of the antiracist-multicultural curricula within the context of the various subject areas. (2) They enhanced their respect for other cultures and learned to better appreciate domestic and global differences. (3) Students were better able to contextualize learning when they engaged in "hands-on empathy and/or experiential lessons, [when they] experienced the lesson more holistically" and when varied teaching techniques were employed, including cooperative learning and discovery, student-centered assignments, student portfolio assessment, as well as when multicultural concepts studied included examining social justice issues. (4) Students became more equipped to handle bias and prejudice at their regular schools and were quicker to step in to articulate the importance of sensitivity to others. Coming in to the project, many of the students were quite reserved. They said they were too afraid to meet new people. They were also somewhat selfish and often fought over seating or made negative comments about other children in class. By the end of the school year these same students were reminding each other to "treat your neighbor as you want to be treated," saying, "Don't be prejudiced," and so on.

The pre- and posttest administered by the statistical project analyst complemented the common theme findings of the qualitative data. For instance, the ethnicity, multicultural awareness, and learning style tests indicated major development for most of the students over the year. Most students coming in to the program did not have a deep sense of cultural appreciation, know their ethnicity, or understand what the term meant. One student who learned the meaning of the term through the program gave it as a spelling word in her regular classroom. The student's teacher was unable to pronounce, spell, or define the word. The student received special points for the day, and her teacher commented to one of the investigators that she had to challenge him to learn and to teach more about ethnicity and culture.

The learning styles of the students were typical of classroom students everywhere, for students come to school with a variety of learning styles (Gardner, 1993). It is our job as teachers to recognize and to teach according to those multiple learning and cultural styles.

The school psychologist viewed videotapes of classes and focus group discussions and observed very positive learning experiences. She commented that teaching styles and the curriculum design and implementation observed in the project could prove beneficial to the U.S. student populace at large.

The results of the investigation suggests that an antiracist-multicultural curriculum approach to academic learning can improve student's self-efficacy and serve as a model for educators seeking to improve the learning and development of their students.

The article "Kuumba 'Creativity' Multicultural Experimental School Research Project: A Model for Antiracist-Multicultural Education School Reform" (Donaldson and Tartakov, forthcoming), will give technical details on the first two years of curriculum implementation, research methodology, data collection, and analyses and findings for the purpose of promoting large-scale school reform.

The purpose of this chapter was to exhibit evidence that education that is multicultural makes an obvious difference for elementary school children. If teachers and school systems understand these positive implications, perhaps they will become greater supporters of antiracist-multicultural education. This chapter also adds to antiracist-multicultural education research. Frequently, multicultural education scholarship is accused of not being grounded in empirical research. Opponents to multicultural education scholarship view the discipline as being unable to prove that transforming the curriculum to become multicultural has a positive effect on student achievement. The ongoing efforts of the KMES Research Project strives to add significantly to this growing body of research, and we encourage implementing more projects of this nature. The more research available, the better we are able to make our case to move beyond a reform movement into the worldwide practice of education that is multicultural.

Conclusion

This book has gone to great lengths to reveal, through research and practice, the possibilities of addressing and reducing racist practices in our schools. It has featured an Antiracist Education Teacher Study that assisted in providing baseline figures of teacher perceptions of racism, and has demonstrated how teachers can successfully implement antiracist concepts in their classrooms. Findings further indicated that such teacher involvement makes a difference in student acceptance and attitude. As teachers display enthusiasm for teaching their subject areas multiculturally, and having an intolerance for racist behavior, many students have shown greater respect and appreciation for their teachers who are willing to expose life's realities. Educators in the Antiracist Education Teacher Study became role models for their students. This role modeling empowered students in positive ways to address issues of racism from the student perspective.

This book has also focused on shattering the denial of teachers who doubt the existence of racism in schools and how student learning is adversely affected by it. It has uncovered the difficulty of teachers having to come to grips with the realities of racism. In light of these difficulties, those who endured have become empowered to be better teachers.

The geographical data have provided us with insight to varying outlooks of teachers by region but by and large it reflected the harsh fact that most white teachers are not currently willing to participate in self-awareness or curriculum and implementation professional development. This grim factor strongly encouraged the many antiracist projects, courses, and studies presented in this book. Teachers need to understand that antiracist education does not mean "attack all the white people"; rather, it means tear down the walls of ignorance and be set free to work toward becoming the best that one can be. Many more teachers may come to recognize the harm they cause students when they ignore or are a part of discriminatory practices in schools. This book challenges teachers who pride themselves as having good teaching abilities to expand those skills in order to reflect more multicultural and antiracist integration within curricula. It also challenges teachers who genuinely care about all students to take an active role in reducing racism. Adhering to these challenges, the needs of all students and preparing them properly for the multicultural world in which they live can be met. Yet, I am curious to know if the efforts in this book will help to change mainstream attitudes of denial and fear. The book contains much data identifying characteristics of denial and ways to break through that denial. There are strategies to move beyond racism, and to become part of the solution; not the problem. However, teachers have all kinds of denial tactics that they cling to. For instance, general attitudes consist of acting as if blind: "Those things don't happen in my school"; blaming the victim: "These students embellish the actual truth" or "There is more racism between students than what's coming from teachers and school policy"; giving someone else the responsibility: "Matters of race should be taught at home"; avoidance & ignorance: "Can't we get beyond the past?" or "Why can't these other groups be like the Orientals and learn without a fuss?" Are teachers willing to insist that educational institutions support opportunities to assist teachers in change? Acknowledging the dense denial from the teacher study, it appears to be a far-off request from the masses.

Teacher education has been the link throughout the book. In-service and preservice teachers, secondary students, graduate student education majors, experimental courses, education study abroad program, and an experimental elementary school research project all attempted to demonstrate that antiracist-multicultural education does make a major impact on student learning and development. For example, some of the major efforts and outcomes that worked included: (1) the teacher antiracist study that revealed the difficulty of getting teachers on board, however, the few that did demonstrated that antiracist strategies make a difference in the education of students; both students and teachers that participated in the antiracist projects agree that such efforts helped to develop non-racist attitudes in the school environment, (2) the pre-service teachers enrolled in the antiracist education study abroad program honed their skills in critical thinking and antiracist teaching, they saw first hand the positive impact that antiracist education made in their lives and their students' lives, (3) graduate students who participated in the antiracist education experimental course demonstrated the need to have an educational platform in which to address and learn about racism in schools and society; they spoke of the relief to have other peers and educators realize the detrimental ef-fects of racism, and the joy of creating antiracist curricula that could actually be put into practice, and (4) the results of the elementary experimental multicultural education project exhibited how antiracist multicultural education can improve self-efficacy and serve as a model for educators seeking to improve the learning and development of their students. These successes (and others that are out there) can shatter teachers' denial of racism and bring forth successful reform efforts in our schools. There is need for more research with teachers and educational institutions at large, if we are to address the issue of racism seriously on both national and international levels. The hope is that this book has contributed to the literature and to the discourse on antiracist education and that there are educators worldwide who will find this book of use in supporting their antiracist education endeavors, enhancing their strategies, and shattering the denial of racism in schools with protocols for the classroom and beyond.

My charge to individuals and schools who want to use this book to assist with change in education would be to: (1) identify and associate with credible "allies," (2) enhance your own knowledge base of multicultural and antiracist education, and (3) take action toward positive change within your classrooms, school faculties, and school communities.

Research with teachers and educational institutions must take place, if major change is going to happen. Some suggestions are to request teacher professional development and research in the area of racism/antiracism. This book along with other available research can be presented to state and local school boards, school departments, school administrators, school curriculum research departments, and school councils. Futher recommendations include linking with national and international multicultural and antiracist projects, organizations, and efforts; and/or seeking funding sources available to create antiracist education programs and projects. In addition, university level institutions can be encouraged to develop multicultural academic components and/or centers that serve all levels of the educational community. Universities should consider expanding core curricula to include multicultural and antiracist education courses, and within their teacher education programs have all courses include multicultural concepts.

Epilogue: Voice of an Author

To put so many projects and studies together in one book was an enormous task. At times I asked myself, Is it worth the effort? So many people reject the actualities of really dismantling racism within our schools and societies. The reality is that racism continues to benefit many, but at the same time it devastates so many others. If we ask the average person if racism will ever be eradicated, the answer will usually be "no" or "not in my lifetime." Why bother if this is true? We must bother because even the smallest of efforts can make a difference in a student's life, and therefore a difference in the world, as that student becomes a productive citizen of our global society.

Perhaps I have overloaded the readers with too much data and too many models for teaching, and perhaps feeling overwhelmed they will put the book down never to read it again. I hope that is not the case. Instead, I hope this book has met its goal of sharing research as ammunition to combat ignorance. Furthermore, I have highlighted some examples of antiracist education at work within a number of educational contexts such as distance education, teacher education, internationalization in education, cohort teaching and staff development, and expansion of preservice teacher education with practical field experiences, demonstrating the vast possibilities for education that is antiracist and multicultural.

I often say to students, "Hum, schools didn't have those concepts, materials, and opportunities when I was attending; education is so exciting today."

And it is. It has been an honor to add to that excitement, knowing that we can provide our students with an educational advantage through the integration of antiracist-multicultural concepts. We can prepare our students better for the real world and give them the skills to communicate and change societies for the betterment of all humankind.

Appendix A

Students' Perceptions of Teacher Race/Diversity Awareness

Name

_____

Preliminary Survey for Grades 3–12
Karen B. Donaldson, Principal Investigator
College of Education
Curriculum and Instruction Department
Iowa State University
Ames, IA 50011

You will be asked to complete another survey at a later date and those answers will be compared to these. It is important that you write in your name each time so we can match your answers. Your teacher will not see your answers and your individual responses will never be reported.

Please circle one of the six possible responses to each statement.
1 = Strongly Disagree
2 = Disagree
3 = Somewhat Disagree
4 = Somewhat Agree
5 = Agree
6 = Strongly Agree

1. My teacher(s) mention contributions   1   2   3   4   5   6
   made by people of color in class.

2. I feel comfortable around my teacher(s).   1   2   3   4   5   6

3. My teacher(s) makes me wish I was born   1   2   3   4   5   6
   into another race.

4. My teacher(s) use classroom activities   1   2   3   4   5   6
   that reflect the history and contribu-
   tions of my racial group.

5. I respect my teacher(s).   1   2   3   4   5   6

6. My teacher(s) won't allow students to   1   2   3   4   5   6
   make jokes or talk badly about people
   who are not of the same race.

7. My teacher(s) only pay attention to stu- 1   2   3   4   5   6
   dents who are the same color that
   he/she is.

8. My school friends feel comfortable   1   2   3   4   5   6
   around my teacher(s).

9. My school friends respect my teacher(s). 1   2   3   4   5   6

10. My teacher(s) make me feel that all peo- 1   2   3   4   5   6
    ple are created equal.

Please complete the following:

Ethnic Background (check one only)
_____ European American
_____ African American
_____ Asian
_____ Hispanic
_____ South Pacific Islander
_____ Native American
_____ White of Hispanic origin
_____ Bi-racial (please specify _____)
_____ Other (please specify _____)

Gender (check one only)
_____ Female
_____ Male

Grade _____

School _____

Thank you for taking the time to complete this questionnaire. Your responses are very important to the success of the study. When you are done, please return this form immediately to the researcher administering the survey.

Appendix B

Teacher Race Awareness Survey I

ID _____

Dr. Karen B. Donaldson, Principal Investigator
College of Education
Curriculum and Instruction Department
Iowa State University
Ames, IA 50011

The goal of this survey is to explore (3–12 grade) teachers' awareness and attitudes about racism in schools. Specifically, it is to examine teachers' abilities to address racism with themselves, their students, the curriculum, and total school environment. This survey is the first phase of a multicultural/antiracist interdisciplinary curriculum implementation study with teachers. It will be disseminated in four regions of the United States and will anonymously include urban, suburban, and rural school teachers' responses from each region. The goal of this wide coverage is to discover and compare outlooks and needs of U.S. teachers in a variety of geographical settings.

You will be asked to complete another survey at a later date and those answers will be compared to these. It is important that you fill in the ID blank in the upper right hand corner with *the last five digits of your social security number* each time so we can match your answers. Be assured that all responses will be reported in terms of group summarizations. Your individual responses will never be reported.

Listed below are a number of statements relating to issues of racism and curriculum development. Please circle one of the six possible responses to each statement.

1 = Strongly Disagree
2 = Disagree
3 = Somewhat Disagree
4 = Somewhat Agree
5 = Agree
6 = Strongly Agree

1. Racism is defined as a system of privilege   1   2   3   4   5   6
    and penalty based on one's race.

2. Targets of racism are usually people of   1   2   3   4   5   6
    color.

3. Racism is largely manifested in schools   1   2   3   4   5   6
    through biased curriculum and instruc-
    tion.

4. Racism exists within most U.S. schools.   1   2   3   4   5   6

5. Racism in schools ended with the Civil   1   2   3   4   5   6
    Rights Movement of the '60s.

6. Being an anti-racist teacher means pay-   1   2   3   4   5   6
    ing attention to the *curriculum* in
    which some students may be favored
    over others.

7. Being an anti-racist teacher means pay-   1   2   3   4   5   6
    ing attention to the *sorting policies* in
    which some students may be favored
    over others.

8. Being an anti-racist teacher means pay-   1   2   3   4   5   6
    ing attention to the *choice of materials*
    in which some students may be favored
    over others.

9. Being an anti-racist teacher means pay-   1   2   3   4   5   6
    ing attention to the *teacher interactions
    and relationships with the students and
    their communities* in which some stu-
    dents may be favored over others.

10. An example of an anti-racist curriculum   1   2   3   4   5   6
    would be lessons on "race," the roots of
    racism in the U.S., how racist practices
    still continue today, and a student social
    action project to assist in the reduction
    of racism.

11. Anti-racist curriculum is for all students.   1   2   3   4   5   6

1 = Strongly Disagree
2 = Disagree
3 = Somewhat Disagree
4 = Somewhat Agree
5 = Agree
6 = Strongly Agree

12. Most teachers are able to respond com-   1   2   3   4   5   6
    fortably when the subject of racism
    comes up in the school setting.

13. Very often teachers' cultural beliefs are   1   2   3   4   5   6
    transferred to the students in the class-
    room.

14. Racism affects students' learning and   1   2   3   4   5   6
    behavior in numerous ways.

15. Racism is a leading deterrent to students   1   2   3   4   5   6
    of color succeeding in school.

16. Racism in schools causes many adverse   1   2   3   4   5   6
    effects on society.

17. Anti-racist curricula are one key to ad-   1   2   3   4   5   6
    dressing racism issues in schools.

18. Anti-racist curricula can be integrated   1   2   3   4   5   6
    into all subject areas.

19. Most teachers would incorporate an   1   2   3   4   5   6
    anti-racist unit if an *instruction manual*
    was available.

20. Most teachers would incorporate an   1   2   3   4   5   6
    anti-racist unit if *professional training*
    for this area was available.

21. Most teachers would incorporate an   1   2   3   4   5   6
    anti-racist unit if a *demonstration video
    or CD programs* were available.

22. Anti-racist curricula can help to ulti-   1   2   3   4   5   6
    mately reduce racist attitudes.

23. Anti-racist curricula can help to ulti-   1   2   3   4   5   6
    mately reduce racist incidents within the
    school setting.

24. As a teacher, you have directly experi-   1   2   3   4   5   6
    enced at least one racist incident in the
    school setting.

25. During your teaching career, you unin-   1   2   3   4   5   6
    tentionally made a racist/stereotypical
    comment to a student, parent, or fellow
    teacher.

1 = Strongly Disagree
2 = Disagree
3 = Somewhat Disagree
4 = Somewhat Agree
5 = Agree
6 = Strongly Agree

26. Racist beliefs and conditioning cause   1   2   3   4   5   6
    many teachers to deny that racism exists
    in schools.

27. As a child, your family members pro-   1   2   3   4   5   6
    moted racist beliefs.

28. As a child, you directly experienced at   1   2   3   4   5   6
    least one racist incident.

29. As a child, you indirectly experienced at 1   2   3   4   5   6
    least one racist incident.

30. During your *college education* you have   1   2   3   4   5   6
    received training in multicultural educa-
    tion.

31. During your *professional development*   1   2   3   4   5   6
    you have received training in multicul-
    tural education.

32. Most teachers are not concerned about   1   2   3   4   5   6
    racism in schools.

33. Most teachers desire an equitable educa-   1   2   3   4   5   6
    tion for all students.

34. Most teachers desire a comprehensive   1   2   3   4   5   6
    education for all students.

                    *   *   *   *   *

Please complete the following demographic
information:

Teaching specialization

_____

Teaching region (check one only)
_____ West Coast
_____ Midwest
_____ Northeast
_____ South

Teaching grade level _____

Years teaching _____

Ethnic Background (check one only)
_____ European American
_____ African American
_____ Asian
_____ Hispanic
_____ South Pacific Islander
_____ Native American
_____ White of Hispanic origin
_____ Bi-racial (please specify _____)
_____ Other (please specify _____)

Gender (check one only)
_____ Female
_____ Male

Age _____

Birthplace _____

Mother's Occupation _____

Father's Occupation _____

School Population

School location (check one only)
_____ Rural
_____ Suburban
_____ Urban

Thank you for taking the time to complete this questionnaire. Your responses are very important to the success of the study. When you are done, please return this form immediately to the researcher administering the survey.

Appendix C

Teacher Race Awareness Midpoint Survey

ID _____

Dr. Karen B. Donaldson, Principal Investigator
College of Education
Curriculum and Instruction Department
Iowa State University
Ames, IA 50011

It is important that you fill in the ID blank in the upper right hand corner with *the last five digits of your social security number* so that we can match your answers to the previous survey you completed. Be assured that all responses will be reported in terms of group summarizations. Your individual responses will never be reported.

How has the antiracist workshop that you have been exposed to increased your awareness and understanding of racism in United States schools?

How have the antiracist materials you've been exposed to (curriculum handbook, software, and video) increased your awareness and understanding of the roots of racism?

From what you have learned, do you feel that racism is a problem stemming from ...
(check all that apply)
_____ institutional policies
_____ educational programs
_____ home practices
Would you recommend these workshops and materials to other educators?
_____ yes
_____ no

How have the materials you've been exposed to increased your understanding of how children of color may feel threatened in today's "mainstream" educational system?

After viewing these materials, do you believe that racism actually exists? Or do you believe that people who make claims of racism are more or less "crying wolf?" Please explain.

Do you now feel better equipped to implement antiracist education in the classroom?

Now that you have been exposed to these materials, would you like to be exposed to other antiracist education seminars and training programs?
_____ yes
_____ no

Thank you for taking the time to complete this questionnaire. Your responses are very important to the success of the study. When you are done, please return this form immediately to the researcher administering the survey.

Appendix D

Antiracist Curriculum Development and Implementation Study: Handbook Participants Questionnaire

Please enter the *last five digits* of your social security number below:

ID _____

How has this handbook benefited you as a teacher?

What changes (if any) would you recommend?

If you have received additional tools with this handbook such as (a):

Workshop
Computer software
Video presentation

Please give your opinion where applicable. . . .

Any additional comments:
Please write on back if necessary. . . .

Appendix E

Models of Path Analysis Results from the Teacher Race Awareness Study

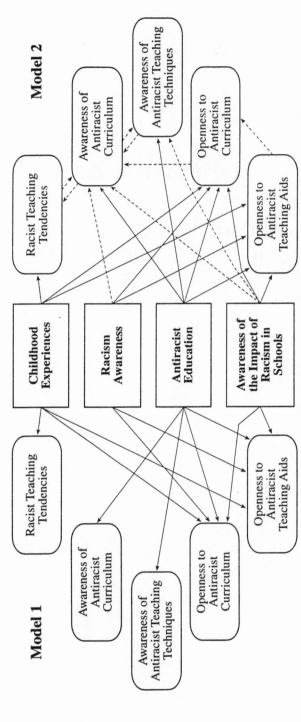

The unique capabilities of LISREL were called upon to estimate the paths of nine constructs resulting from a factor analysis of the questionnaire. The predictor constructs are in bold in the center of the diagram, and the predicted constructs are in the rounded boxes along the outside.

Selected Bibliography

(1994). *Prejudice: Answering Children's Questions*. ABC Television Broadcast & Video.

(1997). Face writing investigated. Associated Press.

(1997). Mock slave auction draws ire of black family. Associated Press.

(1997). Summary of hate crimes statistics for 1997. *Almanac Society-Law Enforcement and Crime*.

(1997). Teacher who wrote on student's face returns to classroom. Associated Press. North Charleston.

(1997). Town tries to smother flames of prejudice: Cross burning in Rushville brings reactions of distress and understanding to family. *Kansas City Star*. A1.

(1997). U.S. Census Bureau Ethnic Identifications. *U.S. Department of Commerce: Bureau of the Census*. Washington, DC.

(1998). Klan rallies at site of black's killing (James Byrd's slaying). *Des Moines Register* (Associated Press).

(1998). Texas men indicted on murder charges in dragging death. *Nando Times News*.

(1999). New Jersey concedes use of racial profiling. *Tribune*. Ames: A4.

(1999). U.S. Justice Department investigates state police discrimination allegation against New Jersey, Florida, Maryland, Connecticut, and other states. Associated Press.

(2000). Columbine massacre report released. APBNews.com.

AAUW Report. (2000). Washington, DC: CNN.

Allen-Sommerville, L. A. & McCormick, T. (1998). *Multicultural education: Aware-ness, strategies & activities*. Madison: Mendota Press.

Anastasi, A. (1988). *Psychological testing*. New York: Macmillan.

Appelbaum, P. E., and Enomoto, E. (1995). Computer-mediated communication for a multicultural experience. *Educational Leadership* 35(6): 49–58.

Aptheker, H. (1993). *Anti-racism in U.S. history*. Westport, CT: Praeger.

Ayalon, A. (1995). Does multicultural education belong in rural white America? *Rural Educator* 16(3): 1–6, 31.

Bacon, J. (1999). Controversial tests. *USA Today*: 3A.

Banks, J. A. (1996). *Multicultural education transformative knowledge & action: Historical and contemporary perspectives*. New York: Teachers College Press.

Banks, J. A. (1997). *Teaching strategies for ethnic studies*. Boston: Allyn & Bacon.

Bayles, Fred. (6/11/99). Standardized exams coming under fire: Protests decry pro-ficiency test madness. Arlington, VA. *USA Today*.

Becker, G. (1997). Retrial ordered for two white officers. *Kansas City Star*. Kansas City, MO.

Bennett, C. L. (1990). *Comprehensive multicultural education: Theory and practice* (2nd ed). Boston: Allyn and Bacon.

Boyle-Baise, M. (1998). Community service learning for multicultural education: An exploratory study with preservice teachers. *Equity and Excellence in Education* 31(2):52–60.

Boyle-Baise, M., and Sleeter, C. (1996). Field experiences: planting seeds and weeds. In C. Grant and M. Gomez (ed). *Making schooling multicultural—campus and classroom*. 371–388. Englewood Cliffs, NJ: Merrill Publishing Co.

Broholm, J. A., and Aust, R. (1994). Teachers and electronic mail: Networking on the network. *Journal of Technology and Teacher Education* 2(2): 167–182.

Brown, P. C., Daniel-Tatum, B. (October 31, 1997). Unpublished Report.

Brown, T. (1995). *Black lies, white lies*. New York: William Morrow & Company.

Carter, R. T., and Goodwin, L. (1994). Racial identity and education. *Review of Research in Education* 20: 291–336.

Cheng, Y.C., et al. (1996). A multi-level and multi-criteria perspective of school ef-fectiveness: A case study. Paper presented at the annual Meeting of the Ameri-can Educational Research Association. New York, NY, April 8–12.

Chinn, P. C., and Gollnick, D. M. (1998). *Multicultural education in a pluralistic so-ciety*. (5th ed). Columbus, OH: Merrill Publishing Co.

Chua-Eoan, H. (2000). Black & blue: The Diallo verdict. *Time*: 24–27.

Clark, C., and O'Donnell, J. (Eds). 1999. *Becoming and unbecoming white*. Westport, CT: Greenwood Publishers.

Cleary, L. M., and Peacock, T. D. (1998). *Collected wisdom: American Indian educa-tion*. Needham Heights, MA: Allyn and Bacon.

Cooper, A., Beare, P. and Thorman, R. (1990). Preparing teachers for diversity: A comparison of student teaching experiences in Minnesota & South Texas. *Ac-tion in Teacher Education* 12(3): 1–4.

Cooper, Michael. (9/22/97). 3 Teenagers are arraigned in an attack. *New York Times*. V146n265pb5 (L) col 1 (10 col in) article A19784085.

Cross, W. E. (1991). *Shades of black: Diversity in African American identity*. Philadel-phia: Temple University Press.

Cummins, J. S., and Sayers, D. (1995). *Brave new schools: Challenging cultural illiteracy through global learning networks*. New York: St. Martin's Press.

Curriculum 2005. (6/15/97). *Wits EPU: Quarterly review of education and training in South Africa*. Vol. 4, No. 4.

Damarin, S. K. (1998). Technology and multicultural education: The question of convergence. *Theory into Practice* 37(1): 11–19.

Daniel-Tatum, B. (1997). *Why are all the black kids sitting together in the cafeteria?* New York: Basic Books.

Doctor, R. D. (1992). Social equity and information technologies: Moving toward information democracy. *Annual Review of Information and Technology* 27: 430–496.

Donaldson, K. (1996). *Through students' eyes: Combating racism in United States schools*. Westport: CT. Greenwood Publishing Group.

Donaldson, K. (September, 1997). Antiracist education: A few courageous teachers. *Equity and Excellence in Education*. Vol. 30, No. 2. 31–38.

Donaldson, K., and Carter, L. (July, 2000). Voices of varied racial ethnicities enrolled in multicultural/antiracist computer and telecommunication courses: Protocols for multicultural technology education reform. *International Journal of Educational Reform*. Vol. 1, No. 3. 234–248.

Donaldson, K., and McShay, J. (forthcoming). Strengthening teacher education programs through multicultural education courses, field experiences, and leadership.

Donaldson, K., and Tartakov, C. (1997). Multicultural education: An answer to racism. *Des Moines Register*.

Donaldson, K., and Tartakov, C. (forthcoming). Kuumba "creativity" multicultural experimental school research project: A model for multicultural antiracist education school reform.

Donaldson, K., and Verma, G. (1997). Antiracist education definition. In Grant and Ladson-Billings (Eds). *Dictionary of Multicultural Education*. Phoenix, AZ: Oryx Press.

Feagin, J. R., and Sikes, M. P. (1994). *Living with racism: The black middle-class experience*. Boston: Beacon Press.

Feagin, J. R., and Vera, H. (1995). *White racism*. New York: Routledge Publishers.

Ford, D. Y. (1996). *Reversing underachievement among gifted black students: Promising practices and programs*. New York: Teachers College Press.

Foster, M. (Ed). (1993). Resisting racism: Testimonies of African American teachers. *Beyond Silenced Voices*. Albany: State University of New York Press.

Fry, F. (1990). Living our commitments: A handbook for whites joining together to identify, own and dismantle our racist conditioning. Unpublished handbook.

Gallavan, N. P. (1998). Why aren't teachers using effective multicultural education practices? *Equity & Excellence in Education* 31(2): 20–27.

Galloway, J. L. (1999). Into the heart of darkness: A Texas prison's racist subculture spawned the grisly murder in Jasper. *U.S. News Online*.

Garcia, J., and Pugh, S. L. (1992). Multicultural education in teacher education preparation programs: A political or an educational concept? *Phi Delta Kappan* 74(3): 214–219.

Gardner, H. (1993). *Multiple intelligences: The theory in practice*. New York: Basic Books.

Gillette, M., and Boyle-Baise, M. (1996). Multicultural education at the graduate level: Assisting teachers in gaining multicultural understandings. *Theory and Research in Social Education* 24(3): 273–293.

Goodwin, W. L., et al. (Fall, 1994). The puzzle of redesigning a preparation program in an evolving, fast changing field. *Teacher Education and Special Education.* Vol. 17, No. 4.

Gordon, R. (1998). *Education & Race: A journalists's handbook.* Oakland, CA: Applied Research Center.

Grant, C. A. (1994). Challenging the myths about multicultural education. *Multicultural Education.* 12(3) 5–11.

Grant, C. A., and Sleeter, C. E. (1998). *Turning on learning: Five approaches for multicultural teaching plans for race, class, gender, and disability.* (2nd ed.). Columbus, OH: Merrill.

Grinter, R. (Ed). (1985). *Bridging the gulf: The need for an antiracist multiculturalism.* Multicultural Teaching. Warwick, NJ: Trentham Books.

Grinter, R. (Ed). (1990). Developing an antiracist national curriculum: Constraints and new directions. *Race relations and urban education: Contexts and promising practices.* London: Falmer Press.

Grinter, R. (Ed). (2000). Multicultural or antiracist education? The need to choose. In *Foundational perspectives in multicultural education.* New York: Longman.

Guba, E. G., and Lincoln, Y. S. (1989). *Fourth generation evaluation.* Newbury Park, CA: Sage Publications.

Harris, J. F. (5/16/97). Clinton seeking to move beyond rhetoric on race issues, aides say. *Washington Post.* P1 A12.

Hayduk, L. A. (1987). *Structural equation modeling with LISREL: Essential and Advances.* Baltimore: Johns Hopkins University Press.

Heinmann, H. (1992). Effects of using early pre-service teachers' field experiences in urban settings to prepare teachers to meet the challenges of multicultural urban schools. *Research in Education*: 13.

Helms, J. E. (1990). *Black and white racial identity: Theory, research and practice.* Westport, CT: Greenwood Press.

Hoffman, D. L., and Novak, T. P. (4/17/98) Bridging the digital divide on the Internet. *Science.*

International Journal of Health Services. (1996). Vol. 26, No. 3.

Jackson, C. (1991). AHS students' of color perceptions of climate. Unpublished Report.

Kocieniewski, David. (8/13/97). Injured man says Brooklyn officers tortured him in custody. (Haitian immigrant Abner Louima in New York City). *New York Times.* V146n225pb1 (L) col 2 (22 col in) article 19689845.

Ladson-Billings, G. (1994). *The dreamkeepers: Successful teachers of African American children.* San Francisco: Jossey-Bass Publishers.

Lancy, D. F. (1993). *Qualitative research in education: An introduction to the major traditions.* New York: Longman.

Larke, P., Wiseman, D. and Bradley, C. (1990). The minority mentorship project: Changing attitudes of pre-service teachers for diverse classrooms. *Action in Teacher Education* 12(3): 5–11.

Lawrence, S. M. (Mar–Apr 1997). Beyond race awareness: White racial identity and multicultural teaching. *Journal of Teacher Education* 48(2): 108–17.

Lawrence, S. M., and Tatum, B. (1997). Teachers in transition: The impact of antiracist professional development on classroom practice. *Teachers College*. Vol. 99. No. 1. 162–78.

Leach, J. (1997). English teachers "on-line": developing a new community of discourse. *English in Education*. 31(2) 63–72.

Leavell, A. G., Cowart, M., and Wilhelm, R.W. (1999). Strategies for preparing culturally responsive teachers. *Equity & Excellence in Education* 32(1): 64–71.

Lee, S. J. (1996). *Unraveling the model minority stereotype: Listening to the voices of Asian American Youth*. New York: Teachers College Press.

Lefferts, J. (1997). School investigates teacher who taped student's mouth. Massachusetts: *Cambridge Chronicle*.

Leigh, P. R. (Fall 1999). Electronic connections and equal opportunities: An analysis of telecommunications distribution in public schools. *Journal of Research on Computing in Education* 32(1): 108–127.

Lyndsey, Henry. (4/16/2000). Lovelady allies believe justice denied. Des Moines Register.

Mahan, J. (Mar 1984). Cultural immersion for inservice teachers: A model and some outcomes. Paper presented at the Annual Meeting of the Association for Supervision and Curriculum Development. New York, NY.

McCall, A. L. (1995). We were cheated! Students' responses to a multicultural, social reconstructionist teacher education course. *Equity & Excellence in Education* 28(1): 15–24.

McCann, Herbert. G. (5/2/97). Beaten youth heads home, faces additional therapy. *Associated Press*.

McCormick, T. E. (1990). Collaboration works! Preparing teachers for urban realities. *Contemporary Education* 61(3): 129–134.

McCormick, T. E., and McShay, J. C. (1996). Field experiences bring reality to preservice teachers in multicultural education courses. *Proceedings of the Annual National Association on Multicultural Education Proceedings*. Minneapolis, MN.

McMurray, J. (1999). Racist or free speech? Professor draws ire. *The Tribune*. Ames, IA: A1, A4.

McShay, J. C. (1996). The effects of multicultural-based field experiences on preservice teacher attitudes. *Unpublished master's thesis*. Iowa State University: Ames, IA.

Medina, N. N., D. M. (1990). *Fallout from the testing explosion*. Cambridge, MA: Fair Test.

Mizell, L. (1992). *Think about racism*. New York: Walker and Company.

Montecinos, C. (1994). Teachers of color and multiculturalism. *Equity & Excellence in Education* 27(3): 34–42.

Murray, C.B.C., and Clark, R.M. (1990). "Targets of racism." *American School Board Journal* 17(6): 22–24.

National Center for Education Statistics. (1990–91). Schools and staffing survey (SASS). U.S. Department of Education.

Nieto, S. (1992). *Affirming diversity: The sociopolitical context of multicultural education* (2nd ed.). New York: Longman.

Nieto, S. (1999). *The light in their eyes: Creating multicultural learning communities*. New York: Teachers College Press.

Nieto, S. (2000). *Affirming diversity: The sociopolitical context of multicultural education* (3rd ed.). New York: Longman.

Phinney, J. S. (Ed). (1983). A three stage model of ethnic identity development in adolescence. In *Ethnic identity: Formation and transmission among Hispanics and other minorities.* Albany: State University of New York Press.

Phuntsog, N. (1995). Teacher educators' perceptions of the importance of multicultural education in the preparation of elementary teachers. *Equity & Excellence in Education* 28(1): 10–14.

Pohan, C. A. (1996). Preservice teachers' beliefs about diversity: Uncovering factors leading to multicultural responsiveness. *Equity and Excellence in Education* 29(3): 62–69.

Pollard, D. S. (Oct 1989). Reducing the impact of racism on students. *Educational Leadership* 47(2): 73–75.

Rex, J. (Ed). (1989). Equality of opportunity, multi-culturalism, anti-racism and education for all. In *Education for all—a landmark in pluralism.* Lewes, PA: Falmer Press.

Romiszowski, A.J.M., and Mason, R. (1996). *Computer-mediated communication. Handbook of research for educational communications: A Project of the Association for Educational Communications and Technology.* David H. Johassen (Ed). New York: Simon & Schuster/Macmillan.

Rotary "6000" International Handbook. (1998). *Rotary Foundation Handbook.* (see www.rotary.org/foundation/training/index.htm#training).

Ruenzel, D. (1994, Aug). Blackflight. *Teacher Magazine*: 19–23.

Seidman, I.E. (1991). *Interviewing as qualitative research: A guide for researchers in education and the social sciences.* New York: Teachers College Press.

Sleeter, C. E. (1992). *Keepers of the American dream: A study of staff development and multicultural education.* London: Falmer Press.

Sleeter, C.E. (1994). White racism. *Multicultural Education* 1(4): 5–8, 39.

Sleeter, C. E. (1996). *Multicultural education as social activism.* New York: Falmer Press.

Sleeter, C. E. (Ed.). (1993). How white teachers construct race. In *Race identity and representation in education.* New York: Routledge.

Sorenson, C., and Sweeney, J. (1994). *Focus group interview procedures.* Research Institute for Studies in Education. Iowa State University: Ames, IA.

Soudien, C. (1994). Dealing with race: Laying down patterns for multiculturalism in South Africa. *Interchange* 25(3): 281–294.

Spring, J. (1997). *Deculturalization and the struggle for equality: A brief history of the education of dominated cultures in the United States.* New York: McGraw-Hill.

Stevens, A. (1996). Project Analyst Report. Unpublished document.

Tartokov, C. (1995). *Ethnicity awareness intervention: Effects on attitudes and behaviors of science educators.* Ames: Iowa State University.

Tatum, B. D. (1992, winter). Teaching the psychology of racism. *Mount Holyoke Alumnae Quarterly*: 19–21.

Teachers are Researchers: Reflection and Action. (1993). International Reading Association. Newark, DE.

Tran, M., Young, R., and Dilella, J. (May–June 1994). Multicultural education courses and the student teacher: Eliminating stereotypical attitudes in our ethnically diverse classroom. *Journal of Teacher Education* 45 (93): 183–189.

Verma, G., Zec, P., and Skinner, G. (1994). *The ethnic crucible: Harmony and hostility in multi-ethnic schools.* London: Falmer Press.

Walt, Kathy. (9/16/97). Controversy grows at UT over professor's remark. *Houston Chronical.* Section A: 1.

Weinberg, M. (1990). *Racism in the United States: A comprehensive classified bibliography.* Westport, CT: Greenwood Press.

Zaichner, K., Melnick, S., and Gomez, M. L. (Ed). (1996). *Currents of reform in preservice teacher education.* New York: Teachers College, Columbia University.

Zeichner, K., and Gore, J. (1989). Teacher socialization. *National Center for Research on Teacher Education.* East Lansing, MI.

Index

About the Author

KAREN B. McLEAN DONALDSON is an Associate Professor and Systems-wide Program Director of the Cross Cultural Studies Institute for the School of Education at Alliant International University. Dr. Donaldson has received numerous awards and notoriety for her work in antiracist-multicultural education. She is the author of *Through Students' Eyes: Combating Racism in United States Schools* (Praeger, 1996).